Disaster and Human Trafficking

Human Trafficking is complex, layered and lies at the intersections of multiple vulnerabilities, gender being among the most significant ones. This gets exacerbated during both natural and human made disasters. Any attempt to either understand or address it will be fraught with challenges if women and girls' unique vulnerabilities, as well as their needs, voice, choice, agency and safety is not centre-staged in any effort. Mondira's book does exactly that...it succinctly and in simple words explores the compounding discriminations, including structural inequalities, that cause and result in women and girls differential gendered vulnerabilities to being trafficked during disasters. Once this is understood, the solutions can be specific, gender responsive, and sustainable.

- ***Anju Dubey Pandey***, *Gender Responsive Governance and Ending Violence against Women Specialist, UN Women, New Delhi, India*

Mondira Dutta

Disaster and Human Trafficking

Springer

Mondira Dutta
Jawaharlal Nehru University
New Delhi, Delhi, India

ISBN 978-981-16-1629-7 ISBN 978-981-16-1630-3 (eBook)
https://doi.org/10.1007/978-981-16-1630-3

This Springer imprint is published by the registered company Springer Nature Singapore Pte Ltd.
The registered company address is: 152 Beach Road, #21-01/04 Gateway East, Singapore 189721, Singapore

भारतीय सामाजिक विज्ञान अनुसंधान परिषद्
शिक्षा मंत्रालय, भारत सरकार
INDIAN COUNCIL OF SOCIAL SCIENCE RESEARCH
Ministry of Education, Government of India

सत्यमेव जयते

V. K. Malhotra
(Professor of Economics)
Member Secretary

Foreword

Disasters are increasingly getting more and more intricate impacting life, property and livelihoods. When a disaster takes place, it typically devastates the most vulnerable sections of the population to the gravest extent. Such people usually belong to the lower socio-economic strata. Even in a demographically homogeneous community, the impact leads to completely varied results as the severity depends on the magnitude with which a disaster affects different strata of population, both in terms of livelihood and environment (J. Drolet et al, 2015[1]; A. Gurung and Clark, 2018[2]).

Disasters provide a conducive condition for abuse and forced confinement, aiding the exploiters to find a perfect situation which is further accentuated by prevailing weak law enforcement mechanism and poverty-caused vulnerability. When livelihood options for men and women start depleting during a disaster, it provides just the kind of opportunity that traffickers are looking for to exploit children who are orphaned or separated from their parents, the women who are in distress and the men that are frantically in search of livelihood options post disaster. Mostly communities get marginalized due to lack of awareness and improper dissemination of developmental policies, schemes and disaster packages. Data from the anti-trafficking organizations show that trafficking gets suddenly heightened during disasters (UNODC reports). Some studies on the recent COVID 19 pandemic have shed light on this aspect as to how children from the vulnerable areas get abused and trafficked for labour and sexual exploitation (UNODC, 2021[3]; R. Nayar, Arab News, August 9, 2020[4]).

The book on 'Disaster and Human Trafficking' is an outcome of ICSSR supported research, and is a pioneering effort towards highlighting the link between Disasters

[1]Julie Drolet, Lena Dominelli, Margaret Alston, Robin Ersing, Golam Mathbor & Haorui Wu (2015). 'Women rebuilding lives post-disaster: innovative community practices for building resilience and promoting sustainable development,' Gender & Development, 23:3, pp 433-448.

[2]Anuj Gurung & Amanda D Clark, 2018. 'The perfect storm: The impact of disaster severity on internal human trafficking,' International Area Studies Review, vol. 21(4), pp 302–322.

[3]UNODC (2021). 'COVID-19 Impact exposes millions to the risk of trafficking,' UN News, February.

[4]Ranvir Nayar (2020). 'Pandemic portends a tsunami of human trafficking,' Arab News, August 9.

जे. एन. यू. इंस्टीट्यूशनल एरिया, अरुणा आसफ अली मार्ग, नई दिल्ली - 110067
JNU Institutional Area, Aruna Asaf Ali Marg, New Delhi 110067
दूरभाष / Tel: 91-11-2641833, 26742059 (Off.), फैक्स /Fax: 91-11-26742109, ई-मेल/ email: ms@icssr.org

and Human Trafficking. The findings of the book were researched during the two-year period of ICSSR senior fellowship of the author which enabled the study's final field visit in 2018 to validate and authenticate the ground realities. The text contains rich experiences from the field to compile and analyse for achieving the logical conclusions.

Disaster researches from the social science perspective have been rather limited and these limited studies have suffered from inadequacy of data and deficiency in terms of establishing a strong causation between disasters and human trafficking (Bowersox, 2017[5]). There have been studies by scholars and also stories by well acknowledged media confirming the threat of trafficking during and post disasters. Many stories or articles have appeared in media on scores of peoples from Bangladesh, India, Sri Lanka and other countries being trafficked for livelihood options following the 2004 tsunami (The Guardian, January 5, 2005[6]; The New York Times, January 13, 2005[7]). Porous international borders with these countries having poverty, vulnerability and socio-economic instability push young girls from Nepal, Bangladesh, Myanmar and other such countries to be sold off to traffickers (B. Gyawali et al, 2017[8]; M. Dutta, 2020[9]; N.M. Sajjadul Hoque, 2010[10]; M.A. Mirza, 2010[11]; G. Qiu, 2019[12]). The total number of registered cases is just the tip of the iceberg as a far greater number of cases go unreported than the reported ones.

As per the Immoral Traffic (Prevention) Act, trafficking is the process of recruiting, contracting, procuring or hiring a person for commercial sexual exploitation. It could be used for other types of violation such as developing pornographic material, sexual exploitation under the disguise of bar tenders, promoting sex tourism and even for exploitative labour with or without sexual abuse. This situation warrants addressing and reforming the social, political and power structures that cause inequality, exclusion and oppression of people in the first place.

---

[5]Zack Bowersox (2017). 'Natural disasters and human trafficking: Do disasters affect state anti-trafficking performance?', International Migration, 56(3), pp 196–212.

[6]The Guardian (2005). 'Criminals may be Trafficking Orphans,' January 5.

[7]The New York Times (2005). 'The tsunamis and child trafficking (Editorial),' January 13.

[8]Bishal Gyawali, June Keeling and Per Kallestrup (2017). 'Human Trafficking in Nepal: Post-earthquake risk and response,' Disaster Med Public Health Preparedness, 11, pp 153–154.

[9]Mondira Dutta (2020), 'Human Trafficking and Disaster Risk Reduction: A Cross Cutting Link in SDGs,' in V. K. Malhotra et al (eds), Disaster Management for 2030: Agenda of the SDG, Springer, Singapore, pp 121–133.

[10]N. M. Sajjadul Hoque (2010). 'Female Child Trafficking from Bangladesh: A New Form of Slavery,' Canadian Social Science, 6(1), pp 45–58.

[11]Mashhood Ahmad Mirza (2010). 'The menace of human trafficking—Pakistan's response to the problem?,' Pakistan Journal of Criminology, 151(2), No. 4, pp. 151–164.

[12]Geping Qiu, Sheldon X. Zhang & Weidi Liu (2019). 'Trafficking of Myanmar women for forced marriage in China,' Crime, Law and Social Change, 72, pp 35–52.

In this regard, India's establishment of a large number of anti-human trafficking units (AHTU) in the vulnerable areas has been extremely encouraging. The role of AHTU offers opportunities to bring together communities for a collective action, mobilising society to express their demands by voicing concerns at local, national, regional and international levels. They have often contributed towards the development of laws and policies with regard to human trafficking in an active, constructive and positive manner. Nevertheless, without the help of CSOs and NGOs it would be next to impossible to contain the menace. According to the Trafficking in Persons (TIP) Report, India has shown a slight improvement in 2019 and 2020 as compared to 2018. It is inTier2 at present.

India's "Disaster Management Act" enacted in December 2005 was further modified in 2016 to be in sync with the "Sendai Framework for Disaster Risk Reduction" and community resilience. The Sendai Framework aims to achieve substantial reduction in risk of lives, livelihood and health, along with lessening of risk of the economic, physical, social, cultural and environmental assets of persons, communities, business firms and countries over the next 15 years, 2015–2030.

The National Disaster Management Plan (NDMP), released on June 1, 2016 by the Hon'ble Prime Minister, aims to make India disaster resilient and reduce the loss of lives and assets. It takes care of all major aspects of disaster management such as prevention, mitigation, response and recovery. It also identifies the foremost tasks like—early warning system, dissemination of information, preparation of medical care, search, rescue and evacuation, and so on. It made India one of the first countries to chalk out a plan of action in tune with the Sendai Framework. Robert Glasser, the Head of U.N. Office for Disaster Risk Reduction, went on to say "The challenges of reducing disaster risks in a country of the size of India are formidable but the Indian government is demonstrating that where there is a will there is a way." In this context, some critics have suggested changes in "top down" approach, while supporting a greater role for NGOs and local communities.

The subject matter of the present book is yet another generous contribution to the hitherto slender collection of disaster research from the social science perspective. Various perspectives based on ethics and values in the book make our understanding much deeper, greater and simpler. The theme of natural disasters has been researched well in the work from the perspective of political, social, economic and anthropological approaches. It involves the emotional and psycho-social stress factors including weak implementation of laws and policies at various levels that would strategize the New Education Policy under a robust framework.

This book is an attempt to highlight the root cause of human trafficking and tries to address the basic factors of vulnerability among the marginalized, especially during and after a disaster. It provides a detailed journey of disaster research starting from the Yokohama Strategy to the Sendai Framework of Action making it a significant read for scholars and students interested in the subject. The book examines the most likely impact of disasters on human trafficking and its links with the human rights abuse. It is a timely contribution, particularly during the period of a pandemic that is afflicting the world. It explores the synergy of existing theories, laws and approaches through a common platform of relevance, ushering in achievable decision-making within the evidence-based perspective. This book is an endeavour to bring forward a study that unveils disaster research in the social science perspective, highlighting the trafficking of human beings. I am sure that the book will prove itself to be of great utility to interested scholars, academicians, policy makers, community leaders and front-line workers.

V.K.Malhotra

V K Malhotra (Professor)
Member Secretary, ICSSR

Preface

Writing this book has been extremely fascinating and rewarding as well. Indeed this exercise has been a dream come true! Studying Human Trafficking has not only been my passion but a most captivating subject to research upon. The more one delves into it, the more complex it gets. The subject has too many tentacles and needs to be handled from different perspectives and each time this research takes you onto a new dimension. It has been more than one and half decades, trying to investigate how things move, understanding the internal mechanisms of human trafficking, but as the years go past, it seems to mutate itself bringing out a new perspective that has altogether not been or much less researched. Working on several opportunities that came along, it is evident that the various aspects related to human trafficking has widened its definition and scope. The understanding of its routes, sources, destinations and the hardships faced by the victims are much more complex and complicated. Indeed the subject with its multi-disciplinary in nature has always brought out a newer perspective that requires to be studied much deeper from different prisms. The more intricately one gets involved, the wider its angle of research gets inculcating a lot many aspects that triggers human trafficking into the scope and subject matter of human trafficking.

Way back in 50s and 60s, as a child, memories come flooding remembering how my mother and grandmother were concerned about my safety in returning back home in the evening after playing with friends. We used to be warned that there were child pickers who may catch us and maim us to beg from people on the streets or be exploited for others. Hence it was made clear as to how important it was that as a child we should not be talking to strangers. Returning home promptly before the street lights gets on was the first priority. Little did we realise then that, how true the warnings were and how genuine the concerns were from the senior women folks of our family. Therefore this is not something new but has been existing since generations. Only its nature has become much more complex and difficult to understand. Trafficking in persons affects almost the entire world as one keeps seeing cases emerging on a regular basis.

Years of research clearly showed that Human Trafficking certainly does not survive in solitude, but is a typical case that gets exacerbated due to situations of vulnerability created naturally or as a result of other factors. It becomes pertinent therefore to address the root cause rather than finding the prescription for the cure. People with vulnerabilities and living under difficult situations are the ones who become an easy prey to human trafficking even before they can realise this fact. Whenever there is chaos in the society arising as a result of natural disaster, ethnic cleansing, political instability or any such abnormal situation, people in most vulnerable situation are the worst sufferers. Natural disasters in particular does not restrict itself to administrative boundaries or to a particular community. The impact is felt by one and all. However the most vulnerable who live in difficult circumstances belonging to a lower socio economic strata become the worst victims. A natural disaster impacts the livelihood and hardships of human beings forcing them to run helter-skelter in search of livelihood options or to protect their young ones. This becomes an opportunity for the traffickers who are quick to make hay while the sun shines! In the absence of proper disaster mitigation policies, a lack of good governance, unawareness, people are simply forced to grab whatever so called opportunity comes their way. Thus this particular lot become the gullible trafficked victims who willingly believe in the false promises offered by the traffickers. Such cases of human trafficking among the men, women and children have been rampant especially during times of disaster and post disaster.

As a result of structural gender inequalities existing in the society women in particular become a part of the excluded and discriminated groups who are victims of human trafficking in most of the disaster prone regions. The multiple impacts that trafficking has on the women and child survivors creates a lifelong impairment besides retarding the human capital, development opportunities and growth of the overall scenario. This results in mass scale vulnerabilities and violence. Undoubtedly it includes forced labour, bonded labour, debt bondage, child soldiers, camel jockeying, and organ trade; besides begging, illicit adoption, circus bondage, forced marriages, sex trafficking or "prostitution", children exploited in commercial sex, child sex tourism and much more newer trends of human trafficking or modern day slavery.

Determining the magnitude of trafficked persons is extremely difficult due to the secretive nature of the crime. Studies and surveys sponsored by the Ministry of Women and Child Development (MWCD) gives a rough estimate of the crime. There are millions of prostitutes in the country and importantly it is estimated that 40% of them are probably minors. Studies have also estimated that fifty percent of all female trafficked victims for sexual exploitation in South Asia have been less than 18 years of age at the time of exploitation. The estimates on the magnitude of trafficked victims are uncertain due to a lack of documentation and methodological flaws. As a result, more qualitative analysis is considered for studying this important issue. Case studies and qualitative data have therefore dominated the empirical research. Estimating the degree and depth of human trafficking has thus become hard to measure. The normal regular process of data collection is arduous due to the secretive nature of operations, besides the anonymity demanded by clientele. There is a low visibility of exploitation and an overwhelming fear of information sharing by the involved persons. Without proper documentation and non-availability of data it is difficult to prove or disapprove a point and develop a clearer picture of the scenario. With a slender collection of authentic documentation on the subject, it gets even more tougher to research upon such a complex issue.

The National Commission for Women identified 1794 places of origin or source areas besides another total of 1016 places, where commercial activities flourish. Such an exploitation of a person typically through force, fraud or coercion for the purpose of forced labour, involuntary servitude or commercial sexual exploitation is a humanitarian concern for Governance, International Institutional Collaboration and Law. Cases of human trafficking are now being increasingly recognized and presented in several studies especially in the disaster prone areas. Although 'prevention is better than cure', unfortunately most of the research focus in addressing a trafficked victim at the destinations like the brothels and the markets areas rather than at the place of origin. It is the source areas that needs to be emphasized taking into account the impact of disaster in an area specific context.

Research is in deficit while studying this important relation between disasters and human trafficking. South Asia has been a vulnerable area in terms of major disasters and human trafficking. India, Bangladesh, Nepal, Maldives, Pakistan and Sri Lanka have all been majorly hit by disasters resulting in trafficking of men, women and children. India happens to be both a source, destination and also a transit point. With porous border areas, India along with Nepal and Bangladesh faces large scale cross border trafficking. During Tsunami a large number of men were trafficked to Maldives for labour not only from India but Bangladesh and Sri Lanka as well. An indepth research on this important topic becomes of utmost significance particularly in the South Asian context.

With millions of Asian women, men and children, get trafficked every year for slavery-like practices and forced labour, more rich and reliable data needs to come from the field. Studies and analysis are constantly demonstrating the changing scenario in the methodology adopted by the traffickers and the illegal trade of trafficking particularly in the South Asian region. Countries in South Asia sharing long international boundaries, witness transnational trafficking movements over the last several decades. These countries have a common culture and history. Their boundaries being porous, is difficult to restrict illegal movements. This trend has gradually become more integrated and imbibed within the trans-national criminal activities. The demand for trafficked labour and commercial sexual exploitation gathered momentum adjusting itself well within a globalized economy. No one even realized how and when this illicit trade got acceptance in becoming perfectly normal and legal.

Having worked on this sensitive topic for the last 17 years, the entire research would remain incomplete without the assistance received from the **Indian Council of Social Science Research** (ICSSR). As a ICSSR senior fellow for two years (from 2018 to 2020), this was an absolute opportune moment when I could totally devote to compiling and documenting my years of research on the subject, incorporating some of the latest untouched areas to make it complete. The outcome of this research finally culminated into the form of this book entitled *Disaster and Human Trafficking*. The ICSSR gave me the opportunity to take up this huge research with a focus on the social science perspective of how disasters have often led to human trafficking and how the gaps between institutions and the civil society organization needs to be looked at from a gender perspective. What is special in this book is its coverage, based upon a rich and reliable series of field visit experiences. It includes various perspectives of human trafficking from different angles all based on field experiences undertaken from 2003 to 2018. My previous field visits had been victim centric and community based preventive measures. It identified the popular routes, origin and destinations as well as the challenges faced by the civil society organizations. However an understanding of the gaps that create hurdles in ushering in a hundred percent successful implementation of policies and strategies was of significant importance. The implementation needs to address the cross cutting edges between institutions and the Civil Society organization especially within the parameters of the 2030 development agenda. All the field visits undertaken earlier had mostly ignored this aspect. Therefore another field visit was essential to be undertaken in order to address the perspectives of the institutions vis-à-vis the Civil Society Organisations. I was fortunate to have been facilitated by the ICSSR within the given limitations of time and resources. I am indeed most thankful to ICSSR for reposing faith and trust in me to take up this important research. Mention needs to be made to the Ex-Chairman Late Shri Braj Bihari Kumar and the Member Secretary Prof. Virendra Kumar Malhotra. I deeply appreciate Prof Malhotra for his constant support and encouragement throughout the study. His pleasing mannerisms makes him easily approachable, always ready to spare time for resolving any issue that crops up, be it academic or technical. The entire span of two years with ICSSR gave me an opportunity to interact with almost all its officials and staff members. I soon realised how comfortable and at home I was amidst the helpful and polite staff at the ICSSR.

Words fail me in appreciating the two years of my affiliation at the Special Centre for Disaster Research (SCDR) of the Jawaharlal Nehru University. The interaction and discourse with the first batch of post graduate and research scholars was extremely satisfying. Teaching them was most rewarding. My sincere gratitude extends to the former founder Chairperson of the Centre, Prof. Amita Singh. Her endless contribution to develop the centre and organize series of conferences and international discourse was a learning experience altogether. I also like to extend my sincere thanks to the present Chairperson Prof. P. K. Joshi and all the concurrent faculty members, staff and students of the Centre. I am indeed honoured to have been a part of this centre.

I take this opportunity to express my sincere gratitude and appreciation for UN Women with whom I have been associated for almost over ten years and have been engaged in some project or the other on human trafficking and Gender. This long span of opportunity gave me the time to grasp the nitty gritty of the issues and made me sharper in understanding the various perspectives of the subject as it evolved over time. A special mention needs to be made for Ms. Anne F. Stenhammer—the former Regional Programme Director UN Women, South Asia, Ms Madhubala Nath, the former Regional Advisor for Asia and the Pacific & Senior Advisor at UN Women, as well as Ms. Anju Dubey Pandey from UN Women, New Delhi. It has been most motivating to have been involved in research with them. My latest work with UN

Women on COVID-19 from July to October 2020, was a unique experience involving disaster of a new dimension, referred to as a pandemic!

My sincere thanks and deep appreciation to the various non-governmental organisations whom I have been interacting from time to time such as Prajwala (Ms. Sunitha Krishnan), Sanlaap (Late Ms. Indrani Sinha, Mr. Pinaki Ranjan Sinha, Mr. Souvik Basu and other staff members), Shakti Vahini (Mr. Ravi Kant), Manav Sewa Sansthan (Mr. Jata Shankar and team), Banglanatak.com (Ms. Ananya Bhattacharjee) and several others. I owe my deep appreciation to all the victims of human trafficking who have been kind enough to share their stories with me and help me in understanding the challenges they faced in the proper perspective. In addition, I am extremely thankful to the government institutions such as the State Commission for Protection of Child Rights, West Bengal (SCPCR) (Ms. Ananya Chakraborty), Anti Human Trafficking Units (AHTU), Lal Bazar, (Ms. Niru Shelpa, IPS), the West Bengal Task Force (Ms. Madhumita Haldar, Director) the ADM South 24 Parganas (Mr. Sagar Chakravarti, ADM) among many others.

A special thanks to my former research scholar Ms. Sanchita Chatterjee for her timely help. I am eternally grateful to my academic family—my husband Prof. Bupinder Zutshi for his constructive suggestions, my daughter—Dr. Ipshita Zutshi for her constant patience and tolerance in listening to my pages of writing bringing in much clarity to my draft and my son—Dr. Aneesh Zutshi for helping me to overcome all my technical difficulties from time to time. For all this I must owe my gratitude to my late mother who has been the actual motivating factor throughout!

New Delhi, India Mondira Dutta

Contents

About the Author

Mondira Dutta has a teaching and research experience spanning over four decades, She has been the Founder Chairperson of the Centre for Inner Asian Studies, School of International Studies, Jawaharlal Nehru University (JNU), New Delhi. India. Her research focuses on gender studies, disaster research and human security. Her research is based on the varied experiences collected from her widely travelled field visits among the various remote areas of South Asia including Afghanistan, Central Asia and other parts of the world. She has been an ICSSR (Indian Council of Social Science Research) Senior Fellow at the Special Centre for Disaster Research, JNU and has been the India Chair under the Indian Council of Cultural Relations at Dublin City University, Ireland in 2019. She was awarded the 'Lifetime Achievement Award', in 2009 at the International Congress of Women for Justice, Equality, Peace and Progress, sponsored jointly by the United Nations Information Centre for India and Bhutan. As a Consultant to UN Women, her work on Human Trafficking is widely acclaimed. Her most recent study as a Consultant cum Senior Researcher to the UN Women was on the 'Socio Economic Impact of COVID-19—Gender Perspectives' (a forthcoming publication) in collaboration with NITI Aayog, October 2020.

Acronyms

ACD	Association for Community Development
ADB	Asian Development Bank
AGF	Adolescent Girls Forums
AHTU	Anti-Human Trafficking Unit
ATSEC	Action Against Trafficking and Sexual Exploitation of Children
BDO	Block Development Officer
BDR	Bangladesh Rifles
BNWLA	Bangladesh National Woman Lawyers' Association
BPFA	Beijing Platform for Action
BSF	Border Security force
CACT	Campaign Against Child Trafficking
CBATN	Cross Border Anti-Trafficking Network
CBO	Community Based Organization
CDPO	Child Development Project Officer
CEDAW	Convention on the Elimination of all Forms of Discrimination Against Women
CENWOR	Centre for Women's Research
CID	Crime Investigation Department
CINI	Child in Need institute
CRC	Convention on the Rights of the Child
CRED	Centre for Research on Epidemiology of Disasters
CSE	Commercial Sexually Exploited
CWC	Child Welfare Committee under the Juvenile Justice (Care and Protection of Children) Act, 2015
DCM	Deputy Chief of Mission
DCPO	District Child Protection Officer
DDMA	District Disaster Management Authority
DI	Differentiated Instruction
DLSA	District Legal Services Authority
DRM	Disaster Risk Management
DRR	Disaster Risk Reduction
DSWO	District Social Welfare Officer

DWCD	Department of Women and Child Development
FWLD	Forum for Women Law and Development
GDP	Gross Domestic Product
HFA	Hyogo Framework for Action
HLPF	High level Political Forum
HPC	High-Powered Committee
IAHTU	Integrated Anti Human Trafficking Unit
ICDS	Integrated Child Development Services
ICPS	Integrated Child Protection Scheme
IDNDR	International Decade for Natural Disaster Reduction
IETC	Information, Education, Technology & Communication
IEWP	International Early Warning Programme
IFRCS	International Federation of Red Cross Societies
IOM	International Organisation for Migration
IRPF	Inter Religious Priest Forum
ITPA	Immoral Trafficking Prevention Act
KSY	Kishori Shakti Yojana
LHRD	Lawyers for Human Rights and Development
MDG	Millennium Development Goals
MGNREGA	Mahatma Gandhi National Rural Employment Guarantee Act
MSS	Manav Seva Sansthan
MWCD	Ministry of Women and Child Development
NALSA	National Legal Services Authority
NCPCR	National Commission for Protection of Child Rights
NCRB	National Crime Record Bureau
NDMA	National Disaster Management Authority
NDMP	National Disaster Management Plan
NDRF	National Disaster Response Force
NEC	National Executive Committee
NIDM	National Institute of Disaster Management
NIPCCD	National Institute of Public Cooperation and Child Development—schemes like Swadhar, Short Stay Homes, Ujjawala, setting up of women help lines for women in distress etc.
NJA	National Judicial Academy
NNAGT	National Network Against Girl Trafficking
NSS	National Statistical Systems
PIL	Public Interest Litigation
PLV	Para Legal Volunteers
PRI	Panchayati Raj Institution
RSBY	Rashtrya Swasthya Bima Yojana
SAARC	South Asian Association for Regional Cooperation
SACG	South Asia Coordinating Group
SAF	South Asia Forum
SAFAHT	South Asia Forum against Human Trafficking
SAPAT	South Asia Professionals against Trafficking

SCPCR	State Commission of Protection for Child Rights
SDG	Sustainable Development Goals
SDMA	State Disaster Management Authority
SFDRR	Sendai Framework for Disaster Risk Reduction
SHG	Self Help Group
SLSA	State Legal Services Authority
SSB	Sahastra Seema Bal
TIP	Trafficking in Persons
TVPA	Trafficking Victims Protection Act
UNDP	United Nations Development Programme
UNDRR	United Nations Office of the Disaster Risk Reduction
UNICEF	United Nations International Children's Emergency Fund
UNIFEM	United Nations Development Fund for Women
UNISDR	United Nations International Strategy from Disaster Reduction
UNODC	United Nations Office on Drugs and Crime
UNTOC	United Nations Convention against Transnational Organised Crime
VAW	Violence against Women
VLCPC	Village level Child Protection Committees
WBSCPCR	West Bengal 'State Commission of Protection for Child Rights'
WHO	World Health Organization
WIP	Women in Prostitution

List of Figures

List of Tables

List of Maps

List of Exhibits

Chapter 1
Introduction

Context

Exploitation of men, women and children for obtaining financial gains by fraud is a harsh crime against humanity. This is called human trafficking. It is a major systematic violation of one's fundamental human rights. Both human trafficking and disaster do not recognize any administrative and international boundary! Victims get trapped under difficult situation and are lured or abducted from the comforts of their homes. Subsequently, they are forced, under severe stress to work in prostitution, agricultural and manufacturing settings, or in domestic servitude, including organ trade and other transnational crimes. Human trafficking inflicts grave personal damage on the victims, often undermining government authority. It fuels organized criminal groups and gangs, resulting in social and public health costs. All human trafficking cases follow a similar pattern. Traffickers use acquaintances or false advertisements to rope in men, women and children from or near their homes. Further, they are quickly transferred elsewhere where they can safely be exploited far away outside their city, region or country.[1] However, the crime of human trafficking can vary in different forms in diverse regions and countries around the world.

Structural gender inequalities essentially lead to human trafficking. This inequality particularly makes women a part of the most excluded and discriminated groups in their own region. Trafficking has multiple negative impacts on the lives of trafficked survivors. It includes the women and children survivors, besides taking a

---

[1]The UN Convention on Trafficking (Palermo Convention 2000) defines trafficking in persons as the recruitment, transportation, transfer, harbouring, or receipt of persons, by means of the threat or use of force or other forms of coercion, of abduction, of fraud, of deception, of the abuse of power or of a position of vulnerability or of the giving or receiving of payments or benefits to achieve the consent of a person having control over another person, for the purpose of exploitation. Exploitation includes, at a minimum, the exploitation or the prostitution of others or other forms of sexual exploitation, forced labour or services, slavery, or practices similar to slavery, servitude, or the removal of organs.

M. Dutta, *Disaster and Human Trafficking*,
https://doi.org/10.1007/978-981-16-1630-3_1

toll on the human capital, growth and development opportunities. The outcome is in terms of a series of vulnerabilities and violence, inflicting forced labour, bonded labour, debt bondage, child soldiers, camel jockeying and organ trade. It also leads to illicit adoption, begging, circus bondage, forced marriages and sex trafficking or 'prostitution'. There are newer trends of children exploited in commercial sex, child sex tourism and many other trends and forms of human trafficking commonly witnessed on a daily basis. Studies conducted in the metropolitan cities reveal that there are about 100,000 commercial sexually exploited (CSE) women and children as per 1998 records. This study was undertaken by the Department of Women and Child Development, Government of India, for six cities of Delhi, Mumbai (Bombay), Kolkata (Calcutta), Hyderabad, Chennai (Madras) and Bangalore. Out of these, it was estimated that almost one-third of the CSE group belonged to a tender age of below 20 years. A total of about 40% had been forced to take up prostitution when they were minors. A study of three major cities of India indicated that a total of 497 raids were conducted and 2219 girls were rescued from brothels of Delhi, Mumbai and Kolkata during 1999–2002. Majority of these belonged to the states of Andhra Pradesh, Karnataka, Tamil Nadu, West Bengal, Maharashtra and Uttar Pradesh. It is tough to estimate the magnitude of trafficked victims given the highly confidential and clandestine nature of the crime. However, other studies and surveys sponsored by the Ministry of Women and Child Development (MWCD) put the estimate to the tune of about three million prostitutes in the country, majority of them being minors (Dutta 2010). Andhra Pradesh, West Bengal, Maharashtra, Tamil Nadu, Karnataka, Bihar, Jharkhand, Orissa and Delhi were identified as the most impacted among all the states. However, among the CSE, more than five out of every 100 women in Indian brothels happened to belong to Nepal and Bangladesh. These sources also suggest that the average age of the trafficked victims is on the decrease. Moreover, estimates suggest fifty percent of all the women trafficked victims in South Asia belong to below 18 years of age at the time of their sexual exploitation. Those belonging to the most disadvantaged social economic strata of the country are exceptionally vulnerable particularly to forced or bonded labour and sex trafficking. Besides internal trafficking, Indian women and children are trafficked to the Middle East, South East Asia and the West for purposes of forced labour and sexual exploitation. In recent years, newer trends have emerged such as sexual exploitation through sex tourism, child sex tourism and paedophilia. There are other trends like prostitution in pilgrim towns and other tourist destinations, besides trafficking for organ transplantation and forced marriages, not excluding the cross-border trafficking from Nepal and Bangladesh.

Every year, millions of Asian children, women and men are being trafficked for slavery-like practices and for forced labour. Studies and analysis are demonstrating certain changes in the process and economy of trafficking at present particularly in the South Asian region. This trend gradually becomes more integrated into transnational criminal activities, and the demands for trafficked labour adjust to a globalizing economy when the illegal started to feel absolutely normal and legal. Soon, no one ever noticed how trends like colonization crept in and millions became slaves of a few (Dutta 2011a).

Methodological weaknesses prevail in estimating the number of trafficked victims. The data thus obtained is always under the scanner and is questionable. Hence, most of the research studies tend to be based on either case studies or empirical research reducing the studies to limited size. However, it has been observed that trafficking of women and girls as one of the criminal activities has increased over the years. It is apparent that under such situation the magnitude of human trafficking is difficult to be measured. Regular data collection mechanisms simply do not work due to the stealthy nature of operations. The low visibility of exploitation besides the desired anonymity by clientele, as well as an overwhelming fear of information sharing by involved persons, makes it all difficult for acquiring the correct picture.[2] The National Commission for Women had earlier identified places of origin from where women are trafficked in the first place. A total of 1794 places of origin and 1016 destination places where the commercial activities thrived were identified.

Human trafficking is thus a heinous crime involving exploitation of a person typically through force, fraud or coercion for the purpose of forced labour, involuntary servitude or commercial sexual exploitation. It is a humanitarian concern for governance, International Institutional Collaboration and Law. Trafficking in Persons affects almost the entire world as either a country of origin, transit or a destination for victims. UNODC, as guardian of the United Nations Convention against Transnational Organized Crime (UNTOC) and the protocols thereto, contributes in assisting the world towards their efforts. Implementing the Protocol to Prevent, Suppress and Punish Trafficking in Persons is referred to as the Palermo Protocol. Every government's efforts are annually measured and presented in the Trafficking in Persons (TIP) Report. These measures are displayed in four categories in terms of the 3P paradigm of prosecuting traffickers, protecting victims and preventing the crime. This is the US government's principal diplomatic tool based on world's most comprehensive governmental anti-trafficking efforts to engage foreign governments on human trafficking. In the TIP Report, the Department of State places each country into one of the three categories of tiers based on their governments' efforts to comply with the 'minimum standards for the elimination of trafficking' found in Section 108 of the Trafficking Victims Protection Act (TVPA) of 2000. This is the first comprehensive federal law to address Trafficking in Persons. The uniqueness of the law is to provide a three-pronged approach of prevention, protection and prosecution in India. In the year 2019, the TIP Report focused on capturing the effective ways of local communities that addressed human trafficking proactively and on how national governments were supporting and empowering them. Although Tier 1 is considered as the highest rank, rather the best category that a country could be in, it does not imply that the country has no problem of human trafficking. These ranks only mean that the governments of that country are addressing the issue of trafficking well. Every year, the governments of each country need to demonstrate that they have made significant progress in tackling the problem and maintaining their ranks. India

---

[2]The Global Report on Crime and Justice published by the United Nations Office for Drug Control and Crime Prevention suggests that although statistics were limited, trafficking in women and children particularly in Asia, Europe and Latin America have increased significantly.

has been put in Tier 2 in the TIP Report of 2019 which is a slight improvement over the last year situation where it was pushed down to Tier 2 watch list. This implies that the Indian government is still in deficit to fully comply with the *Trafficking Victims Protection Act* (TVPA) and does not qualify to the minimum standards for elimination of Trafficking in Persons (TIP 2019). However, such of the countries are also considered in making significant efforts towards bringing themselves into compliance with these standards. However, the dearth and inconsistency in the overall victim identification and protection continue. The government sometimes have been found to be penalizing the victims by arresting them for crimes committed rather than for being victims who are subjected to human trafficking. This is despite the fact that the Ministry of Home Affairs has made its act victim-friendly through Articles 20 and 8 in 2010, which clearly states that the victims be treated as victims and not culprits. Moreover, the government's conviction rates have been abysmally low. So are the number of investigations, prosecutions and convictions in relation to the scale of trafficking happening in India, especially those that come under the cases of bonded and forced labour.

Countries in South Asia share long international boundaries, which have witnessed transnational trafficking movements during last one and a half decade. These countries have common culture and history, and their boundaries are porous; hence, it is difficult to stop illegal movements. The understanding on human trafficking received a further clarity with the adoption of a comprehensive understanding on trafficking at the 'Consultative Meeting on Anti-Trafficking Programs in South Asia' held at Kathmandu in September 2001.

At the intergovernmental level in South Asia, the signing of the SAARC Convention on Combating the Crime of Trafficking in Women and Children for Prostitution by the member countries in January 2002 by all the South Asia governments was a major achievement. This was followed by the Council of Ministers' 23rd Session, in which the amendments to the SAARC convention based on civil society feedback were presented as part of the Secretary General's Report. This process was facilitated by UN Women (formerly known as UNIFEM) under the Regional Anti-Trafficking Program. It signed a MoU with SAARC in 2002, which provided it with the mandate to addressing issues pertaining to women's human rights with SAARC as an institution as also with governments in the region.

South Asia is home to the second largest number of internationally trafficked persons, highest of them belonging to South East Asia (UNFPA 2006). A major source country undoubtedly directs towards Bangladesh. For the purposes of sexual exploitation, involuntary domestic servitude and bondage of debt, the women and children mostly come from Bangladesh. Estimates reveal that every year millions of women and children are trafficked (intra- and cross-border combined) to India alone. In 2008, it was estimated that half of all female sex trafficking victims in South Asia were under the age of 18 years at the time of exploitation (Trafficking in Persons Report 2008). Among all the trafficking victims, it has been found that the majority of the cases were victims of labour trafficking or for sexual exploitation.

Methodology and Field Visit

Researching on human trafficking often brings one to face case studies that seem to be a fiction and too painful to comprehend. However, modern-day slavery are not hidden in some faraway tunnel, but are practiced in broad daylight, exploited in open public spaces and probably within the neighbourhood itself. Forced labour is predictable, and one can easily see them working in factories, agricultural fields, restaurants, homes or simply trapped in a foreign country working in the construction world inside the sea. It is important to create a large-scale awareness among the communities and create an instant Task Force against trafficking. Creating awareness is a preventive measure, and 'prevention is always better than cure'. It is better to have an informed public that ends the demand rather than a public which lacks awareness. Unfortunately, this is a very serious and under-researched topic in the society. Many of us have no idea how worldwide human trafficking works. Human traffickers buy and sell people, unlawfully detaining people for others' use. This in the present times is referred to as modern form of slavery. This is a business with an unending nature of demand worth multi-billion dollars. Importantly, human trafficking can occur anywhere in the world. As stated earlier, this is the third most frequently committed crime worldwide. Moreover, it is illegal to hold persons in an involuntary servitude. Various studies undertaken in South Asia, based upon field visit amply display as to how disaster played an important role in contributing towards human trafficking. Unfortunately there is, however, little empirical research towards an understanding of the link. While several laws, MoUs, protocols and UN conventions keep coming to the forefront, but somewhere there is a disconnect between disaster and human trafficking or this link tends to get undermined while undertaking a research on human trafficking or for disaster risk reduction strategies.

The present study aims to highlight the dangers that lurk men, women and children during a disaster and even after a disaster has happened. Before even anyone can realize, the vulnerable, unaware and illiterate people get trafficked away to distant places for being exploited for various purposes. The study attempts to highlight how such a link can be broken and the nexus between the two be arrested so that people and community are aware of the danger and risks that looms large in the air during a disaster and post disaster. The synergy of international framework of actions on disaster and human trafficking needs to be merged for better impact addressing the needy and the vulnerable. Unfortunately, there is a dearth of trafficking data based on empirical studies in general. This becomes even more thinner when trafficking is studied in the context of a disaster. South Asia has been a source, origin and destination for trafficked victims (Dutta et al. 2010). The vulnerable areas are the borders and places which often witness a landslide, earthquake, floods, drought or some natural calamity. Such areas are extremely vulnerable for labour trafficking, trafficking of children and commercial sexual exploitation (CSE) among the women. The existing socio-economic profile of such regions also goes to show how it further enhances the vulnerability of the people especially when a disaster hits the area impacting the region severely. To add fuel to the fire, the cross-border trafficking is governed and bound by different laws across the international borders which results very often in confronting the trafficked victims as culprits and several such people are languishing in the prisons of India, Bangladesh and Pakistan for years on end.

The lack of empirical data has been one of the biggest constraints for analysing and understanding the trend pattern between human trafficking and natural disasters. Several studies undertaken earlier suggest how mass scale women from disaster hit areas land up in the brothels or how large number of people get trafficked as forced labour to faraway destinations without any social security measures or without the support of their near and dear ones around.

Studies exclusively on human trafficking or disaster mitigation and risk reduction do exist, but there are hardly any studies which study the link between the two and address the issues that arise out of the link. This is an area where institutions and civil society organizations play a significant role. They need to be in a compatible mode supporting each other rather than in competition with each other. The gaps between the two need to be identified and studied in order to implement a proper policy framework wherein institutions and CSOs can work in connivance with each other. Their roles are crucial in combatting human trafficking especially when disaster strikes. The present study attempts to highlight the interlinks between disaster and human trafficking. It is an attempt to understand how disaster mitigation and human trafficking can supplement and complement each other in the establishment of preventive and protective measures. The present research attempts to study the gaps in the overlapping areas between disaster and trafficking and attempts to highlight their links through field-based experiences in South Asia particularly in the Indian context.

The Hyogo Framework of Action was established in 2005, for a period of ten years followed by the Sendai Framework of Action in 2015 over the next fifteen years. It is important to relate these with the Palermo Protocol on trafficking, which was formed in the year 2000. Individual Protocol and Framework of Action have their own strength, but the implementation will hold better when the synergy of all these actions is compatible with each other and is put together in addressing the overlapping areas. This would help in putting together a strategy which is not only need-based but context and area-specific as well. It is important to weave together the synergy among these protocols within the perspective of the present development agenda of Sustainable Development Goals (SDGs). Since a large proportion of trafficking happens for labour and commercial sexual exploitation, the present study will therefore focus mostly on these two types of trafficking.

In order to study the role of institution and civil society organizations, a field visit was undertaken in the month of November 2018. Kolkata in West Bengal was chosen for the field visit. West Bengal was chosen for the field visit due to a number of reasons. According to the National Crime Record Bureau (NCRB) report, West Bengal had recorded the maximum number of trafficked victims and also the maximum number of rescues. This however does not mean that trafficking is less in other parts of the country, but it could also suggest that the reporting procedures have been more regular and prompt in West Bengal. In addition, West Bengal is also located adjacent to Bangladesh which is a source for trafficked victims in terms of both labour and sexual exploitation. From previous studies, it is clear that there is a high concentration of non-governmental organizations that are located in and around Kolkata itself. This becomes helpful for understanding the collaboration between the government and the non-government organizations without wasting much time in travelling from one place to another. West Bengal has also been vulnerable in terms of natural hazards, like floods. Every year, the occurrence of floods has been a catalyst to trafficking of women and girls. There are studies (Dutta et al. 2010) which have reported how girls within a particular age group land up from Murshidabad to the brothels of Sonagachi in Kolkata. It is important to interview the stakeholders concerned so that policy decisions are not a stand alone independent initiatives for disaster mitigation and human trafficking. They need to stay in compliance with each other.

The present research purports to provide guidelines for NGOs and communities which are need-based, area-specific and context-specific.

The present research attempts to probe the following pertinent questions:

- Which are the vulnerable areas of human trafficking in India?
- Are these areas similar to the disaster-prone areas?
- What would be an estimate of the magnitude of human beings trafficked during/post-disaster? To what extent the post-disaster data reflects the extreme vulnerability of the trafficked victims?
- How does the lack of coordination between institutions and the civil society organizations affect human trafficking in disaster-prone areas?
- Which stakeholders are concerned and responsible in implementing the policies and laws of human trafficking during a disaster?
- Do the policy recommendations provide sustainable solutions to the problem keeping the SDGs in mind?

The premise of the study is based upon the belief that an 'absence of community participation in the decision-making bodies does create a disconnect in the successful implementation of policy decisions'. In addition, the existing 'inter-regional laws on human trafficking and disaster mitigation are fuzzy and create much confusion and delay in the repatriation process of the victims, resulting in a discontinuity and deficit in addressing the issues of cross-border trafficking'. The methodology adopted includes a detailed literature review from secondary sources of information that identifies the vulnerable areas of the country which are not in compliance with the Sendai Framework of Action, 2015, and the Disaster Management Act, 2005. Despite innumerous CSOs and NGOs working in this area, there exists a serious deficit in terms of coordination and monitoring of the implementation processes and institutional mechanisms that clearly lack an involvement of the CSOs. The secondary sources of information, throws light on the magnitude and interlinks between disaster and human trafficking, the policies and protocols, and the crucial role played by community and institutions. It further identifies the origin, destination and some of the routes of human trafficking besides the important stakeholders concerned. Some important studies (both published and unpublished) will be considered for an initial understanding of the issue (Dutta 2011b, Dutta et al. 2010). The entire approach of the present study has been summarized in Table 1.1:

Table 1.1 Indicators of research parameters for disaster and human trafficking

S. no.	Parameters	Indicators
1	Desk review based on thematic classification	• Disaster and human trafficking—the interlinks • Disaster risk reduction and human trafficking—policies and protocols • Community participation and institutional support
2	Identification of vulnerable areas	• Disaster-prone areas • Human trafficking (origin, route and destination) • Cross-border trafficking
3	Identification of important stakeholders	• Victims • Government officials/SDMA/DDMA/BSF/SSB • Local governance/Panchayat members • Media networks • Community members • CSOs, NGOS and GOs
4	Field Visit Survey	• NGOs, CSOs, victims, communities and the local vigilance committees created by NGOs • Whether the interventions were appropriate—need-based and context-specific • Identification of gaps and challenges
5	Lessons learned	• Based on experiences of victims • Quick and effective dissemination process • Awareness generation initiatives • Continuity in joint programmes of institutional implementation and NGOs activities
6	Policy recommendations	• Protective and preventive outcomes within the framework of Sendai Framework of Action

It was important to rely on field visit experiences for the lack of authentic data availability. Therefore, the study relies on a series of field visits undertaken earlier as well as the last field visit undertaken in November 2018. The latest field visit of 2018 was undertaken in order to understand the role of institutions and the civil society organizations and the procedures adapted for disaster risk reduction in combatting human trafficking. The rationale for selecting Kolkata for field visit has already been explained earlier. It was important to observe the institutional mechanisms in operation within the state for rescuing the trafficked victims. The survey also included a focused group discussion of 22 women victims who worked in the brothels of Kolkata and had been trafficked for commercial sexual exploitation. The field study aimed to identify gaps existing in the implementation processes. A majority of the concerned stakeholders from the government and non-government organizations were interviewed directly or through focused group discussion. Some of the critical stakeholders interviewed in the field have been displayed in Annexure No V.

The interview with stakeholders was extremely significant in understanding the chaos that sometimes gets created as a result of misunderstanding between the governmental and the non-governmental organizations. The border areas are the most vulnerable whether it is a preventive, a protective or a rehabilitation measure that is being implemented. Due to existence of fuzzy legal procedures on both sides of the border, victims sometimes get doubly penalized from either side of the border. Long waiting time for clearance of bureaucratic hurdles and red tapism too scuttles the prospects of the victims' repatriation process and sometimes even gets trafficked back into the hell as the traffickers are only waiting to capture the vulnerable, tired and gullible people, who give up all hopes of ever getting repatriated. This survey is based on qualitative detailed interviews held with the various government and the non-governmental organizations.

The main objective of the qualitative survey was to capture the causes, consequences and impact factors. The major types of trafficking prevalent in the region were also assessed. The mitigation factors through interviews were deliberated upon, and gaps were identified as to how it helps the traffickers to exploit men, women and children in the first place. Based on these gaps, the major places of origin, destination and the routes through which trafficking takes place in the disaster-prone areas were identified. The field survey through the interviews of stakeholders focused on how disasters impacted differently on men, women and children among people belonging to the lower socio-economic background. The discussion with stakeholders revealed how the laws operating on both sides of the borders at times create conflicting situation and how the international laws have hardly been in compliance with the local laws. They more often seem to be in conflict with each other. There remains a deficit in the understanding process creating more confusion in the repatriation process.

The focused group discussion with the trafficked women victims in Sonagachi area of Kolkata revealed how women who were migrating in search of livelihood options during floods got trafficked and became a prey in the hands of the traffickers for commercial sexual exploitation. Such examples were also found earlier from studies undertaken by UN Women (Dutta et al. 2010). It corroborates how the macro-level data fits into the micro-level scenario. Areas such as Murshidabad in West Bengal, Kishanganj in Bihar, the Indo-Nepal and Indo-Bangladesh border areas and a few other extremely vulnerable areas clearly show how trafficking was carried on during and post-disaster. The focused group discussions, interviews and detailed survey in the brothels of Sonagachi among the trafficked women victims and the second-generation 'at-risk' children revealed the huge exposure of human rights abuse that they faced.

Information collected from the stakeholders had to be authenticated through triangulation and validation of data. The focused group discussion held among the trafficked victims with the help of NGOs clearly revealed why and how the age-specific sex ratio in certain disaster-prone areas depleted and gradually got enhanced as the age group started to increase. The field visit also attempted to understand whether the instruments of disaster mitigation were in sync and effective with the activities undertaken by the help of civil society organization and NGOs. This would lead to establishing effective preventive and protective measures with positive outcomes. The lessons learnt from the experiences of the trafficked victims before and after a disaster will go a long way for policy recommendation. Some simple statistical tools like tabulation and graphical representation of data were utilised to analyse the trend patterns and magnitude of trafficked victims.

Disaster and Human Trafficking—Interlinks

Human trafficking thrives mostly in almost all the vulnerable areas. These may be poverty stricken areas, or where the population belonged to a lower status of the socio-economic profile, lacked awareness, were mostly illiterate or were located in a disaster-prone area. When a disaster happens, it hits those the most who are from a low socio-economic profile. The impact may lead to completely different outcomes even though the communities may be demographically homogeneous. It is the most vulnerable groups that tend to suffer the maximum. Research (Miko 2007; Finn 2016; Dutta 2015) further authenticates facts that disasters only make it doubly sure for more hardships and increase in exploitation and gender inequality, thus creating worse situations worser specially for the women. As a result, targets get created where exploitation and forced labour and slavery are easily enforced (CdeBaca 2010). Such a situation aids traffickers to flourish under an environment of weak law enforcement measures and extreme economic hardship (Finn 2016). The United Nations International Strategy for Disaster Reduction (UNISDR) aims to offer a clear guidance for gender mainstreaming under their policy in situations of disaster risk reduction (DRR). A set of actions required to implement the Hyogo Framework for Action (HFA) have been detailed out in subsequent sections. The present UN Office for Disaster Risk Reduction (UNDRR) (formerly known as the UNISDR) is the pivotal point of the United Nations system for disaster risk reduction. Besides, it is the custodian of the Sendai Framework and has been supporting countries and societies in implementation, monitoring and review of progress. It is well known that disaster risk reduction (DRR) aims in reducing the damage caused by natural hazards like earthquakes, floods, droughts and cyclones, through a series of preventive measures. The magnitude of the impact that a hazard creates on the society and the environment determines a disaster's severity. The impact gets manifold based on the choices we make for our lives and for our environment. Any DRR policy necessarily includes subjects like disaster management, mitigation and preparedness, notwithstanding that DRR is an integrated part of the sustainable development. Reducing disaster risk is essential for development activities to be sustainable. Contrarily, an unsound development policy will only enhance the disaster risks and eventually disaster losses. Every part of society, every government and every part of the professional and private sector form the intrinsic core of any DRR policy (UNISDR).

The potential contributions of a woman towards disaster risk reduction are overbearing around the world, but they are often overlooked and female leadership in building community resilience to disasters is frequently disregarded. Several organizations (UNDP, IUCN and UNISDR) have now come together to synergize their effort towards this regard. The World Health Organization (WHO) has also expressed concern over the vulnerabilities especially when children get separated from their families and livelihood options for men and women start to deplete during a disaster creating an ideal situation for the traffickers. Traffickers wait for such opportunities and get tempted to specially target children orphaned or separated from their families, women in distress or even the men who are in search of livelihood options during a disaster. Such cases are rampant and frequently witnessed in countries that have been often hit by natural calamity impacting the most vulnerable sectors of the society such as migrants, job seekers and the poorer families. Several studies and field-based research undertaken earlier show how Maldives, Tajikistan, Nepal, India, Bangladesh and other parts of the world have been a victim of sexual exploitation, labour trafficking, agricultural worker and domestic servitude during a natural disaster. These have been explained in the subsequent chapters. The negative impact of a trafficked victim lasts for a lifetime as compared to property damaged or even lives lost.

Disasters and human trafficking do not confine to the administrative borders, rather spills much beyond. Studies (Dutta 2011b; Samuels 2015) show that whenever there occurs a civil war or a natural calamity resulting in disasters, ethnic conflict, political instability or any unpredictability, the traffickers make the most out of such a situation. The best time for the traffickers to 'make hay while the sun shines' is a period when people are the most vulnerable. The more the community is unprepared, the better it is for the traffickers. Poverty, natural calamity, epidemic, despair, war, crisis and ignorance all add fuel to the fire resulting in enhancement of human trafficking (Miko 2007). Any disaster thus will only pave a smooth path for the traffickers. Although disasters do not discriminate among people, it exacerbates the pre-existing vulnerabilities which are often ignored in the disaster risk reduction policies. One such vulnerability leads to human trafficking. The already existing socio-economic conditions imply that disasters can lead to different outcomes even for demographically similar communities. Nonetheless, the most vulnerable groups suffer the maximum.

Human trafficking is among the top three biggest criminal enterprises in the world. It follows drug trafficking and counterfeiting which are the other two largest criminal activities. Even in terms of organized crime, human trafficking also ranks third in the que after drugs and arms smuggling. This is evident that human trafficking is no doubt a gross violation of human rights. Victims suffer from not only physical and mental abuse but social stigmatization lifelong. They become isolated and lonely. They are completely detached from their former lives and families. Generally, trafficking is a destabilizing factor for any development efforts, instead of raising social and health costs. Today, trafficking of women and children is a major challenge for the international agencies and the United Nations to tackle. It is a root cause and is an indicator displaying poverty and human deprivation. However, there are always challenges and gaps in terms of participatory democracy and governance that are encountered in fulfilling an agenda. This is particularly so, in fulfilling the subgoals of developing efficient, effective, accountable and transparent institutions at all levels. Thus, it is of importance to ensure ushering in an approachable, inclusive, participatory and demonstrative decision-making process at all levels. Over the years following the Palermo Protocol to human trafficking in 2000, it has been observed that disaster not only plays havoc on the lives of human beings but impacts the people disproportionately. This results in an enhancement in the magnitude of human trafficking particularly from the most vulnerable areas.

Communities get largely marginalized due to lack of awareness and improper dissemination process of developmental policies and schemes. It was not until 2005 that the Disaster Management Act (DMA) came out with its policies, plans and guidelines for disaster management ensuring an appropriate and timely response to disaster. The Act led to the establishment of the National Disaster Management Authority (NDMA). Every state had its own State Disaster Management Authority (SDMA), and every district had its own District Disaster Management Authority (DDMA). Additionally, the National Disaster Response Force (NDRF) was particularly created for handling a threatening disaster situation. For addressing the disaster mitigation at various levels, the National Institute of Disaster Management (NIDM) got established which was to mandate funds for such a situation. However, the DMA has not been proactive and has been slow and slack in its implementation process. At the global level, the Hyogo Framework for Action (HFA) was adopted in 2005, and global reports suggest that countries and relevant stakeholders acknowledge that some success was achieved in terms of reducing disaster risk at various levels such as the local, national, regional and global levels, thus leading to a decrease in mortality during hazards. Undoubtedly, the HFA has been attested as an important device for raising public awareness and institutional changes. This has generated political commitment and brought about appropriate actions by a wide range of stakeholders at all levels. This is so, while simultaneously a heavy toll due to disasters continued. As a result, the well-being and safety of persons, communities and countries have been affected.

An estimate suggests that over 700 thousand people lost their lives. The injured were to the tune of more than 1.4 million, and around 23 million people became homeless due to disasters. It has been estimated that more than 1.5 billion people on the whole have been impacted in some way or the other. Disasters have hit women, children and people disproportionately in various vulnerable situations. As far as the total economic loss is concerned, it is estimated to be more than $1.3 trillion. Between the years 2008 and 2012, there were about 144 million people who got displaced due to disasters (UN 2015). This figure excludes another 21 million people (IFRC 2014) which is a rough estimate of those that have been trafficked during a disaster. Field-based studies suggest that this is only the tip of the iceberg.

Based on the experience gained through the implementation of the Hyogo Framework for Action, the states at local, national, regional and global levels felt an urgent need for focused action within and across the sectors. There were four priority areas that were identified:

- Understanding the concept of disaster risk

- Bolstering disaster risk governance to run disaster risk programmes effectively
- Capitalizing in resilience building for disaster risk reduction
- Boosting the disaster preparedness for an effective response and 'Build Back Better' through the three 'R's that is revival, rehabilitation and restoration.

The Sendai Framework for Disaster Risk Reduction, 2015–2030, thus came along outlining the above four priorities. The main objective is to achieve a substantial reduction in terms of disaster risk and losses in lives. This is to be accomplished within the economic, physical, social, cultural and environmental assets of persons and businesses among the communities and countries in the next 15 years. The current framework will apply to all kinds of risks whether it is a small-scale or the large-scale disasters. It may be the frequent and the infrequent, sudden types or the slow—onset disasters that are caused by natural or man-made hazards. It also includes the technological and biological hazards and risks too. It necessarily targets to monitor and supervise at all levels, the multi-hazard management of disaster risk within and across all sections.

Magnitude of Human Trafficking

Each and every instance of human trafficking takes a common toll. Each crime is an insult to the basic ideals of human dignity, inflicting grievous harm not only to the individuals concerned but also to their near and dear ones within the communities. According to Ambassador Richmond, 'If it were possible to hold human trafficking up to a light like a prism, each facet would reflect a different version of the crime, distinct in context but the same in essence' (Annexure No III, TIP Report 2019). When studied in totality, they reflect a wide range of methods that the traffickers use to coerce both the grown-ups and children from all genders, belonging to any and every education level, nationalities, immigration status, in terms of licit as well as illicit segments. Sometimes, the coercer may be a close family member, a recruiter, employer or simply strangers who exploit vulnerability of any kind forcing the victims to engage in commercial sex or cheat them into forced labour or for their personal gain. These crimes are committed through well-developed plans that take victims miles away from their dwellings or even sometimes within the same neighbourhoods especially among the children who are born there itself. For centuries and decades on end, millions of men, women and children ventured to newer pastures, from various parts of the world, sometimes even daring to migrate to another country without proper documents. They may be driven due to poverty, social exclusion, disaster hit or even as a result of a civil unrest. Their only goal at that point of time is how to survive and earn a livelihood for their family members. Many a times, these journeys end tragically, sometimes even disproportionately (particularly for women and children), if they happen to become a prey for the eagerly awaiting traffickers.

Estimating the magnitude of trafficked victims is hard to come by, and most of the studies are based on qualitative research such as case studies and micro-level research. Estimates therefore need to be taken with a pinch of salt. As per one estimate (USAID 2019), traffickers at present rob a population to the tune of 24.9 millions in the world from their freedom and basic human dignity. Other estimates (IFRC 2014) suggest around 21 million are victims of people trafficked and modern-day slavery. Another global estimate (ILO 2019) puts the figure at 40.3 million victims who are trapped in modern-day slavery. There are 5.4 victims of modern slavery for every 1000 people in the world. Out of these, 24.9 million were trafficked for labour exploitation, while another 15.4 million were trafficked for forced marriage. Women and girls constitute around 71% of the trafficked victims around the world with only 29% being the men and boys. It also states that about 75% (30.2 million) are aged 18 or older, with the number of children under the age of 18. This implies almost 25% (10.1 million) are the children below 18 years in age. Almost 37% of the trafficked victims for forced marriage happened to be children. Moreover, 21% of the victims of sexual exploitation were children.

UN Women's anti-trafficking programme in South Asian region had begun in 2000 (under the name of UNIFEM) to promote preventive, protective and rehabilitation measures for combating trafficking. UNIFEM's programme synchronized with the launching of the Millennium Development Goals (MDGs) adopted by 189 nations in the year 2000. In corroboration to MDG's mandate for ensuring gender equality and empowerment, UNIFEM initiated a broad range of programme to combat 'violence against women' (VAW). Under such a programme, the anti-trafficking measures in South Asian region aimed to promote policy advocacy with the regional governments and multi-stakeholder partnerships suitably addressing the issue of trafficking.

Trafficking in women and children is reported to be on the rise in South Asia and its neighbouring regions. Studies suggest 150,000 trafficked victims are from South Asia alone and 225,000 are from South East Asia. As per the TIP Report, the Government of India officially abolished bonded labour in 1976, but the system of forced labour continues. 'For example, under one scheme prevalent in granite quarries in India, quarry owners offer wage advances or loans with exorbitant interest rates, trapping workers in debt bondage—in some cases for their entire lives' (Annexure No III, TIP 2019). The region of South Asia has been a source, origin and destination for trafficking at vulnerable points such as the borders where trafficking of women and children are most common.

The interlinks between disaster and human trafficking have been mostly a neglected field of research. It is amply clear that a natural disaster can increase both physical and economic insecurities. At the same time, it may disproportionately impact the most vulnerable sectors of society. This includes the migrant labourers, women, children, job seekers and poorer families. Disasters therefore have the potential to create not only targets for exploitation but enslavement as well (CdeBaca 2010). It helps in making situations easier for victims to become a prey in the hands of traffickers. There has not been much attention to this important link between disaster and its impact on human trafficking. Fortunately, over the recent years the concern for this neglected field of research is growing. It is being more and more realized as to how traffickers wait for such opportunities and get tempted specially to target an orphaned child or children separated from their families, women in distress or even the men who are in search of livelihood options during a disaster. Such cases are rampant and frequently witnessed in countries that are often hit by natural calamity.

An absence of poor law implementation or even an absence of laws and lack of governance adds further to the deteriorating situation. Hazards when combined with poor implementation of laws lead to a disaster! Borders and boundaries go unrecognized. They remain as mute spectators displaying the fragments of destruction in the region's 'once upon a time' vibrant ancient history, geography and culture. The more the community is unprepared, the better it is for the traffickers. Poverty, natural calamity, epidemic, despair, war, crisis and ignorance are all recognized as adding fuel to the fire resulting in human trafficking (Miko 2007). Disaster and human trafficking are closely related, but when it comes to research and actions they seem to be studied independently. They seem like parallel lines working irrespective of each other with no common objective. Research in disaster and human trafficking complements each other rather than supplementing the cause. They are studied in a world of their own completely oblivion of the synergy of risks and danger that loom large over the community. Studied as a stand-alone subject, it defeats the very purpose of addressing the issue of human security, human rights and human trafficking. The UN protocols, conventions and MoUs need to synergize their efforts towards this grey area and address the links between the two.

According to the US Department of State, the 2010 earthquake in Haiti and the 2016 Hurricane Matthew, traffickers laid a trap to kidnap orphans for illegal adoptions. They forced the impoverished children to work in domestic bondage in families. Exploitation was at its peak during the drought of 2011 and famine in the Horn of Africa as well as during the 2013 typhoon in the Philippines.

In South Asia, many of the jails of India, Bangladesh and Pakistan are full of such trafficked victims who are not claimed by anyone as in most cases their families back home are eliminated in disasters or are untraceable. Studies and field-based research (Dutta 2011c; Dutta et al. 2010) show how Maldives, Tajikistan, Nepal, India, Bangladesh, Sri Lanka and other parts of the world have been a victim of sexual exploitation, labour trafficking, agricultural workers and domestic servitude during a natural disaster.

In Maldives, there were several hundred men who were trafficked from Rajasthan and other parts of India to undertake construction work to rebuild the country that was devastated after tsunami struck in 2004. These men were trapped, and during their interview they revealed their state of affairs and were desperate to return home. The after-effects of the trauma last a lifetime as compared to property damaged or even lives lost. Maldives is a typical example of labour trafficking following the disaster of tsunami where one-third of the entire population consists of immigrants mostly from India and Bangladesh and partly from Sri Lanka. The contribution of migrant workers in the development of Maldives post-tsunami has been significant in the sectors of education, tourism, health, construction and aviation. In 2010, the data on immigration by the Immigration Office in Maldives showed a total of 87,178 legal migrant workers, 30,000 illegal migrant workers, 10,000 undocumented workers, 18,233 new expatriate employees and 35,710 on re-entry work visa permits. Field study showed (Dutta 2011c) that unfortunately many of the legal migrants become illegal overnight due to their vulnerable conditions where workers are not paid for days on end and they are forced to take up illegal work for their survival. There is clear evidence of such trends being repeated again and again based on various case studies and field-based research. It may be recollected how in 2004, following the tsunami, voices were raised by several non-governmental organizations expressing concerns and reports stating trends of vulnerability to sexual violence, abusive violent behaviour and trafficking (Miko 2007). It is crucial that the facts behind the phenomenon need to be understood in order to grasp and respond to the magnitude of this issue. A clear understanding helps in developing sustainable projects mostly for curative and preventive measures, as well as for rehabilitation and re-integration of the trafficked victims.

The 2004 Indonesian tsunami left 35,000 children without one or both parents. Authorities in Aceh had banned children from leaving the province unless they were with a proper family member who could be verified in order to guard against predators. Again the Palu earthquake and tsunami that hit Palu in Central Sulawesi of Indonesia in September 2018 resulted in a death toll of 4340 people. Cases of child trafficking were confirmed by several organizations and NGOs. Children who lost both their parents' life was a day-to-day struggle. The United Nations Children's Fund and the International Organization for Migration (IOM) have confirmed cases of child trafficking. Some of the non-governmental organizations expressed suspicion as well especially when the couple were not consistent in their story as to where the child was being taken.

Similarly, studies (Dutta et al. 2010) undertaken earlier suggest how mass scale women from Murshidabad, West Bengal, land up in the brothels of Sonagachi in Kolkata during floods every year. Macro-level data shows (Census of India 2001) that the age-specific sex ratio for a particular age group 10–24 was alarmingly low in districts such as Murshidabad, Kishanganj and a few others in the Indo-Nepal border areas in comparison with the other age groups. This fact got further attested from the primary survey in the Sonagachi brothels. The victims revealed that every women trafficked to Sonagachi eventually brought a friend along and the process continued. Thus, the micro-level field visits corroborated the macro-level data depicting why the age-specific (10–24 years) sex ratio was low in these districts as displayed in the Census of India, 2001. As the age group was enhanced, the sex ratio also increased accordingly.

In Bangladesh, the return of 120, 4–5-year-old children who were trafficked to UAE as camel jockey were being repatriated. This was a horrendous scene. They had been trafficked for the purposes of entertainment and hardly remembered their parents' details or where they belonged to (Dutta et al. 2010). Such children had injury marks all over as a result of their fall from the camel's back during the sports event. The trauma was large and loud on their faces, and they all huddled up together in a corner of the room not touching a single toy that was there to entertain them.

Trafficking is surely an outcome during and post-disaster. Though closely related, the two issues are so apart. They seem like parallel lines complementing each other. They are usually studied in a world of their own completely oblivion of the synergy of risks and danger that loom large over the two. The several UN protocols, conventions and MoUs need to synergize their efforts towards this grey area and address the links between the two. Unfortunately, this important interlink between disaster and human trafficking has been mostly a neglected field of research.

The need of the hour is to incorporate all international treaties into one disaster law. The existing municipal laws of countries providing guidelines for mitigation, protection, rescue and rehabilitation will all merge under the said law and help in guiding the implementation of strategies. The 'International Disaster Response Law is found in treaties, municipal law and regulations. Its development is facilitated through resolutions adopted by the International Conference of the Red Cross and Red Crescent, the UN, other intergovernmental organizations and learned societies, and through public and private codes and standards adopted to guide humanitarian action' (IFRC 2003). The Disaster Management Act of India forms the fortification of the disaster response law (Dutta and Kamthan 2017). Thus, the disaster response law scope is much wider than merely those laws which directly relate to disasters. Although not specified clearly, several other laws remain hidden within its framework that can be applicable under different circumstances depending on the nature and depth of the natural disaster.

'A gender perspective should be integrated into all disaster risk management policies, plans and decision-making processes, including those related to risk assessment, early warning, information management and education and training' (UNISDR 2005–2015). The UN General Assembly's 23rd Session was entitled 'Women 2000: Gender equality, development and peace for the twenty-first century'. It called for an approach of disaster prevention, mitigation and recovery strategies and natural disaster assistance that were gender-sensitive in nature. This was adopted by the UNISDR.

It was conspicuous that the Disaster Management Act of 2005 had unfortunately not even mentioned the word 'women' or 'gender'. Unfortunately, the special needs of women tend to get ignored in the absence of gender-specific post-disaster studies. Although the topic of gender mainstreaming is now very much a part of the disaster discourse, it remains far from being represented in strategy formulation. Gender still does not form part of neither the mainstream disaster risk reduction nor the response practices (Bradshaw and Fordham 2013). Even today, cultural practices sanctioned by the society force the girls to either be owned as the property of the rich men or become a petty wage earner for her family through prostitution.

Among human trafficking, labour trafficking constitutes the largest proportion of all cases of human trafficking followed by commercial sexual exploitation. Most of the studies however focus on sexual exploitation. Despite the existence of several field-based authentic sources on disaster and human trafficking, there continues to be a deficit of empirical data on trafficking in disaster-prone areas, neither before, during nor after a disaster. This creates a big hurdle in constructing policy strategies.

Violence Against Women (VAW)

Trafficking, in fact, has been an issue of concern within the development sector for the past years. The UN Conferences of the 1990s and developments ever since have attempted to cement the issue of gender equality. The Vienna Declaration of 1993 and Programme of Action have both declared unequivocally affirming that the human rights of women must be protected. The 1994 International Conference on Population and Development also recognized the inextricable links of violence against women to reproductive health and rights.

One of the most critical developments has been the focused attention on the issue of trafficking in the Beijing Plus 5 agenda. In 1995, the UN Fourth World Conference on Women in Beijing generated renewed commitment towards issues of inclusion, gender equality and women's human rights from the international community. These changes have further put increased pressure on development agencies. Appropriate policies in the normative and policy environment for gender equality were developed. Resource allocation and accountability for demonstrating progress in the areas of violence against women were made mandatory. The international discourse for increasing human rights-based approaches to development offered hope that women's inequality and violence issues will get targeted. The changing social, political and power structures of inequality, exclusion and oppression were the processes that were expected to bring about such a change. Rights-based approaches recognized women as 'claim-holders' and establish duties or obligations for those against whom a claim could be made.

The UN International Day for the Elimination of Violence against Women was designated in the year 1999 on 25 November. This was of a major significance. It was here that the UN adopted the document entitled 'Women 2000: gender quality, development and peace for the twenty-first century'. Violence against women especially human trafficking was clearly spelled out along with the action needed to address the challenge. In the year 2000, another important Convention against Transnational Organized Crime got adopted in November by the United Nations. It had incorporated two more optional protocols which were of significance. The two optional protocols were important for countries to undertake measures at length for combatting not only smuggling of migrants but also trafficking of women and children. Thus, the protocol, namely '*Prevent, Suppress and Punish Trafficking in Persons*', became one of the first to have addressed Trafficking in Persons of women and children. Based on the in-depth understanding of the term trafficking, this got adopted in a comprehensive manner with its multiple dimensions.

The passing of the 'Victims of Trafficking and Violence Protection Act of 2000' was an equally important development contributing to the issue of trafficking by the US Senate. The reviewing of progress on anti-trafficking initiatives on a regular basis became easier. It provided an assessment framework for multiple agencies to address trafficking in the global process. The report on Trafficking in Persons (TIP) is produced annually by the US government. It relies on inputs given by the government and civil society organization and the actions that each country has initiated to combat trafficking. Different categorizations in terms of 'tiers' are allocated to the countries based upon the interventions taken by the governments concerned for combatting the problem of trafficking. A significant advocacy event in the Asia-Pacific region has been the Asia Region Initiative Against Trafficking of Women and Children. This was held at Manila in March 2000. It provided a platform for sharing expertise and experiences and designing collaborative efforts to address trafficking. Significant influence has been noticed on the global trends for aid modalities. The Paris Declaration on Aid Effectiveness (2005)[3] has been instrumental in harmonizing approaches. Optimal efficiency and effectiveness of investments towards addressing violence against women are now ensured.

The 2000 UN Millennium Declaration geared up to fight all forms of violence against women. Subsequently, the first ever 2004 Security Council Open Debate held at the 2005 World Summit devoted exclusively to sexual and gender-based violence in conflict and post-conflict situations. Finally, the momentous Security Council Resolution of 1820 got adopted in June 2008. The UN Women's (formerly known as UNIFEM) anti-trafficking programme in the South Asian region began in 2000 to address the political, social, economic and severe human rights violation challenges leading to human trafficking of girls and women. Addressing trafficking was the major way of programming on violence against women (VAW) in the region. Initially, trafficking was basically considered as a simple crime issue by most agencies. Gradually, realization dawned that it was an outcome the existing structural gender inequalities that pushed women into the excluded and discriminated groups in the region. The programme started on a plane where there were ambiguity, mistrust and divergence of actions. Issues of primary concern at the start of the programme in 2000 were national government's indifference and denial of the existence of human trafficking, ineffective implementation of the existing legal systems and rise in transnational human trafficking magnitude among South Asian countries, particularly for sexual exploitation of girls aged below 18 years. 'Governments were in denial to accept human trafficking. There was even neglect when it comes to either reporting on or prosecuting cases of human trafficking'. The immediate task was to act as a catalyst for

- Enhancing research, information systems and data base on different aspects of trafficking
- Strengthening legal and policy frameworks especially improves legal perspectives and provisions for tackling the transnational trafficking issues
- Policy advocacy and policy planning processes with all stakeholders for enhancing political will and commitment
- Strengthening the lobbying groups working towards advocacy on issues related to trafficking
- Capacity building of groups in prevention, rescue, rehabilitation and prosecution in different areas
- Create awareness about the issue of trafficking at multiple levels of governance

---

[3]https://www.oecd.org/dac/effectiveness/45827300.pdf

- Implement programmes through effective civil society–government and institutional partnerships adding value to the national-level activities
- Rehabilitation and re-integration processes need to be facilitated with community of the survivor victims.

The UN Women had carried out numerous programmes and projects delivering to make a difference to the existing scenario. The beneficiaries of the regional anti-trafficking programmes included:

- Survivors of gender-based violence (trafficking)
- Vulnerable and at-risk communities, especially second-generation potential child victims, children, adolescents and women
- Concerned government departments, especially local government (national and regional)
- Other stakeholders and civil society at large
- Network coalitions
- Mainstream institutions (law institutions, academic institutions, SAARC Secretariat).

The entire conceptualization of the issue of trafficking in women and children is based on the CEDAW, the CRC and the optional protocol and the larger Human Rights-Based Framework. The internal context of UN Women over the past years has characterized a number of corporate initiatives towards ending violence against women through accountability mechanisms like the Beijing Platform for Action (BPFA) and the SAARC. Efforts were made to broaden the base at all levels of different partners that it works with. Besides the traditional partners, women's NGOs, CSOs, other UN agencies and bilateral donors, this was an addition.

The Yokohama Global Commitment 2001 midterm assessment in 2004 on trafficking and commercial sexual exploitation of children provided an opportunity for UN Women to collaborate with other UN agencies, governments and civil society on the issue. It has been playing a greater role in its implementation from January 2005, as chair of the interagency group called South Asia Coordinating Group (SACG) on Action Against Violence. The SACG is supporting the work of the South Asia Forum (SAF), a regional interministerial body formed to respond to the recommendations of the Yokohama MTR and the UN Secretary General's Study on Violence against Children.

The UN Women through the sustained efforts has been instrumental in getting the Asian Development Bank (ADB) involved in addressing the issue of trafficking through their larger economic development programmes in South Asia. This resulted in the ADB sending a mission to South Asia for designing a regional strategy for ADB to provide value-added inputs to ongoing interventions in the region. The ADB mission to South Asia was in collaboration with UN Women (UNIFEM). At the biennial meeting held in Bhutan in 2003, all regional governments, represented by Ministers and Senior Bureaucrats, from South Asia gave their commitment to—*taking forward the SAARC Convention on Trafficking; strengthening processes towards regional, bilateral and national dialogue involving NGOs and initiating legal reforms and promoting technical exchange.*

Policies and Protocols

Some of the international protocols developed such as the Palermo Protocol on trafficking and the MDGs both evolved in the same year in 2000, but these seem to be divergent and apart from each other. The factor of gender equality and empowerment of women have been emphasized in the third goal of MDG and continues to be a focus area under the SDG. The fifth goal under SDG states '*Eliminate all forms of violence against all women and girls in the public and private spheres, including trafficking and sexual and other types of exploitation*'. Subsequently after five years, in 2005 the Disaster Management Act and the Hyugo Framework of Action were also formulated, followed by the Sendai Framework of Action in 2015–2030. It is important that these protocols be developed in a manner such that there is a connect among them and can strengthen from the synergy of each other. Individual Protocols and Framework of Action have their own strength, but the synergy of all these become stronger in addressing the overlapping areas. It becomes a need-based strategy which is area and context-specific as well. Unless these protocols supplement each other, the main issue remains unanswered. The Sustainable Development Goals (SDGs) on the other hand have emerged as the linking factor among many of the protocols and goals. In fact, the SDG 16, that is, 'Peace, Justice and Strong Institutions', is an important goal which seemed to have been an omission during the MDGs, like that of governance, inclusion, participation, rights and security. SDG 16 seems to be both an end in itself and a crucial part of delivering sustainable development in all countries. It would not be incorrect to state that SDG 16 is the transformational goal and key to ensuring accomplishment of the agenda.

The UNISDR has also expressed concern over vulnerable children especially during a disaster. When children get separated from their families and are left on their own, they become extremely vulnerable. It elaborates about the chaotic environment that gets created in the absence of a humanitarian aid. The system of emergency that follows a disaster can be easily exploited by criminal elements. The sale of children was also noted by the UN Special Rapporteur. It stated that 'the collapse or absence of a state system during and after an emergency will result in a protection vacuum for children who may become separated from their families' (Samuels 2015).

On the other hand, women's potential contributions to the disaster risk reduction are often ignored. Building community resilience to disasters under the female head is frequently disregarded. Several organizations (UNDP, IUCN and UNISDR) have now come together to synergize their effort towards this regard. The World Health Organization (WHO) too expressed apprehension over the vulnerabilities that children face during a disaster. Not only the children but even men and women become vulnerable when livelihood options begin to deplete post-disaster. This creates an ideal situation for traffickers to prey upon. In fact, a 'protection vacuum' gets created particularly for the children (Samuels 2015). The World Health Organization noted that when women's options for a livelihood get restrained like in the case following a disaster they would do anything to feed their young ones. Therefore, sexual exploitation and trafficking are bound to increase (WHO 2005).

The regional programme has been implemented through well-defined, multi-pronged preventive, protective and rehabilitation strategies in the South Asian region to combat trafficking of women and children. The programme adopted a three-pronged strategy to combat trafficking in women and children. It included different types of trafficking such as sex tourism, paedophilia, commercial sexual exploitation and forced labour. Several programmatic outputs were promoted. These mostly belonged to areas of advocacy and lobbying. Besides, it included other areas like creation of a knowledge base, awareness generation and media. The thrust of human rights programming and project initiatives started to get clearly defined through capacity development/networking and piloting best practices. The objectives, thrust and expected outcome have been geared towards achieving the same common goal of reducing weaknesses of women and children in becoming a prey to trafficking and exploitation.

Some of the major strategies from the study (Dutta et al. 2010) show:

- A holistic, process-centric response to address trafficking by understanding and analysing the context, including socio-economic and political environments, in which trafficking occurs after undertaking the relevant research in the countries concerned
- Strengthening community initiatives at the grass-roots level and facilitating capacity building of community groups to create vigilant communities
- Strengthening cross-border vigilance measures to protect vulnerable groups from transnational trafficking
- Engaging with government functionaries at various levels for building institutions for implementing existing legal laws, policy frameworks and regional plans
- Engaging with professionals and other multi-stakeholders in combating trafficking
- Building strong advocacy and lobbying initiatives for accountability of various stakeholders in combating trafficking of women and children
- Engage partner organizations to address the issue of alternative sustainable livelihoods especially introducing new skills among vulnerable groups and victims
- Create opportunities to enable women escape situations of violence against them. This implies creating economic security and autonomy for the women in terms of protection, comprehensive care and access to laws and justice system
- Adopting measures of sustained multifaceted and mutually reinforcing interventions in ushering in changes in discriminatory practices
- Replicating and up-scaling of good practices that helped combat trafficking.

Some of the major perceived outcomes of the regional anti-trafficking programmes of UN Women during the period 2000–2008 were to:

- Validate the human trafficking magnitude and its manifestation analysis through supporting and sponsoring country research studies, so that appropriate strategies

and partnerships with government, NGOs and CBOs are developed to reduce the incidence of trafficking in women and children in South Asia
- Facilitate the work of NGOs/CBOs, government institutions and agencies, and other relevant partner organizations; to develop and implement holistic strategies and programmes to combat human trafficking; and to promote well-defined and multi-pronged strategies for prevention, rescue and rehabilitation in the South Asia region
- Enhance the commitment and institutional capacity of cross-border institutions to rescue trafficked victims before they reach their final destination, through increased engagement of the community and law enforcing agencies
- Reduce the demand for and incidence of sex tourism through increased advocacy, awareness and rescue operations in Goa and decrease the use of Goa as a transit point for traffickers transporting victims to Mumbai
- Several regional forums were formed. These include South Asia Forum against Human Trafficking (SAFAHT), South Asia Professionals against Trafficking (SAPAT) and ATSEC to enable and support activities at all levels. The national, regional and local networks, besides the interchange of available information and experiences, the professional know-hows and deliberations among intra-faith groups all got included
- Development of Regional Resource Centre with a wide collection of information resources on the issue of human trafficking
- Development of website covering the issue of trafficking comprehensively and providing useful links to other important sites.

The United Nations Protocol to Prevent, Suppress and Punish Trafficking in Persons was implemented in December 2003. The response was widespread. By 2008, a large majority of the 155 countries (63%) had passed laws against Trafficking in Persons. All major forms of trafficking had been addressed. In comparison with the year 2003, 2008 was a huge success. In 2003, only one-third of the countries had passed the legislation against human trafficking. The anti-trafficking legislation among the countries more than doubled as compared to 2003, in response to the passage of the protocol. Basic rights such as 'the freedom from coercion at work, the freedom to set up associations and bargain collectively, and the freedom from discrimination at work' gets violated as a result of human trafficking. ILO defines trafficking of children, as one of the worst forms of child labour. This leads to serious impairment in the growth and development of the child mentally and physically.

ILO adopted four core principles in 1998. This is in the ILO Declaration on Fundamental Principles and Rights at Work. Two out of the eight core conventions in their declaration are closely related to the Palermo Protocol (No. 29 on Forced Labour and No. 182 on the Worst Forms of Child Labour) (ILO 2008). Countries ratifying the ILO Forced Labour Convention, 1930, commit 'to suppress the use of forced labour or compulsory labour in all its forms within the shortest possible period'. The term 'forced or compulsory labour' was defined as 'all work or service which is exacted from any person under the menace of any penalty and for which the person has not offered himself voluntarily'. The State Parties to the Convention needed to ensure that ‘the illegal exaction of forced or compulsory labour shall be punishable as a penal offence’ and ‘that the penalties imposed by law are really adequate and are strictly enforced’ (ILO 1930). The ‘Elimination of the Worst Forms of Child Labour, 1999’ mandates ratifying member states to take ‘immediate and effective measures in securing the prohibition and elimination of the worst forms of child labour’ on an urgent basis. The Convention for ‘Suppression of the Trafficking in Persons’ and of ‘Exploitation of the Prostitution of Others (1949)’ has already been ratified by South Asian countries. They include Afghanistan (1985), Bangladesh (1985), India (1953), Pakistan (1952) and Sri Lanka (1958). These countries therefore need to imbibe into their national laws all the provisions stated in the convention for achieving an end to human trafficking.

The National Crime Record Bureau (NCRB) of India has now started to collect information regarding the trafficked victims since 2016. The 2016 Crime in India Report states that some investigations have been taken. Out of a total of 5217 trafficking cases, 587 prosecution cases were complete, while 163 conviction cases and acquittal of 424 individuals had been undertaken in trafficking cases (TIP 2019). However, the position displays a dismal picture of India when it comes to prosecution and conviction rates.

According to Kofi Annan, the former Secretary General of United Nations, a culture of prevention is not easy to build. The costs of prevention are always in the present tense, while benefits are in the future tense. Thus, there is always a mismatch in assessing the cost-benefit analysis. Efforts are on in order to minimize the damages caused by disasters. Despite the involvement of the government and international communities including the donor agencies, several of the disaster management programmes do not become sustainable at the micro-level after the completion of the project. Therefore, the policy decisions for a disaster management need to inculcate community participation as an integral part of policy decisions. Community involvement in terms of partnership, participation, empowerment and ownership is of significance. The basic idea is to make people aware of the post-disaster scenario and how trafficking can start operating even before one can realize it.

The Government of India has come forward with comprehensive laws, covering trafficking offences, together with a range of protection measures and support services for victims/survivors, including establishing a special police, Anti-Human Trafficking Units and/or other prosecution units. The training programme, materials on human trafficking and guidelines for investigation and prosecution are being provided to police and the prosecutors with the help of partner organizations. The adoption of the Palermo Protocol in 2000 did set the ball rolling when the world community got active. More legislation criminalizing all forms of human trafficking, collaboration efforts among the civil society and human trafficking survivors have been introduced ever since. Despite the best efforts, traffickers around the world leave no stone unturned to exploit millions of victims particularly the vulnerable for forced labour and sex trafficking. Although governments continue to bear the primary responsibility for addressing human trafficking, support comes pouring in from the civil society and international organizations who have no doubt significantly contributed towards evolving a more holistic and effective anti-trafficking solution. Not only community participation but enhancing the community preparedness programmes can be introduced at regular intervals as an advance capacity of a community to respond to the consequences of an adverse event so that people know what to do and where to go if a warning is issued or when a hazard is ensuing.

The role of community participation and institutions is significant in connecting the top to the bottom. The NGOS, CSOs and government officials need to work in conformity to get the message home! Community-based preventive measures form an integral part of any strategy for eliminating trafficking in women and girls and go a long way in addressing the gendered dynamics of demand at the destinations. This also enables achieving gender equality and women's human rights while eliminating violence against women, stopping of sexual exploitation and forced labour particularly during a disaster as well as post-disaster. Preventive measures highlight the socio-economic and cultural background that makes men, women and children vulnerable in the absence of disaster risk mitigation strategy to being trafficked in the first place. These measures provide a platform for the target group to access the rights-based redressal mechanisms.

India has emerged as one of the biggest source, route and destination country for victims of trafficking. India has ratified the Palermo Protocol, but it did take more than 11 years to do so. India has been in the Tier 2 watch list of the TIP Report and has marginally improved to Tier 2 in 2019. It still has a long way to go although it is making an earnest effort towards this regard. The Government of India also adopted a multi-pronged strategy for preventing and combatting Trafficking in Persons. It has built strong linkages and partnerships involving various stakeholders. They include the civil society organizations, NGOs, international organizations, the corporate sector and many others. This helps in creating an integrated response to combat trafficking especially that of labour and sexual exploitation. The UN with the help of its partner organizations has been actively engaged in implementing programme on anti-human trafficking in areas of vulnerability in India.

The 'Convention on Preventing and Combating Trafficking in Women and Children for Prostitution, 2002' of the South Asian Association for Regional Cooperation (SAARC) has already been ratified by India. The Ministry of Women and Child Development (MWCD) was the nodal agency for SAARC Gender InfoBase in India. Besides, a Central Advisory Committee was also constituted. The Chairperson of this Advisory Committee is the Secretary, Ministry of Women and Child Development. It included members from Central Ministries like the Ministry of Home Affairs, External Affairs, Tourism, Health, Social Justice and Empowerment, Information Technology and Ministry of Law and Justice. This was to help fight the menace of 'trafficking in women and children for commercial sexual exploitation' as well as to rehabilitate the trafficked victims and improve legal and law enforcement mechanisms.

Community Participation

A study (Dutta 2017) undertaken by the UN Women on the community-based preventive measures clearly shows five important subheads. These are 'Awareness and Sensitization', 'Networking, Advocacy and Media', 'Training and Capacity Building', 'Vigilance, Prosecution and Conviction' and the last component being 'Information, Education & Communication (IEC)'. Each category contains further subdivisions which become most effective during and post a disaster. The importance and successful implementation of these has been discussed in detail in later sections. A brief of these have been stated below.

Awareness and Sensitization programme for anti-human trafficking covers a wide range of activities which include information campaigns through publications, airing of radio and television programme, videos, creating websites, screening of films and documentaries, plays, exhibitions, holding of seminars, workshops and lectures, border vigilance lifeguards, organizing camps, formation of pressure groups consisting of adolescents, women and young girls and other programme that target the second-generation victims and the 'at-risk' population. These programmes not only involve stakeholders such as NGOs, Cross-Border Anti-Trafficking Network (CBATN), community-based organizations, Border Security Forces, members of the civil vigilance committees, local leaders, police, district/village officials, teachers and schools but also simultaneously address the marginalized population such as the women and girls belonging to India's most disadvantaged socio-economic strata that are vulnerable to trafficking for commercial sexual exploitation. Those community-based preventive measures that generate awareness and sensitization can be further subdivided into the following categories:

(a) Rallies, campaigns, camps
(b) Research, seminars and workshops
(c) Street plays, puppet shows, films and documentaries
(d) Formation of groups
(e) Second-generation victims, vulnerable people and 'at-risk' population.

Besides the above, it is important that the correct community partners be identified. They must represent a full demographic range of the community. Considering the elements that make a community function on a regular basis such as puja, entertainment, fairs and so on are the best places to continue beyond the event, the community will surely be aware of trafficking and become disaster resilient as well. Many of the successful initiatives have been with the involvement of folk troupes, ventriloquisms, volunteers, fairs, socio-religious platforms and emergency operating centres.

For example, following the Gujarat earthquake in 2001 January, the Patanka New Life (PNY) Plan was initiated. It was a joint initiative of diverse organizations that included not only the government but also the non-governmental organizations, academicians and international organizations for community-based effective rehabilitation. The aim of the initiative was to train and empower the local masons and community members based on local tradition and culture. The proper earthquake-safer technologies were based on these. Ensuring confidence building and long-term use of traditional technologies were emphasized. The local communities are more familiar with knowledge of the local geology, the hazard context and the livelihoods options available. Given this fact, it is essential that the local communities must be involved in disaster management programmes from the initial stages of the project. They need to be supported to develop the capacities and linkages that help them overcome the challenge.

Networking has been found to be an extremely effective tool in addressing cross-border trafficking of women and girls. It contributes significantly to all the measures that are adopted for prevention, protection, rescue and repatriation. Networking has been considered as one of the best means of effective advocacy. A networking initiative is usually considered as a strong representation and one which enjoys the support from the communities they work with. This ushers in urgency among the concerned governments to attend to the issues raised. Donor agencies have the advantage of working with a wider base of NGOs bringing about a stronger impact. A network organization ensures greater effectiveness and efficiency in the use of resources and also in reaching out to the masses.

Training, Capacity building and upgradation of skills are a must where education and training becomes of serious consequences. It is necessary to make available materials for policymakers, administrators, trainers, engineers, etc., in order to achieve the same. Planning for and mitigating against natural disasters have incorporated basic and detailed training modules in disaster preparedness. Training methodologies have been evolved for trainers, community preparedness and manuals for training at district, block, Panchayat and village levels.

The vast nature of activities imparted under training and capacity building involves nearly all major concerned stakeholders ranging from the grass-roots to officials that belong to the decision-making bodies and strategy implementers. Activities include vocational training, skills building, micro-credit and support for formal or non-formal education. It also includes training for awareness generation among the law enforcement and security personnel, parliamentarians, PRIs, bureaucrats and other officials. However, there seems to be a disconnect between the capacity building measures of disaster management and trafficking, while it would be brilliant to combine the two together before being implemented.

Two types of operation are currently in practice—the anti-trafficking training and the capacity building measures. At the grass-roots level, building the capability of different segments of the local communities is addressed. They in turn would be responsible to prevent trafficking at the source itself. On the other hand, the capacity building measures are basically to strengthen the capacity of law enforcement, border control and immigration authorities in apprehending traffickers and rescuing trafficked victims during disasters. The present section can therefore be divided into two categories, (a) capacity building, skill development and livelihood opportunity and (b) policy strategy implementers.

Vigilance, Prosecution and Conviction is an important factor in the study of human trafficking. Justice delayed is justice denied. Without prosecution and conviction, the cases of trafficking become meaningless. Apprehension and prosecution of recruiters/traffickers and brothel owners can be the most important preventive measures. Only such measures can deter the traffickers from any future trafficking. Strengthening the national criminal justice systems has been a major goal for the regional governments and to see that a greater number of convictions are achieved globally. However, the enactment of the law, training of border and law enforcement personnel, and apprehension and prosecution by criminal justice authorities are considered state's responsibility. Hence, these are largely under the purview of the state. They are also expected to act as deterrents to trafficking. So networking with the Border Security Force (BSF), the Sashastra Seema Bal (SSB) and police personnel is expected to translate into active prosecution and conviction rates. The present section has also at least four subsections for a better understanding. These include:

1. Prosecution
2. Conviction
3. AHTU
4. Community surveillance.

In the border areas, several successful case studies show that the civil vigilance committees are extremely effective especially in the Indo-Nepal and Indo-Bangladesh borders. These committee members range from a barber, a tea shop owner, an adolescent school boy and even a stranger who are located at the border and can keeps an eye on all who looked suspicious.

The Ministry of Home Affairs has compiled/prepared a set of resource materials. These were developed by various organizations/institutions for being replicated and disseminated by state governments. This would enable the state governments to activate and strengthen their capacity building and awareness generation. It would help in learning from past experiences including sharing of best practices. The state government could translate the available voluminous material of about 10,000 pages into the local language. This has been divided into 4 broad sections covered under 7 volumes. Depending upon the vulnerabilities, the state government could widely distribute these materials translated in the local language. The various sections covered include education and training; construction toolkit and planning to cope with disasters. It also includes information, education and communication toolkit including multimedia resources on disaster mitigation and preparedness. The planning section contains material for analysing a whole range of mitigation activities. These are assessing community's risk, development of preparedness, mitigation and disaster management plans, coordinating available resources and implementing measures for risk reduction. Besides the model bye-laws, DM policy, act and model health sector are all included into the planning section.

There are other school safety programmes for almost 4105 schools with 130,000 (UNDP India 2009) enrolled school children. In India, the disaster management has been integrated within the education curriculum for middle and higher secondary schools under the Central Board of Secondary Education (CBSE). The Delhi schools are in the process of imbibing their school disaster management plans within their curriculum. Their planned hazard preparedness activities are regularly practised through drills. Even teachers, school managers and education department officials of the CBSE and the state boards participate actively in the extensive disaster management trainings. The state government of Uttar Pradesh have decided to design and construct 80,000 primary and upper primary classrooms. These are to be located in the seismic zones VI, III with earthquake proofed design features. Engineers and architects from government departments are being trained to use earthquake proof designs and codes for construction of new schools and modifying existing school buildings. A model school design guideline is already in place for various seismic zones in India.

The plethora of Information, Education Technology and Communication (IEC) materials which are available in plenty is of immense significance. The IETC strategies have frequently been implemented, targeting individuals, communities and other stakeholders. Several useful knowledge products and resources in the form of films, interactive materials, calendars, puppet shows, *nukkad nataks*, handbooks, CDs, resource materials, ready reckoners, marches, posters, films, training manuals and standard operating procedures for creating effective awareness, investigation and rescue as well as care and attention post-rescue of the victims have been developed. IEC materials have been developed for religious leaders, media sensitization for the print and electronic media. The IEC materials have been distributed at the village level. There are many training modules and other booklets designed and produced by partner organizations in collaboration with Government of India and international donor agencies in order to target stakeholders like police, law enforcing agencies, border security personnel and parliamentarians. Simultaneously, various resource materials are available for the communities, women and girls, at-risk and potentially vulnerable, NGOs/CBOs, 'Panchayats' (members of the local governance) and other stakeholders. These are available in the form of pictorial displays such as posters, banners, wall paintings, music, cassettes, TV/radio talks, cartoon films, dance and so many other displays which are educating and provide information and awareness to the community and the most vulnerable. The entire material under this subhead similarly needs to be categorized into the following segments:

(a) Print
(b) Audio
(c) Audio-visual
(d) Internet.

Although the above parameters show well-planned policies are in place, there seems to be a gap in the implementation of these policies. The understanding of disaster risk is multi-layered with several offshoots. These need to be factored into the planning policies. The policies though well meaning seem to be a stand-alone factor trying to implement without taking into consideration area and context-specific perspectives. They need to be intertwined with human trafficking issues at the grassroots level in order to create the necessary impact. The impacts are not uniformly spread over space, and hence the planning strategy needs to have a thorough understanding of the situational analysis of the region before being implemented. Institutions have a huge role to play, and the vulnerable marginalized communities need to be involved at every stage. The policy framework needs to be intertwined with the initiatives of the civil society organizations who are closest to the vulnerable population. Studies in this regard have so far been few and scanty.

The present study attempts to bring together years of field-based research on various aspects of human trafficking in the context of disaster research under a common roof. Based on the present study, it is important to understand how the role of institution which must be in conformity with the initiatives undertaken by the civil society organizations. Such a study would throw light on the policy building mechanisms for overcoming the vulnerability of men, women and children that become a prey in the hands of the traffickers during and after disasters. This study will be an important contribution to the hitherto slender collection of research on human trafficking and disaster.

References

Bradshaw, S., and M. Fordham. 2013. *Women, Girls & Disasters: A Review for DFsID*. https://www.gov.uk/government/uploads/system/uploads/attachment_dat.

CdeBaca, Luis. 2010. *Best Practices: Human Trafficking in Disaster Zones*, U.S. Department of State, May 24, 2010. https://www.state.gov/j/tip/rls/rm/2010/142160.htm.

Dutta M, et al (2010): Evaluation study undertaken for UNIFEM Regional Anti-trafficking Programme in South Asia, (2000–2009). UNIFEM South Asia Regional Office, New Delhi, February 2010. http://www.unwomensouthasia.org/2012/evaluation-of-regional-anti-trafficking-programme-2000-2009-2/

Dutta, M. 2017. *Trafficking of Women in India—Community Based Preventive Measures*, LAMBERT Academic Publishing, an imprint of OmniScriptum GmbH & Co. KG Bahnhof straße 28, 66111 Saarbrücken, Germany, March 2017, ISBN: 978-3-330-04701-3

Dutta, Mondira, and Manika Kamthan. 2017. Gender and Trafficking in Disaster Law—The Emerging Threshold Edited by Amita Singh. Oxford: Routledge, August, 2017. https://www.routledge.com/Disaster-Law-Emerging-Thresholds/Singh/p/book/9781138036437.

Dutta, Mondira et al. 2010. *Evaluation study on the UNIFEM Regional Anti-trafficking Programme in South Asia, (2000–2009)*. UNIFEM South Asia Regional Office, New Delhi, February 2010. https://www.unwomensouthasia.org/2012/evaluation-of-regional-anti-trafficking-programme-2000-2009-2/.

Dutta, Mondira. (2011a). *India—Afghanistan: Options for Access and Trade*, in 'Central Asia and South Asia, Energy Cooperation and Transport Linkages' Edited by K. Warikoo, Pentagon Press, August 2011, New Delhi. ISBN: 978-81-8274-555-1.

Dutta, Mondira. (2011b). A Study on '*Mapping Vulnerability to Trafficking of Women and Children in India*', sponsored by UN Women and the National Commission for Women, March 2011, UN Women, New Delhi.

Dutta, Mondira. (2011c). *Situation of Human Trafficking in the Maldives—A Rapid Assessment*, sponsored by UN Women and Human Rights Commission, Maldives, May 2011.

Dutta, Mondira. 2015. *Understanding Maldives in the Context of Trafficking*, in Development and Regional Cooperation in Central and South Asia: Euro-Asian Perspectives, Edited By Henrik Berglund, Mondira Dutta & Per Hilding, Pentagon Press, Oct 2015, New Delhi.

Finn, Joshua. 2016. Human trafficking and natural disasters—exploiting misery. *International Affairs Review* XXIV.

IFRC. 2003. *International Disaster Response Laws, Principles and Practice: Reflections, Prospects and Challenges*, Geneva.

IFRC. 2014. https://www.ifrc.org/en/news-and-media/opinions-and-positions/opinion-pieces/2014/statement-on-migration-by-francesco-rocca/.

ILO. 1930. *Article 25 of Forced Labour Convention.* https://www.ilo.org/dyn/normlex/en/f?p=NORMLEXPUB:12100:0::NO::P12100_ILO_CODE:C029.

ILO. 2008. *ILO Action Human Trafficking.*

ILO. 2019. *International Labour Organization.* https://www.stopthetraffik.org/about-human-trafficking/the-scale-of-human-trafficking/.

Miko, Francis. 2007. *International Human Trafficking,* in Transnational Threats, Edited By Kimberly Thachuk. Westport, CT: Praeger Security International.

Samuels, A. 2015. *Narratives of Uncertainty: The Affective Force of Child-Trafficking Rumors in Post disaster Aceh,* Indonesia, American Anthropologist.

TIP. 2008. *TIP (Trafficking in Persons Report),* US State Department.

TIP. 2019a. https://www.state.gov/wp-content/uploads/2019/06/2019-Trafficking-in-Persons-Report.pdf).

TIP. 2019b. Country Narrative, India.

TIP Report. 2019. https://www.state.gov/wp-content/uploads/2019/06/2019-Trafficking-in-Persons-Report.pdf, June 2019.

UN Security Council Resolution 1820. 2008. *Women, Peace and Security,* S/RES/1820 (2008). New York: United Nations.

UN. 2015. *Sendai Framework for Disaster Risk Reduction, 2015–2030.* https://www.preventionweb.net/files/43291_sendaiframeworkfordrren.pdf.

UNDP India. 2009. *GOI—UNDP, Disaster Risk Management Programme, 2002–2009.* https://sdmassam.nic.in/pdf/publication/undp/gd_practices_in_cbdrm.pdf.

UNFPA. 2006. *State of the World Population Report, United Nations Fund for Population Activities,* 45.

UNISDR. *UNISDR.* https://www.unisdr.org/asiapacific.

UNISDR. 2005–2015. *Hyogo Framework for Action 2005–2015.* www.unisdr.org/2005/wcdr/.../Hyogo-framework-for-action-english.pdf. Accessed on 3 Mar 2015.

USAID. 2019. *Secretary of State, US Agency for International Development.* https://www.usaid.gov/trafficking.

WHO (World Health Organization). 2005. *Department of Injuries and Violence Protection, Violence and Disasters.* https://www.who.int/violence_injury_prevention/publications/violence/violence_disasters. Pdf, 2005, a/file/236656/women-girls-disasters.pdf. Accessed on 5 Mar 2015.

Chapter 2
Links Between Disaster and Human Trafficking

Disaster and Human Trafficking—The Perception

It is now an established fact that natural disasters can take far more lives in comparison to wars, genocide or terrorism. The year 2013 has been the most horrendous year for conflict and disasters. A total of 22 million people had to become homeless due to floods, hurricanes and other hazards. A study of the Norwegian Refugee Council found that twice as many people lose their homes during a disaster making themselves vulnerable and an easy prey in the hands of exploiters. It is believed that over the last decade, 27 million people lost their homes due to natural disasters. This increased to 42 million in 2010. The typhoon Haiyan in Philippines had killed 4000 people and displaced four million in the year 2013 (The Guardian 2013). The risk is even higher for developing countries. It was found that more than 80% of the displaced population during the last five years lived in Asia. Sometimes, the disasters occured in such quick succession that people hardly got the time to recover before a new one hit. Such mass scale despair spreads across the borders and administrative boundaries. In Africa, widespread displacement was seen in places like Niger, Chad, Sudan and others due to floods. While in America, nearly 220,000 people lost their homes to tornadoes in Oklahoma. The fact is such risks are on the rise outpacing not only population growth but even the rapid urbanization. Since the 1970s, the global population has doubled while the urban population seems to have tripled. Thus, the mass migration from rural to urban cities has even put a greater risk for the people particularly among the mega-cities of Asia, making them vulnerable and disaster prone.

Disclaimer: The presentation of material and details in maps used in this book does not imply the expression of any opinion whatsoever on the part of the Publisher or Author concerning the legal status of any country, area or territory or of its authorities, or concerning the delimitation of its borders. The depiction and use of boundaries, geographic names and related data shown on maps and included in lists, tables, documents, and databases in this book are not warranted to be error free nor do they necessarily imply official endorsement or acceptance by the Publisher, Editor(s) or Author(s).

M. Dutta, *Disaster and Human Trafficking*,
https://doi.org/10.1007/978-981-16-1630-3_2

Thus, a lasting stability among the lives of the people cannot be achieved until people are protected from disasters that create a negative impact such as violence, abuse of human rights, safety and absence of protecting the lives of the vulnerable. A disaster approach has to be necessarily people oriented and people centric. Such an approach will fill in the void that is created due to disasters and help in achieving sustainable development. A people-centric approach, as a means of security, can protect as well as empower the people and societies. The realization of disaster risk reduction necessarily warrants a broader and deeper participation of regional and international organizations, non-governmental organizations, government and the local communities. Disaster mitigation and sustainable development are interconnected and necessarily people oriented. A lack of disaster mitigation will result in imbalanced development involving 'horizontal inequalities' which will remain short in achieving the 2030 development agenda

Four critical factors matter in linking natural disaster with human trafficking. These are,

(a) Compounding of the pre-existing vulnerabilities
(b) Children separated from guardians or children orphaned
(c) Displaced population
(d) Deficit in rescue resources

(a) Compounding the pre-existing vulnerabilities—The pre-existing vulnerabilities get exacerbated as a result of natural disasters. Thus, weaknesses that are already present in a community or in the family gets compounded further. A natural disaster can make a family lose all their assets—their homes, jobs and transportation all in a jiffy. The main family owner who runs the family may get injured or lose their lives. Rebuilding or purchasing basic necessities, expenses on account of ongoing medical needs may all require capital which the family is unable to afford. Starting the lives all over is not only traumatic but impacts the disaster survivor's existence and the future. As the options before the families start depleting, they get desperate to feed their young ones. Managing to survive itself becomes an ordeal. These are the families that fall preys in the hands of the exploiters. The traffickers do not miss this opportunity to cast a spell over their prey during the chaos that prevails in the disaster-prone region. An example can be cited here. The 2015 earthquake that had struck Nepal showed how several young girls got trafficked by frauds who posed as aid workers. The helpless people having lost their homes and livelihoods were in a position only to grab any straw of hope that comes their way. All the disaster victims believed that the traffickers are actually trustworthy aid workers and were offering them a better life. Any job opportunity offered to them is likely to be willingly accepted irrespective of whether the job existed or not. Sometimes, the traffickers bribed the family members with cash as an advance for the work that their child will be undertaking. This tempts the family to allow their wards to accompany the trafficker to another city willingly. The cash offered ensures confidence among the family members that there would be a regular supply of such cash every month. Families remain ignorant about the fraudulent nature of this job. Thus, their child soon becomes a trafficked victim.

(b) Children separated from parents/orphans—Children are most vulnerable during a disaster, especially if he/she happens to be an orphan or are those who have got separated from their parents/caregivers. The traumatized children gets easily trapped as they tend to be unsuspecting and trust any helping adult that come to their rescue during a disaster. A child can never distinguish when an adult had malicious intentions at heart and is not genuine while promising to find the child/youth's family. Besides legal adoptions are a common scene during disasters. The traffickers are quick to send pictures of the child to willing families for adoption. The families believe that they were trying to help the child. An 'adoption fee' is collected by the traffickers, and the child gets promptly sold to an altogether new and unfamiliar family where the child has no chance of ever being reunited with his birth family.

(c) Displacement population—Any kind of displacements always causes stress to the person involved. The displaced person is vulnerable and susceptible to trafficking but not all displacement lead to trafficking. Sometimes families are forced to migrate to flee from dangers. They often have to adjust with new surroundings or in refugee camps without social and civic safety nets which would protect the vulnerable people from getting exploited during the crisis period. Amidst new surroundings and alien environment surviving itself becomes a challenge. Even basic needs like obtaining food, shelter and a livelihood option becomes confronting. The disaster survivors are faced with innumerable challenges like differences in language, culture, legalities and unfamiliar rules and regulations. On top of all these if they are without proper documentation, their existence is threatening. When trafficked under these circumstances, they suddenly find themselves as an illegal immigrant even within their own country. Under such circumstances obtaining any kind of service becomes cumbersome and complicated.

(d) Deficit in rescue resources—During a disaster, the availability of resources becomes limited. Countries that have governance issues amplify the miseries of the vulnerable people. Amidst the chaos that looms large over the head of a disaster survivor, dangers of human trafficking get even more magnified. The only priority then is to save lives and undertake rescue operations. Countries with weak governance and development structures are uncoordinated. Most of the government machinery is busy with the rescue operations rather than implementing the law and nabbing the culprits. They remain overworked navigating the rescue operations and are hardly available for any other needed services.

There are several examples of the Indian Ocean tsunami suggesting how trafficking and disasters are closely linked. There were instances of how boats carrying 100 infants were being trafficked away from Aceh Province in Sumatra following the 2004 Indian Ocean tsunami (The Age, 2005).

Another media report (The Guardian, 2014) stated how an Alabama-based company named Signal International recruited 500 Indian men to perform oil rig repairs following the devastating hurricane Katrina that happened in 2005. According to the report, 'The workers paid $10,000 a piece to recruiters and were promised good jobs and permanent US residency for their families... When the men arrived ... they discovered that they would not receive promised residency documents. Signal also charged the men $1050 per month to live in guarded labour camps where up to 24 men lived in single 1800-square-foot units, according to the suit'. A similar situation happened in Maldives where Indian men had been trafficked for labour following the tsunami in 2004. The location of the country Maldives is extremely low. So much so that during the tsunami nearly every inch of the country was inundated by the water from the tsunami barring nine islands. However, Maldives was lucky not to have been hit by the devastating waves like the ones that had hit Indonesia and Thailand. Rather, the tsunami waves were like rising gushes of water that flooded the islands.

The 2010 Haiti Earthquake was of 7.0 magnitude. The earthquake simply shattered the nation of Haiti. An estimation states that the death toll during the six-week period of the earth quake was to the tune of 158,679 people in Port-au-Prince, some of whom died due to injuries or illness that followed the disaster. It is also on record that during this period after the earthquake, 10,813 people were sexually assaulted and majority of them were women. At the same time, another 4645 persons were physically assaulted. Food insecurity during the said period was 18.6% among the households. The study revealed complete destruction of houses by 24.4% of the respondents. Further, 'survivors continued to experience high levels of sexual assault and limited access to durable shelter'. The Prime Minister of Haiti Jean-Max Bellerive observed that orphaned children were trafficked for the purposes of organ trafficking. There were another lot of children who had been orphaned were being illegally sold from the country for the purposes of international adoption. Families remained unaware about their children. Their loved ones just disappeared, and the cases remained hanging in the absence of details (Kolbe Athena et al. 2010).

In Philippines, the 2013 typhoon Haiyan struck the country in the month of November. It affected a total number of 6 million workers. From this, there were a large scale of workers who were already living under the poverty line. Around 2.6 million workers were engaged in vulnerable employment. Following the storm, the child labourers who worked in the rural areas were trafficked to Manila for sexual and labour exploitation. (International Labour Organization (ILO) and International Organization for Migration (IOM) 2015). There was a tremendous increase of child trafficking during that period. Children became a substitute for their injured or deceased family members. Children as young as nine years of age got engaged as labourers in sugar plantations, under traitorous conditions. These areas are the most vulnerable due to their location in the border areas from the viewpoint of different laws that operate on either side of the borders. The laws operating on one side of the border are not applicable on the other side of the border. Therefore, the police get handicapped and the case remains in an unfinished stage.

The year 2018 has particularly been a dreadful year as far as natural disaster is concerned. India too faced a major disaster like other parts of the world. Some of the deadliest ones included the wildfires in Greece, the earthquake of Papua New Guinea, the floods in North Korea, Nigeria, Japan and India), heat waves in Pakistan, the volcanic eruptions in Guatemala and the tsunami in Indonesia. These vulnerable areas unfortunately do not have the data pertaining to trafficked victims. If one considers the number of people that were killed, displaced and missing, one could imagine what would have been the level of vulnerability and desperation among the people. Therefore, the greater the vulnerability, the greater is the risk of getting trapped into trafficking. Such trafficking examples go on, and the list is unending. Human trafficking has no boundaries or borders. It is a systematic well-designed violation of fundamental human rights of women, men and children. Human trafficking or the modern-day slavery is found to be exacerbated during a disaster and post-disaster like poverty and other vulnerabilities. The studies related to this have been rather slender, and not much research has come to the forefront. Though human trafficking has existed over generations, this had been studied in silo. The issue of human trafficking started to gain attention only over the last few decades. The governments and international organizations started to deliberate about the link between disaster and human trafficking more seriously rather late in the day. Whenever there is a chaotic situation such as war, disintegration of a country, a political conflict or a disaster, it becomes a merry time for the traffickers. They are ready to prey upon the unsuspecting victim and exploit the situation for their personal gains. Studies have shown that a major natural disaster is a typically ideal situation for uncertainty and hardships to creep in. During such occasions, the links clearly get accentuated. Human trafficking thrives when disasters hit an already vulnerable region. The Haiti earthquake of 2010 and the typhoon Haiyan of 2013 reveal how poverty and a lack of livelihood options get exacerbated to form as the root causes of human trafficking (Finn 2016). Similarly, media reporting states how Japan's 2011 tohoku earthquake and tsunami had also created similar horrendous situation where trafficking played its role. Tsunami and earthquake in Philippines, Maldives and other parts of South Asia have exacerbated the number of missing children, men and women. It is also true that while all major disasters are documented and reported, there are many smaller ones which go completely unreported. Nevertheless, big or small, they do reinforce the increasing threat of such events.

There are many complex factors like poverty, gender discrimination, lack of awareness, foreclosure of livelihood options, which operate to make people vulnerable to trafficking. In the Indian context, other causes besides the social and economic are the cultural factors that play an important role. Factors such as disparities of wealth, persisting and unescapable inequality as a result of class, caste and most importantly gender biases make the people extremely vulnerable. The gradual breakdown of the traditional family systems and values throughout the region also contribute to the factor of vulnerability. Other sinful social conventions, lack of transparency in regulations governing labour migration (domestic and cross-border) and weak implementation of the enforcement mechanisms of internationally agreed upon human rights standards contribute profusely towards a flourishing business of the exploiters. The enormous profits earned in the trafficking business only guarantee the traffickers further of their share of the profits. There are studies showing how the outlawed religious practices (like 'Devadasi' and 'Jogin' systems) was an exploitation by the temple priests themselves, who exploited their position before disposing the unsuspecting girls into the business of prostitution. The 'Bedia' and 'Bacchara' communities of Madhya Pradesh readily buy the girls from the traffickers. There are many other such communities along the border districts of Uttar Pradesh and Maharashtra besides the Rajnats from Rajasthan, where the whole family gets involved. For them, prostitution is a traditional means of earning a livelihood (Dutta 2001).

Studies have also shown how women in the age group of 10–24 depleted in Murshidabad (West Bengal) (Dutta 2010). Upon further research at the micro-level, it was clearly evident how this particular lot had been trafficked to the brothels of Sonagachi in Kolkata while they were in search of livelihood options. They had been trafficked during the regular rainy season floods in the region. Many such case studies can be quoted suggesting how human trafficking thrives during a disaster. The disaster becomes like an extra burden on the already vulnerable people gradually leading them to a situation where they become weak and weaker to withstand any further, and ultimately, the human traffickers have the upper hand. It is important to identify the concerned stakeholders in the vulnerable areas and seek a greater engagement among them and the community members.

Different sources quote figures differently. The International Labour Organization (ILO 2012) estimates 21 million victims of forced or bonded labourers. The International Federation of Red Cross states around 4 million people who are victims to human trafficking annually (IFRC 2003). The US State Department estimates the number of trafficked victims every year to be somewhere around 600,000–800,000 of people worldwide (US State Department 2004). Women constitute 70% of the trafficked victims. More than half of the trafficked victims are children. It also states that a large number of the women and girls get trafficked for commercial sexual exploitation. The International Organization for Migration (IOM) claims to have assisted around 100,000 men, women and children, who had been trafficked since 1990s. Most of them were either for sexual or labour exploitation. Some of them were for slavery or similar to slavery practices, servitude or for organ trade (IOM 2019).

The purpose of trafficking does vary such as for forced labour, sexual exploitation and abuse, domestic servitude, forced child labour, organ trade, terrorist activities, entertainment and so on. Trafficking that take place mostly during a disaster is for forced labour and commercial sexual exploitation followed by children for various purposes. The impacts of such an exploitation last for a lifetime as compared to property damaged or even lives lost. Trafficking generates billions of dollars, organized crime and disaster is an ideal situation in setting the tone of the situation. The unsuspecting vulnerable communities fall prey to the billion-dollar trade robbing millions of people and children of their human rights and dignity. They are also the victims of mental and physical abuses, besides mental breakdowns, and suffer from sexually transmitted diseases and yet have to survive without any medical care (Miko 2007). During one of the field studies to Maldives (Dutta 2015), it was found that a group of young men from Rajasthan in India had been trafficked to Maldives for labour. Maldives had been hit by a tsunami and were in serious need of people to reconstruct their country. Being illiterate and unaware, they are extremely vulnerable and become an easy prey to the fraudulent recruitment practices. These illegal migrants are often exploited by being forced to work in situations which do not comply with domestic and international labour standards and did not match the job profile that is stated in the work permit. Another common practice is that upon arrival the passports of the migrant workers are taken away by their employers. This makes them even more insecure and vulnerable. Those who were employed complained about this practice as they were unable to leave the country urgently in the event of a death in the family or to meet an emergency, more so if this happens to be a Friday or Saturday which is a weekend in Maldives.

It is estimated according to 2008 records that in Maldives there exists a sum total of 85,000 migrant workers out of which 28,000 are Indians. Bangladesh tops the list in terms of migrant workers. There are more than 50% of the workers who are illegal. They are illiterate and belong to the poorest of the poor from the developing parts of the world. Many of them who arrive in the Maldives are not even aware as to which country they have come to or who their agents are. They sell whatever little they have in order to pay the agent/middleman so that they can enter the foreign country where dollars were supposed to be raining. Such is the understanding that they were given.

A weak law enforcement and economic hardship are the climate ideally suited the traffickers to be successful. This situation of desperation is apparent as the population is in search of a better life elsewhere. The majority of such victims are poor and isolated or are living in a destitute situation. Hence, traffickers get attracted to major economic transitions, natural disasters, situation of ethnic cleansing as well as wars and are ready to exploit the misery of the miserable victims.

Media reports and other documentation there suggest that in 2013 there were more people to the tune of 22 million that were displaced by natural disasters rather than by war. Moreover, these numbers are on the increase (Goldenberg 2014). The push factor of migration that takes place from the rural areas to the cities also exacerbates the problem. Huge masses of people live in dangerous conditions in the slums of the city area. These areas are so highly dense that it may be impossible to get out of the area when a disaster hits. If one compares the economic costs of the 1980s as compared to the 2014, the jump is gigantic. In 1980s, it was about $25 billion per year in comparison to an average of $130 billion per year during the period 2004–2014 (Baur 2015). Thus, a disaster can enhance both the physical and economic insecurities. Simultaneously, it can disproportionately impact the most vulnerable sectors of the society. These are the migrants, job seekers and poorer families. This is the reason it is believed disasters 'create targets for exploitation and enslavement' (Luis 2010). Traffickers also get tempted especially to target children who are weak and fragile due to their orphan status or too confused to fight back without their parents around them to support. Such cases have been attested by the civil society organizations during and after a disaster. The UNISDR has expressed their anxiety in this regard and expressed their concern for children's vulnerability. Several scholars have observed that when a state-run system collapses or is absent altogether, it will proceed towards a stage of frenzied environment during the emergency, which makes conditions conducive for traffickers to go about their business easily (Singh 2012). According to the report, the sale of children was because of 'the collapse or absence of a state system during and after an emergency resulting in a protection vacuum for children who may become separated from their families'. The World Health Organization has also attested the fact that sexual exploitation is bound to get enhanced the moment a women's options for employment get restricted in situations of disasters (WHO 2005). The Harvard's Program on Humanitarian Policy and Conflict Research notes that a natural disaster has the potential to create the primary environment for trafficking, thus 'raising the need for a cogent international response to human trafficking in complex emergencies' (Calkins 2013).

It is not as if the traffickers swoop down in hours after a disaster hits the region, but waits for the right moment to exploit an ideal situation such as when families are completely desperate after losing all their possessions. It is then that the traffickers approach the vulnerable families, and in their vulnerable state, they 'fall prey to the blandishments of traffickers' (Sur 2015). The most important for establishing the link between disaster and human trafficking is the empirical evidence which is in deficit. Most of the data collected are based on qualitative analysis and case studies. However, the magnitude of the data available do pose a constraint in establishing the link fully.

Researchers are now getting more and more apprehensive and are interrogating on this continuous media reporting about the link between human trafficking and disaster. This is particularly gained momentum post-tsunami on the Indian Ocean in 2004. Some experts (Gozdziak and Walter 2014) feel that since there is a lack of empirical data, such a threat may be just an exaggeration. They argue that while the aftershock of a natural disaster is 'considered by many to be prime environments for Trafficking in Persons ... the evidence for this is thin' as there is a total lack of empirical figures. Despite several research and documentation showing an increase in the trafficking cases during and following the 2004 tsunami on the Indian Ocean, there are others who feel it is only an inflated trend hyped up by the Western media (Gozdziak and Walter 2014). Samuels similarly (Samuels 2015) While it is a fact that there is a dearth of data, but at the same time micro-level studies across India has shown how disaster plays an important role in exacerbating the problem of human trafficking (Dutta 2010, 2011, 2015). Other studies undertaken by the civil society organizations and NGOS based on field-based case studies cannot simply be washed away. It is possible that the poorer the country is, disaster is expected to exacerbate human trafficking significantly. Conditions leading to human trafficking are even more shocking in countries that had 'prior histories of armed civil and/or social conflict' (USAID). However, this argument does not hold good in the case of Japan as there were no prior histories of such nature existing. This was, however, in sharp contrast to the situations that existed in Haiti and the Philippines. There were several concerns of human trafficking already existing. A major problem facing the researchers was the deficit in empirical data gathering. Such information was not available either prior or post-disaster. The absence of the exact magnitude of human trafficking cases posed a hurdle in the thorough analysis of concerned legal issues and policy strategies. A UN Environmental Program had suggested on the basis of data obtained from organizations that worked on anti-trafficking issues that trafficking possibly has enhanced to the tune of 20–30% at the time of disasters. Nevertheless, such arguments were brushed aside saying the 'uncertainty regarding the possible elevated levels of exploitation that existed even during political conflicts or climate-related disasters' (Nellemann 2001). Other experts (Samuel 2015) have also confirmed about the trafficking cases post-2004 tsunami. A few other cases had also been confirmed by the Center for Child Protection and Study. This is a local Acehnese organization in Indonesia. Further, it has been attested post-tsunami by the Indonesian government agencies themselves that several hundreds of children were taken away to orphanages located outside Aceh. So much so that the government had put a ban to taking any children out of the country without proper verification. On the other hand, no investigations were undertaken for those cases of trafficking which existed although unconfirmed. This was mainly due to investigation difficulties and lack of capable and skilled officers. Hence, these were often very cumbersome to prove as to whether the adoption was genuine or fake.

India's border with over seven countries is porous in nature. It is thus very easy to enter India from various sides of the border. The support from the border police on either side at times facilitates traffickers in moving across the borders. Undoubtedly, political uncertainty and financial pressures force the young girls from South Asian borders like Nepal, Bangladesh, Myanmar to get trafficked and exploited as minors. There have been cases as far as Uzbekistan who have been trafficked to India. At the micro-level, studies do confirm trafficking cases that has taken place during and after a disaster. Huge number of men from Bangladesh, India and Sri lanka had been trafficked to Maldives following the tsunami, with promises of livelihood options. Some of these men claimed to have been cheated by the agent both in India and in Maldives. Dutta's study (Dutta2015) reveals how the men from Rajasthan had sold off all their assets to come to Maldives for earning a livelihood. They had been shuffled into a 'cage like accommodation' without proper food, rest or wages. Their job skills were ignored and were put to all kinds of labour. They starved for days on end until some of them managed to be back in India with the help of the Indian High Commission. Yet another study revealed (Dutta 2011), how women in the age group of 10–24 left their villages in search of livelihood options during the annual floods that inundate Murshidabad area. Some of these had been trafficked to the brothel for commercial sexual exploitation. The focused group discussion revealed how after one landed in the brothel, she started to feel lonely and gradually managed to bring along many of her other friends.

During the focused group discussion, one-third of the women from among the sixty to seventy women present belonged to the district of Murshidabad. When compared to the macro-level data, this fact corroborated to the age specific (10–24) sex ratio in Murshidabad. The sudden decline of sex ratio in the age group (10–24) was rather conspicuous. As the age group started to increase, the census figures on the sex ratio got enhanced in the district. The micro-level fact authenticated the macro-level data displayed through the Census of India, 2001. This clearly shows that trafficking does happen when natural disaster hits the region. It must be borne in mind that Murshidabad is hit by floods every year during the rainy season when livelihood options simply cease to exist.

Another example is related with the children who are a much easier prey for the traffickers. During a field visit to Bangladesh, it was observed (Dutta 2010) that 120 children had been trafficked to UAE as camel jockey (Dutta 2010). It was overwhelming to find these traumatised children who had just arrived to a rehabilitation centre, in Bangladesh after a gruelling exercise of going through inter-country protocols and the bureaucratic set up. The organisation—Bangladesh National Women Lawyers' Association (BNWLA) handling these children got desperate at their plight as most of these children could not even remember where they lived or who their parents were. Rehabilitating these children was quite a task. They were too scared to speak and remained huddled up in one corner of the room. Many of them had injury marks all over as a result of falling from the camel's back. These children unfortunately were sometimes trafficked by their own relations.

The United Nations Children's Fund (UNICEF) in 2011 started an action plan for disaster risk reduction exclusively for the children (UNICEF 2011). This initiative was distinctive in the sense that affected children due to disasters got straight away involved into the programme. There were several hundreds of children from 21 countries in the world. The children decided the priority areas based upon their experiences of the disaster's impact on their lives. An important priority recognized the importance of child protection throughout a disaster. Other areas that were identified include the requirement to propose a special care centre where children could be trained to deal with the suffering, pain and trauma undergone. They could also learn skills about how to protect themselves from other risks that may occur following the disaster.

Disaster Mitigation and Risk Reduction

India besides being an origin, destination and route for human trafficking has also been a vulnerable country to face disasters year after year. The natural disasters include floods, droughts, cyclones, earthquakes, landslides, avalanches, forest fires and many others. A total of 27 states of India are disaster prone. A major chunk of the disaster prone area are the coastlines where 76 percent of these are constantly hit by cyclones and tsunami followed by drought, landslides and avalanches (Table 2.1).

The National Institute of Disaster Management (NIDM) states that among the ten most disaster-prone countries in the world, India happens to be one of them. The heavy toll on the lives of people is mainly because of the high concentration and regular occurrence of disasters. This impacts the life support system of the people in the country. India can be divided into five distinct geographical regions (Table 2.2) with specific vulnerability in terms of various types of disasters.

Table 2.1 Natural disasters in India

S. no.	Type of disaster	Area affected
1	Earthquake	58.6%
2	Floods and erosion	12% (40 million ha)
3	Cyclones and tsunamis	76% (5700 out of 7516 km coastline)
4	Drought, landslides and avalanches	68%

Source https://nidm.gov.in/easindia2014/err/pdf/country_profile/India.pdf

Table 2.2 Vulnerable regions to natural disasters in India

Geographical regions	Type of disaster
Himalaya	Earthquakes and landslides
Hilly part of Peninsula	Landslides
Alluvial plains	Floods
Coastal zone	Cyclones and storms
Deserts	Droughts and famine

Map 2.1 shows the state-wise multi-hazard disasters of the country in India. As is evident from the map, every part displays a threat to disaster. It may be a natural disaster or a manmade one.

The map reveals the length and breadth of the spread of natural disasters within the country. If one were to exclude the hazard-prone states one by one, not a single state will remain which is not hazard prone in nature. However, all hazards do not become a disaster provided it adopts proper mitigation procedures that would reduce the disaster risks. An estimated 2% of the country's GDP is lost every year due to disasters and around 12% of government's revenue is devoted in aid support and rehabilitation measures. The year 2018 was the toughest year in terms of losses during a disaster. It is considered to be the fourth costliest year for natural disasters in history, incurring a loss to the tune of $160 billion. The floods of 2018 had the most number of displaced people in the world.

Disaster Management Act

Tracing back the history of disaster policies and protocols, the disaster relief Act was the first step adopted in 1974 by the USA. This established the presidential disaster declaration processes based on the series of annual disasters that hit the country. Following this, many conferences have been held on 'disasters' and 'Climate Risk Management'. Notable among them is the 'Yokohama Strategy and Plan of Action for a Safer World' held in May 1994. This was held in Yokohama (Japan). The main

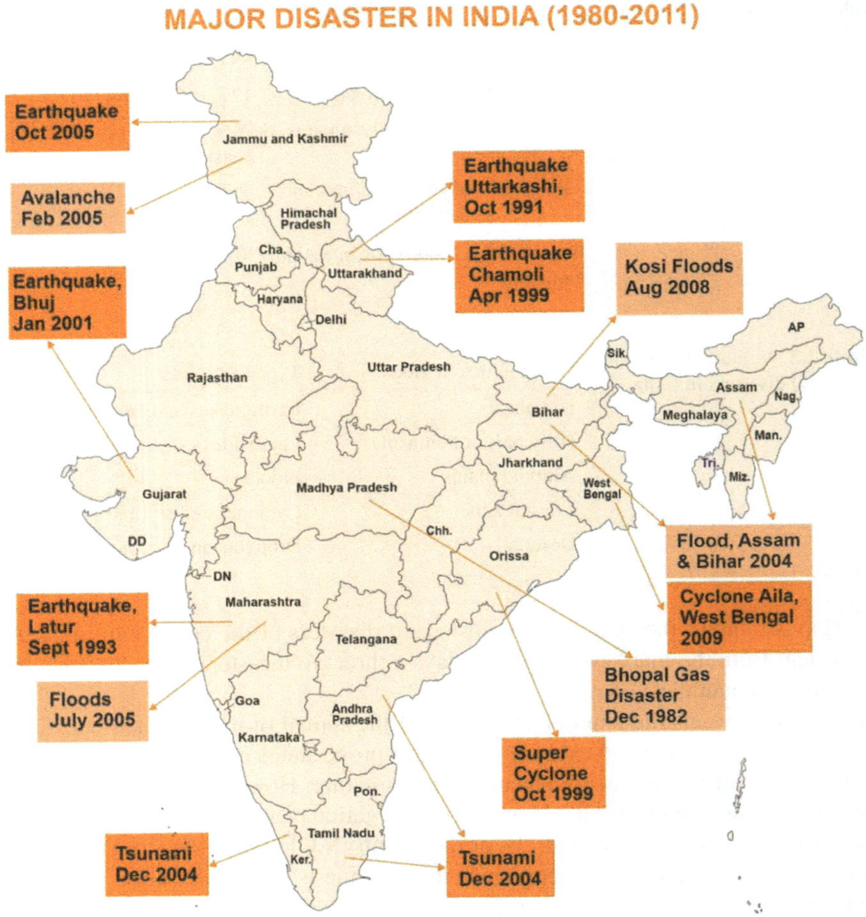

Map 2.1 Major disaster in India (1980–2011). *Source* https://nidm.gov.in/easindia2014/err/pdf/country_profile/India.pdf

outcome was the 'International Decade of Natural Disaster Reduction (IDNDR)' which focused on a set of ten principles. Based on this, the strategy, plan of action, and the follow up were carried out. The ten principles were based mainly on the risk appraisals, disaster deterrence and readiness, capacity building measure, early warnings and preventive and protective measures. The subsequent major conferences were coordinated by the 'United Nations International Strategy for Disaster Relief (UNISDR)' which is now referred to as the 'United Nations Office for Disaster Risk Reduction (UNDRR)'.

Subsequently, the 'Hyogo Framework for Action (HFA)' was held at Kobe in Japan in 2005 in the month of January. A total of 168 governments participated at the world conference. The conference on disaster reduction adopted a 10-year plan aiming for a better and safer world free from natural hazards. It was here that the International Early Warning Programme got further recognition after it was first introduced in 2003 at Bonn in Germany. The concept became of crucial importance following the 2004 Indian Ocean tsunami. This disaster had claimed 200,000 lives besides injuring more than half a million people. This programme besides other tools also included a quick data sharing and educating communities at risk. The major aim was to significantly reduce disaster losses by the year 2015 in terms of lives and assets.

The first major agreement in the post-2015 was 'the Sendai Framework for Disaster Risk Reduction (SFDRR)'. It is based on parameters that guarantee a continuity with the previous researches under the HFA by states and other participants. A number of novelties were discussed during various meetings and dialogues. The most crucial point being a significant shift on 'disaster risk management' rather than simple 'disaster management'. The whole focus is on the risk factor. It brought together a whole range of participants from governments, partner, civil society organizations and communities. There were at least 6500 participants in all. The 'Sendai Framework of Action' prescribes seven global targets. Four of them aimed to significantly bring about a reduction in

- Disaster mortality
- The number of affected people
- Direct disaster economic loss vis-à-vis global gross domestic product (GDP)
- Damages to critical infrastructure and discontinuity of basic services.

The remaining three targets aimed to substantially enhance

- Countries that have national and local disaster risk reduction strategies ready by 2020
- International cooperation to developing countries complementing their national actions
- Assessments to be made available to the people about the multi-hazard early warning system and disaster risk information.

Besides the above, there are four priorities. These are

- Understand disaster risk
- Strengthening disaster risk governance to manage disaster risk
- Investing in disaster risk reduction for resilience
- Enhancing disaster preparedness for effective response and to 'Build Back Better' in recovery and rehabilitation.

Therefore, a series of conferences were held in ushering in disaster risk reduction. The most important ones include

- 1999—the 'Yokohama Strategy'
- 2005–2015—the 'Hyogo Framework of Action'
- 2015–2030—the 'Sendai Framework for DRR' (a successor to Hyogo).

From Yokohama to Sendai, in the two decades, there has been an enormous continuous effort put in by international organizations for a paradigm shift towards disaster management policy framework. The shift has been from ‘response and relief centric’ to ‘mitigation and preparedness’. The approach is now multi-dimensional, multi-sectoral, multi-tier. The emphasis is to incorporate risk reduction measures in development planning. Today, the disaster risk reduction and disaster mitigation measures are being implemented in the country on a war footing results of which are apparent through the Odisha Cyclone called *Foni* that hit the eastern coast of Odisha on 3 May 2019. Compared to the 1999 supercyclone that had hit the state, the casualties were hardly around 25–30 compared to 10,000 people who died during the supercyclone. Within a span of twenty years, the state did well in protecting its people and managed to implement safety and evacuation of places on the basis of early warning system. Nevertheless, there was huge post-disaster devastation in terms of loss in cattle, inundation of agricultural fields, breakdown of infrastructure facilities and so on. Despite all, we lag behind in terms of disaster risk reduction, community resilience building and disaster mitigation. Although we have moved further and transformation is taking place, but we lag behind in disaster mitigation and risk reduction under the Sendai Framework of Action.

The Disaster Management Act of India popularly referred to as the DMA was set up on 23 December 2005, soon after the Hyogo Framework of Action. It provided efficient running of disaster mitigation and all connected matters. The National Executive Committee (NEC) under the Central Government comprises of secretary-level officers from various ministries under the Government of India with the Home Secretary served as the Chairperson. The NEC is the authority responsible for preparedness of the National Disaster Management Plan. It ensures to regularly review and get updated. Way back in 1999, a high-powered committee (HPC) was set up with a national committee after Gujarat was hit by an earthquake. It recommended the preparation of disaster management plans and suggested disaster mitigation through effective mechanisms. Finally, the act was enacted. The Prime Minister, headed the National Disaster Management Authority (NDMA); the State Disaster Management Authorities (SDMAs) were headed by respective Chief Ministers. The committees were to lead and implement the all-inclusive integrated approach of disaster management in India. The State Disaster Management Authority (SDMA) has the states Chief Minister as the Chairperson. Members (a maximum number of 8) are appointed by the Chief Minister. The state disaster management plan is prepared by the State Executive Committee who is also responsible for the national plan’s implementing. The SDMA makes sure that all the state departments are on a common platform and design the disaster management plan according to requirement specified by the National and State Authorities.

Building a safe and disaster-resilient India was incorporated into the National Policy Framework by NDMA. It was prepared after a thorough discussion and deliberation on developing an all-inclusive, practical, multi-disaster and technology-oriented plan for disaster management. This framework is nevertheless in agreement with international strategies. These include ‘the International Strategy for Disaster Reduction’, ‘the Rio Declaration’, ‘the Millennium Development Goals’ and the

'Hyogo Framework 2005–2015'. This all-inclusive policy under the NDMA has the following themes:

- Community-based disaster management
- Capacity development
- Recognition and crystallization of past initiatives and best practices
- National-, regional- and international-level cooperation with agencies
- Compliance and harmonization to generate a multi-sectoral synergy.

Similarly, the district magistrate/collector/deputy commissioner is the chairperson of the District Disaster Management Authority (DDMA). Members of the DDMA are the elected representatives. The act empowers the Central Government to appoint a Director General by establishing a 'National Disaster Response' for handling situations of disaster threat. The National Disaster Response Force (NDRF) played a significant role during the 2014 Kashmir floods. It rescued several people including many tourists. They were awarded for their heroic contribution by the Government of India. The act also addresses the creation of the 'National Institute of Disaster Management (NIDM)'. The NIDM further mandates funds at various levels to mitigate disasters.

The act nevertheless has not been forthright in its implementation. It has been criticized for overlooking the importance of the roles of NGOs, elected legislatures, local groups and municipal group. It is criticized for adopting a top-down approach, nurturing a graded ranking of administrative officers' authoritative control. Such an approach gives undue advantage by transferring sweeping powers to the authorities at the central, state and district levels. It is assumed that this act has 'became a law almost at the will of the bureaucrats who framed it' (DMA 2005). The DMA has been modified in 2016 and made in sync with Sendai Framework for DRR and community resilience. Its act envisages punishments for creating impediments, wrongful demands and embezzlement. There is no favouritism in providing compensation and relief on the basis of caste, community, gender and colour. Some of the important landmarks under disaster management includes,

- Formation of the Disaster Management Act, 2005
- Constitution of NDMA, SDMA, DDMA
- Constitution of NDRF/SDRF
- Provision of migration/legal actions
- Responsibility assigned to each department
- Inclusion into all plans
- Recommendations by 13th Finance Commission
- Inclusion into the Curriculum of the Education System
- Community preparedness/awareness.

Without a disaster management strategy in place, no development policy can be complete. The inbuilt component of disaster management is a must in all the segments and departments of development planning.

Sendai Framework of Action (SFA) and Sustainable Development Goals (SDG)

The UN member states on 18 March 2015 adopted the 'Sendai Framework for Disaster Risk Reduction (2015–2030)'. This was the third UN World Conference on 'Disaster Risk Reduction' and was convened in the city of Sendai, Japan. It is important to understand how 'disaster risk reduction' and 'resilience' impacts the targets of SDGs and the Sendai Framework of Action. The 2030 Agenda for Sustainable Development is being welcomed as a constructive and motivated breakthrough. The Sustainable Development Goals (17) and its global targets (169) set the 2030 development agenda (Fig. 2.1).

The disaster risk reduction is one common factor that cuts through all the different aspects and segments of development. About 25 targets relate closely to disaster risk reduction. From among the 17 goals, there are 10 of them that strongly establish the role of disaster risk reduction as a central policy for development. The ten goals are the numbers 1–4, 6, 9, 11, 13–15. Those that are not directly affected are indirectly affected. The SDGs have been approved as an affirmative and ambitious milestone which will impact all. The 2030 SDG agenda is the final representation for conclusion of efforts. It is developed in a manner so that it becomes a proper replacement of the 'Millennium Development Goals'. Poverty eradication is a predominant objective. At the centre lies the amalgamation of economic, social and environmental dimensions of sustainable development. The document supports the cause that no one will be left behind. It recognizes the pressing issue for reducing the disaster risks urgently. The UN World Conference on 'Disaster Risk Reduction and the Sendai Framework' is an attestation of the methods to be adopted for achieving the SDGs. Lessening the

Fig. 2.1 Sustainable Development Goals (SDG)

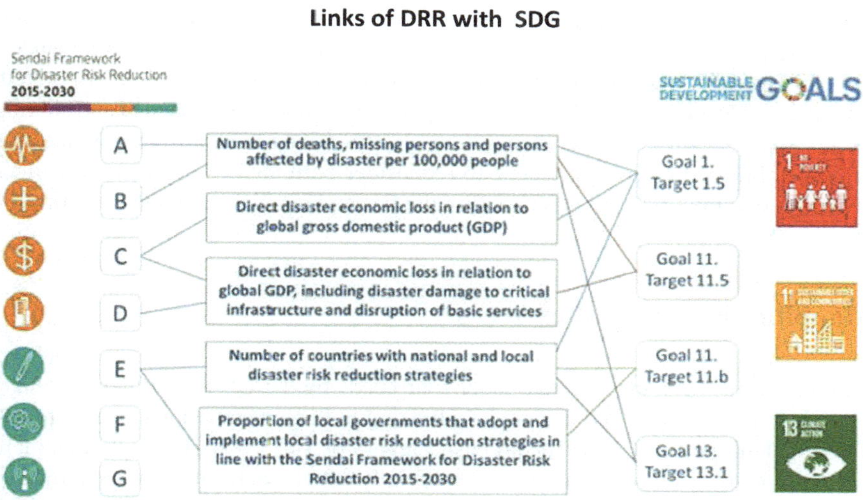

Fig. 2.2 Links of DRR with SDG. *Source* https://www.preventionweb.net/sendai-framework/sendai-framework-monitor/common-indicators

exposure and weaknesses of the deprived to face disasters or to build resilience on the ground will surely reduce disaster risks. Additionally, several goals and targets do contribute in reducing disaster risk even when the language of disaster risk reduction is not explicitly clear. Building resilient infrastructure helps in reducing disaster risks in a better manner. Therefore, the 2030 Agenda for Sustainable Development needs to be observed through different perspectives of disaster risk reduction (Fig. 2.2).

By the mere implementation process of disaster risk reduction, the major portion of the success for 2030 agenda can be clearly measured. Disasters have resulted in an increase in terms of direct economic loss is to the tune of more than 150% over the past 20 years. These losses are not proportionately distributed in the society. Those who are vulnerable and are in the developing countries bear the maximum brunt. A list of the targets under disaster risk reduction has been stated against each SDG, those of which are directly affected with their suggested indicators for assessing the impact (Refer Annexure IV).

The High-level Political Forum (HLPF) receives the annual report each year of the 'Sustainable Development Goals'. It is prepared based on the data collected and as reported by individual countries on an annual basis. The progress report for the year 2019 was received by the HLPF. The progress was reported reporting on progress concerning the shared indicators, those between the Sustainable Development Goals and the Sendai Framework. This information was fed into the High-level Political Forum and the Sixth Global Platform. Over the decades, there has been a major shift from the days of Yokohama Strategy to the present days of Sendai Framework. The shift was from response and relief centric to mitigation and preparedness. This implies implementation of multi-dimensional, multi-sectoral and a multi-tier approach. The emphasis being on incorporating risk reduction measures in developmental planning. It is important that besides promoting technological advances, a focus towards involvement of the local community input must be incorporated. There is a widespread recognition of the significance of local knowledge and sharing of information. This growing recognition of intra-community differences in terms of vulnerability, it is of significance to reconsider both the discourse and practices involving community-level actors within the DRR planning and implementation.

Mapping the Vulnerable Areas

Trafficking has been categorized under four heads by the US Department of State. The categories referred in the annual Trafficking in Persons report are Tier 1, Tier 2, Tier 2 Watch List and Tier 3. The highest category of Tier 1 does not imply that there are no cases of trafficking in those countries. It merely states that the government in these countries attempt in fully complying with the minimum standards of the Trafficking Victims Protection Act. While countries that belong to Tier 2 suggest that although they do not comply fully with the minimum standards, but are making significant efforts to do so. Countries that belong to Tier 2 Watch List are those that suffer from a significantly high number of victims with extreme forms of trafficking. There is a deficit in the show of evidence of *increased* efforts to combat trafficking as compared to previous year. It could also imply that the efforts to comply are merely on

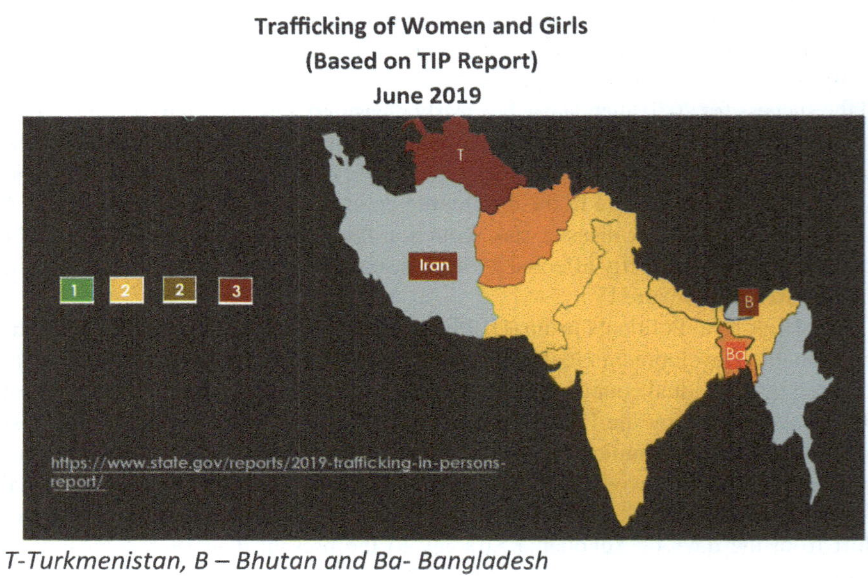

Map 2.2 Trafficking of women and girls (based on TIP Report) June 2019

paper without any action. The last is Tier 3 where countries are not making significant efforts to comply with the minimum standards whatsoever. The recent report of 2019 shows that there are 22 countries in Tier 3 including Iran, Bhutan and others (Map No. 2.2).

Most of the South Asian countries do not fare well as per the Trafficking in Persons (TIP) Report is concerned. According to the 2019 TIP Report, India, Nepal and Pakistan are in Tier 2, while Bangladesh, Maldives, Sri Lanka and Afghanistan are in Tier 2 Watch List and Bhutan is in Tier 3 (US Department of State 2019). This means there is plenty of room for improvement for the entire South Asian region.

This is despite the fact that,

> 'All countries in South Asia have ratified the Convention of the Elimination of All Forms of Discrimination against Women…'—***United Advancement of Women***, Department of Economic and Social Affairs.

It is interesting to glance at the vulnerable areas of human trafficking, especially for girls and women in South Asian region. According to a study (Dutta 2010), the vulnerable areas of trafficking of women and girls have been demarcated on the basis of origin, destination and the routes. Map No. 2.3 shows clearly the concentration of the source areas along the borders of India–Bangladesh, India–Nepal and the areas around Hyderabad in (Andhra Pradesh). The destination points are the red stars which are the demand areas most of them located in the metropolitan centres. The routes are also demarcated along the border areas which are usually porous and are mostly deficit in monitoring and supervision. Especially, during a disaster, the international boundaries are just imaginary lines and people step out in search of livelihood options. It is difficult to document people who are getting trafficked under such situations. They believe the traffickers are actually in support of them and even lie at times when caught in these border areas stating the traffickers are their relatives and friends. Some of the border security officials do nab them and upon cross-examination they might sometimes get the real story. People migrating from Nepal and Bangladesh become the source areas. There is a growing recognition to 'identify the needs of the community, to plan effective interventions and to obtain the necessary support for their implementation' (CdeBaca 2010). Regardless of this, there exists several countries which are yet to adopt the modern anti-slavery laws. This creates a legislative vacuum. It was also important to engage the local stakeholders.

> Violence against women is an issue that cannot wait…. No country, no culture, no woman young or old is immune to this scourge…. And we know that when we work to eradicate violence against women, we empower our greatest resource for development….

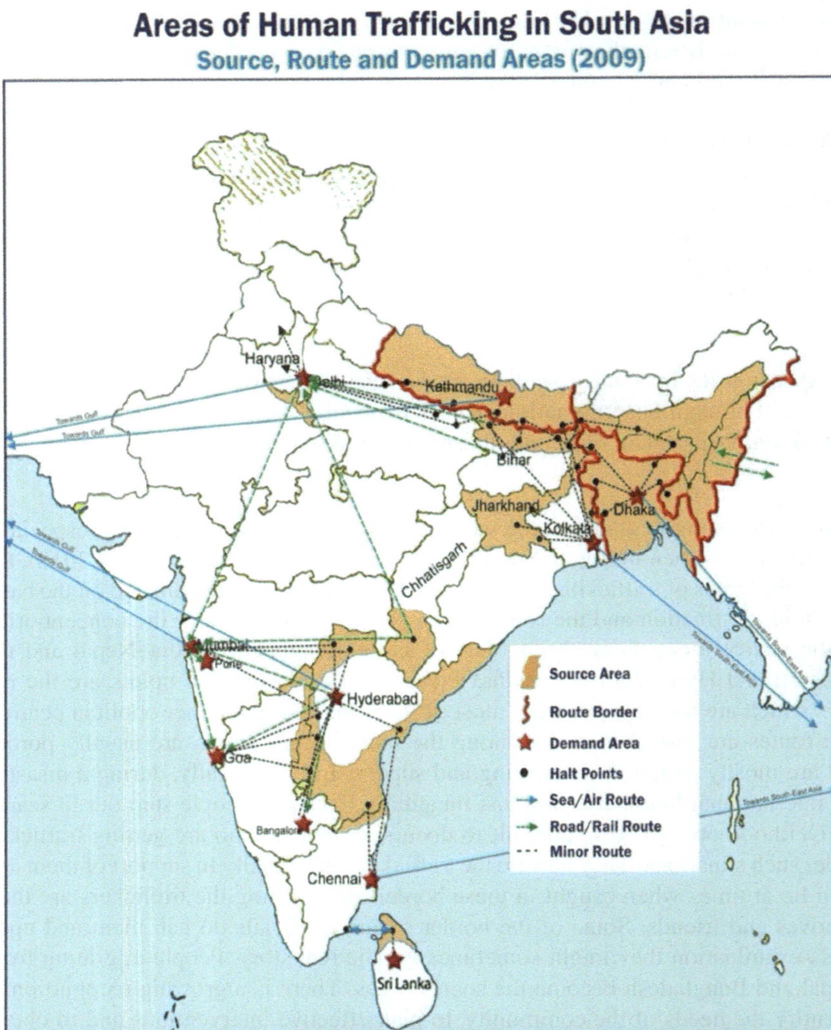

Country	Source	Route	Destination
India	West Bengal, Bihar, Jharkhand, U.P. Andhra Pradesh, North Eastern States of India, Southern Chattisgarh, north Tamil Nadu	Indo-Nepal & Indo Bangladesh Border Districts, Indo-Myanmar Border Areas	Mumbai, Kolkata, Goa, Delhi, Hyderabad, Bangalore
Bangladesh	Rajshahi, Chapainababganj	Indo-Bangladesh Border Districts	Dhaka
Nepal	Interior districts of Nepal	Indo-Nepal Border (Adjoining districts of Nepal with U.P. and Bihar)	Kathmandu
Sri Lanka	Northern Sri Lanka & South India	Indo-Sri Lanka sea route	Colombo, South India

Map 2.3 Areas of human trafficking in South Asia.
Source Route and Destination (2009)

Ban Ki-Moon, UN Secretary-General, remarks to the Commission on the Status of Women

According to CdeBaca, there are several organizations on the ground during the post-disaster situation. They do put in the necessary effort required to fight the problem of a flourishing human trafficking trade. There are officials from UNICEF and Save the Children as well who attempt to reunite children that are separated from their families. The process involves identifying, registering and providing the separated children with interim care. Several aid organizations have recognized the fact that the main urgency during the post-disaster situation is to make sure that children are quickly able to resume normal activities. Especially, activities like returning back to schools, at the earliest instance (Branigan 2013). Availability of safe spaces in the absence of schools which may have been destroyed in the disaster becomes particularly important. Several of the buildings may be in need of urgent repairs so that they may be converted into emergency evacuation centres. Debris clearance becomes important from the view point of physical safety hazards. The children may be at risk. Since the tsunami of the Indian Ocean tsunami in 2004, awareness has enhanced about the role human trafficking plays after the disaster. Despite the lack of data, there is a general agreement that the root cause that lead human trafficking to succeed are instability and poverty. These are often exacerbated in the aftermath of a disaster. Studies show that the future of natural disaster is even more fearsome. They will be more frequent and more severe. This makes the work of organizations even more tough. Organizations such as UNICEF, Save the Children, IOM, ILO, UNDP and others need to seriously bring the aspect of human trafficking into the forefront.

The Disaster Response Plan

According to the Ambassador-at-Large, Office to Monitor and Combat Trafficking in Persons (CdeBaca 2010) there are some crucial initiatives that need to be incorporated within the disaster response plan. These include the following:

- All contingency plans for disaster response must include counter trafficking interventions. Human trafficking does not spring up as soon as disaster hits the area, so if a proper planning is already in place during the initial stages, it would help in curbing and reducing the gaps that traffickers prey upon in order to exploit the situation, especially after the emergency phase is over.
- Coordination among the international community is a must. The United Nation's Trafficking in Persons Protocol needs to be followed both in letter and in spirit both on the ground and at the headquarters. The focus of the Palermo protocol is not whether someone is migrating, but rather it should focus whether the migrants are compelled into services that imply 'enslavement, involuntary servitude, debt bondage, sex trafficking, forced labour or practices similar to slavery'.

- Importance should be to support the government-run institutions. These have a role in effective anti-trafficking response. It includes all those institutions which are responsible for social welfare, education, child protection and the judiciary. While playing its predominant role, the government should be discouraged in fostering dependency on the international community. All efforts should be towards leveraging resources and avoid duplication of efforts. Institutions be strengthened for easy adaptability and be prepared for any other emergency that may crop up.
- Local stakeholders be engaged keeping the cultural factors in mind. All anti-trafficking initiatives will be sustainable provided there exists a robust engagement of civil society and the government. The two together may complement each other but not be in competition with each other.
- Interventions introduced in trafficking issues need to be more careful to the most vulnerable sectors, such as the displaced and migrating workers and identification, registration and providing initial interim care for children who are lost or orphaned. Protection for the women and girls from gender-based violence must be given special attention.
- Assessing of the vulnerabilities that exist. To make sure that policies, legislative tools and social norms are adequate. Education campaigns, awareness to people about the potential for human trafficking, dissemination of information sharing in local languages and obtaining help from relevant quarters are essential.
- All rebuilding efforts and process of economic recovery needs to imbibe codes of conduct. It includes job creations of various kinds, construction, debris clearance, burial of the dead and microenterprise. Strengthening of weak legislation processes on human trafficking need to rewrite the adoption measures and anti-slavery laws.

A balancing act needs to be in place for all disaster response efforts; otherwise, human trafficking will far outweigh the weak institutional set up, poor disaster mitigation with ineffective disaster risk reduction initiatives (Fig. 2.3).

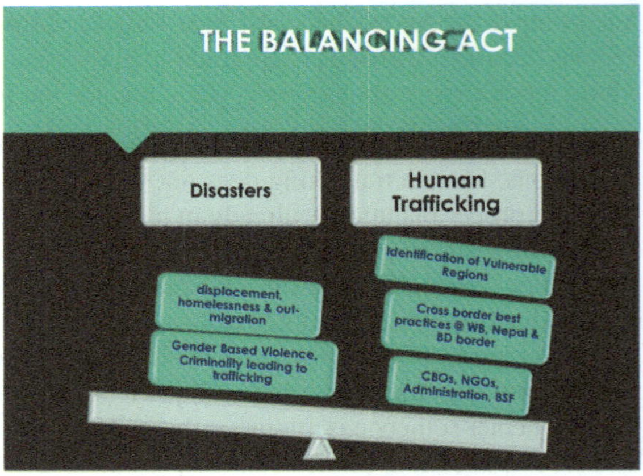

Fig. 2.3 Balancing act

It is important to involve the entire civil society organizations, the NGOs and all stakeholders concerned for an efficient, effective and successful output. Some of the important stakeholders include

- The trafficked survivors themselves
- 'At Risk' Groups—second-generation trafficking
- Police, judiciary and prosecutors
- Civil vigilance committees set up at the border areas, trafficking routes, railway stations and bus stands
- Local administrative officials
- NGOs and civil society organization
- Local governance, parliamentarians
- Trainers to care givers, shelter home officials
- Trainers for trauma and psycho—social counselling, mental healing
- Vocational training for survivor victims
- Border security officers
- Media and network coalition.

Unless and until all concerned stakeholders gear up to synergise their efforts and give that big push, the balancing act between disasters and human trafficking will remain lopsided. Therefore, all disaster mitigation plans necessarily need to incorporate the anti-trafficking parameters.

Crime Against Women

Currently, fully inclusive laws are in place. It not only covers trafficking crimes but includes a wide span of protective measures besides backing the rehabilitation of victims/survivors. A special police and prosecution unit is established. The training programme and documents related to human trafficking are provided. The police offers guidelines for investigation and prosecution, especially to the prosecutors for helping partner organizations. The 'National Crime Records Bureau (NCRB)' of India, under the Ministry of Home Affairs is 'mandated to empower the Indian Police with Information Technology for modernization of Indian Police'(NCRB). The NCRB was established in January 1986 to collect information pertaining to 'crime against women'. Some of the important indicators include kidnapping and abduction of women and girls, molestation, sexual harassment, cruelty by husband and relatives, importation of girls, besides rape, 'dowry' deaths and others. Till 2011, the total number of cases registered under crime against women was to the tune of 228,650 (Refer Fig. 2.4). Today, the total cases of crime against women is to the tune of 4,05,861 cases as per the year 2019. This is almost double. Compared to 2018, this is an increase of 7.3%, the total cases being 378,236. The crime rate registered per lakh women population is 62.4 during 2019 in comparison to 58.8 of 2018, as per the NCRB report (Ghose 2020). Nevertheless, even though the magnitude of the

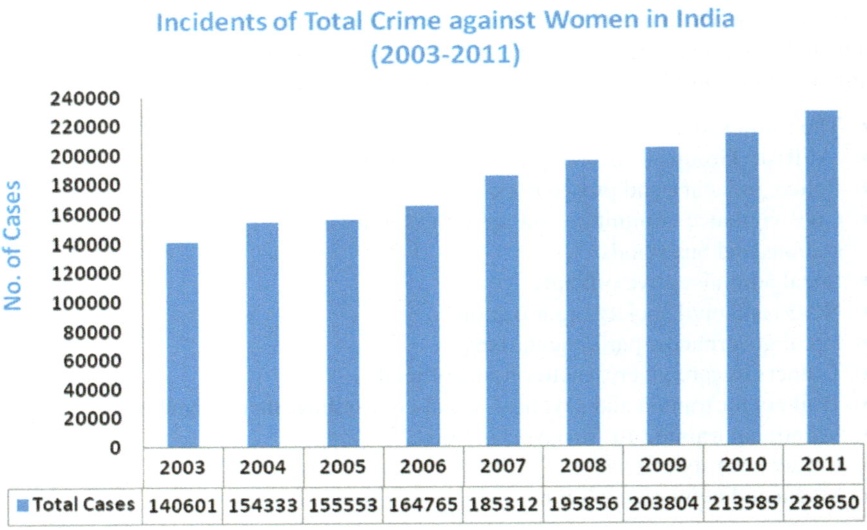

Fig. 2.4 Incidents of total crime against women in India (2003–2011)

total crime seems miniscule, as most of the cases go unreported, this is considered as only the tip of the iceberg and the trend is growing at an alarming rate!

The literature survey reveals that over the last one and a half decade, not only the magnitude of trafficked victims in India have significantly enhanced, but what is alarming is that there has been a substantial fall in the age of these trafficked victims. According to the 'Central Bureau of Investigation', out of three million prostitutes in India, 1.2 million (40%) were children, in 2009. The 'Commercial Sexual Exploitation' of children in India is actually present in great magnitude and in various ways and is one of the chief manifestations (ECPAT 2006).

Among the total registered cases, 24,206 were that of rape cases and 8618 were cases under dowry deaths in 2011 (Refer Fig. 2.5). The figure shows the trend line for various indicators of 'crime against women' during the five-year period. It shows the trend pattern from 2007 to 2011. While there has been a sharp decline in the number of registered cases under the ITP Act, a steady increase was observed in the number of cases under molestation, rape, dowry deaths, sexual harassment, kidnapping and abduction. The largest number of cases that were registered was under 'cruelty by husband and relatives'. Circumstances that were under 'Procuration of Minor girls' shows a steady rise since 2009. The Child Marriage Restraint Act, 1929, shows a drastic fall in the number of cases in 2009 only to pick up equally fast from the subsequent years. Under COVID 19, there are innumerous reports of child marriages and child molestation (UN Women 2020). 'Molestation' has been the second largest section among 'crime against women'. 'Procurement of minor girls' although was to the tune of 862 in 2011, but the trend line shows an alarming increase in the number over the previous two years (Refer Fig. 2.5). This when studied in the backdrop of

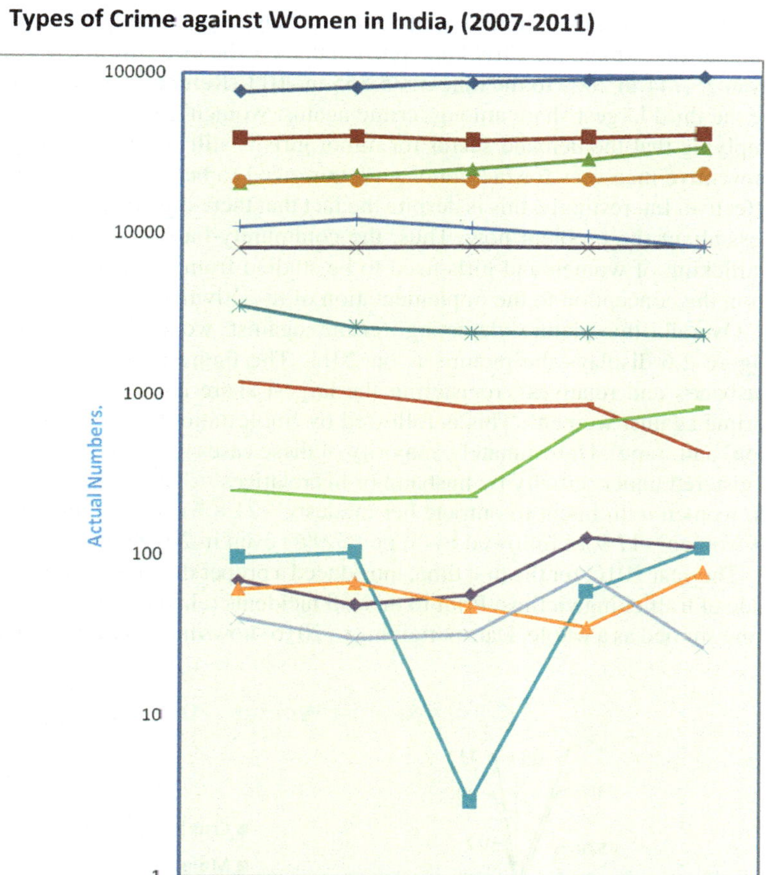

	2007	2008	2009	2010	2011
Cruelty by Husband/Relatives	75930	81344	89546	94041	99135
Molestation	38734	40413	38711	40613	42968
Kidnapping & Abduction	20416	22939	25741	29795	35565
Dowry Deaths	8093	8172	8383	8391	8618
ITPA 1956	3568	2659	2474	2499	2435
Rape	20737	21467	21397	22172	24206
Sexual Harrasment	10950	12214	11009	9961	8570
Indecent Representation of Women	1200	1025	845	895	453
Procuration of Minor Girls	253	224	237	679	862
Selling of Girls for Prostitution	69	49	57	130	113
Child Marriage Restraint Act 1929	96	104	3	60	113
Importation of Girls	61	67	48	36	80
Buying of Girls for Prostitution	40	30	32	78	27

Source: NCRB, Crime in India 2011

Fig. 2.5 Types of Crime against women in India (2007–2011)

the indicator—'kidnapping and abduction'—suggests a similar picture where the number of women and girls kidnapped/abducted shows a disturbing picture rising from 25,741 in 2009 to the tune of 35,565 in 2011 (Refer Fig. 2.5). This happens to be the third largest share among 'crime against women'. Such a trend is dangerous implying that the demand sector for minor girls is still strong and unyielding. The preventive measures for the minor girls thus need to be further activated and made effective. Interestingly, this is despite the fact that there is an increased public awareness about the problem now. Thus, the community-based preventive measures to trafficking of women and girls need to be studied from a holistic perspective right from the conception to the implementation of its activities.

Overall, the picture depicting 'crime against women' has been worrying. Figure 2.6 displays the picture as on 2011. The figure clearly shows 'cruelty by husbands and relatives', registering the largest share among all the indicators of 'crime against women'. This is followed by 'molestation', 'kidnapping and abduction' and 'rape'. Unfortunately, majority of these cases under the IPC continue to be registered under 'cruelty by husband or his relatives' (30.9%), followed by 'assault on women with intent to outrage her modesty' (21.8%), kidnapping and abduction of women' (17.9%) followed by 'rape' (7.9%) even in 2019 (Ghose 2020).

The year 2016, for the first time, introduced a proper documentation on the magnitude of trafficking victims. Prior to this, all incidents related to crime against women were studied as a whole. Data pertaining to 2016 shows human trafficking by purpose

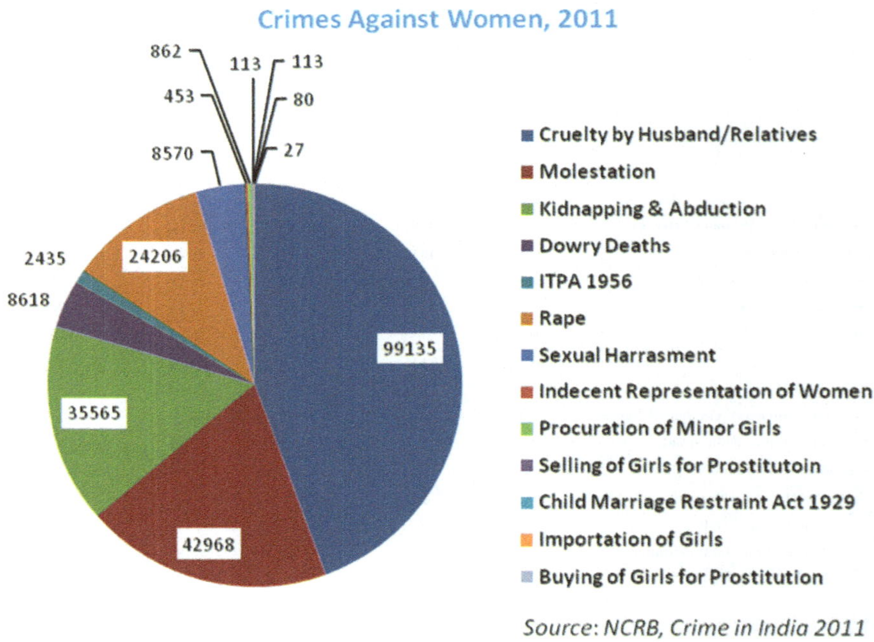

Fig. 2.6 Crimes against women, 2011

Table 2.3 Human Trafficking by Purpose, 2016

Purpose	2016	As %
Forced labour	10,509	45.5
Prostitution	4980	21.5
Other forms of sexual exploitation	2590	11.5
Domestic servitude	412	1.8
Forced marriage	349	1.5
Petty crime	212	0.9
Child pornography	162	0.7
Begging	71	0.3
Drug peddling	8	0
Removal of organs	2	0
Others	3824	16.5
Total	23,117	100

Source Human Trafficking, Crime in India, 2016, National Crime Records Bureau

(Refer Table 2.3). It is apparent from the table that maximum trafficking is for 'forced labour' followed by 'prostitution' and other forms of 'sexual exploitation'. Although a maximum number is trafficked for forced labour, most of the studies focus on the commercial sexual exploitation. This is an area where data documentation is weak for various reasons. However, this is a dark area and preventive measures are always better than cure. Thus, all possible strategies need to be incorporated within the larger policy of disaster management.

A definitional difference of the term trafficking in diverse areas may create more hurdles. Nevertheless, the international cooperation is fundamental. In order to achieve a steady and efficient anti-trafficking response to the initiatives, a strong coordination needs to be in place not only before and after but during the disaster as well. Therefore, under such circumstances, it is recognized that partnerships are key to success in combatting Trafficking in Persons. Otherwise, curbing the menace would be like the ballooning impact. When pressure is applied to one part, the air simply changes its location and goes to another part where there is no pressure. The synergy of all operating at the same time is a necessity if one has to address issues of human trafficking.

Unfortunately, documentation lacks. Evaluation processes to test the monitoring, effectiveness, practicality and sustainability of preventive measures to human trafficking at present are weak. Awareness and sensitization programme seems to be clubbed together to form a general broad-based subset of the greater programme of anti-trafficking strategy development activity. They have been rather irregularly formed to be imposed in bits and pieces and have been rarely studied in depth so as to understand their efficacy and sustainability. Funds for such programme are only a trickle and short lived often aborting the programme in its bud. Such programme needs a thorough understanding of the different methodologies involved and incorporates mechanisms that can adjust to changes as per the situation demands. It needs to comprehend what are the lessons learned and which are the areas that need further research.

Further considering the total magnitude of registered cases, it is obvious and implies that many of the cases does go unreported. Even then among all the crimes, it is the immoral trafficking (prevention) act that over powers the rest. The international discourse for increasing 'human rights-based approaches' offers hope that women's inequality and violence issues will get targeted. There will be a change in social, political and power structures of discrimination, segregation and coercion. International donor agencies have come forward in large scale to support many of the anti-trafficking programmes that are currently being implemented in India, instrumental among them being the UN Women, UNODC, UNICEF and many others such as ILO, IOM and UNDP which directly/indirectly contribute to curbing the menace. As a result, pressure has mounted to usher in gender equality on the development agencies. They are responsible for building apt strategies, distribute resources and be liable to bring in growth and progress in areas of violence against women besides human trafficking.

References

Baur, Esther, and Martyn Parker. 2015. GRF Davos. Building Financial Resilience. April 5, 2015, https://planet-risk.org/index.php/pr/article/view/173/299.

Branigan, Tania. 2013. Typhoon Haiyan: Children in disaster zone are vulnerable, Warns Unicef. *The Guardian*, November 20, 2013.

Calkins, Kelly. 2013. *Haiyan, Natural Disasters and Human Trafficking*. BORGEN, November 27, 2013, http://www.borgenmagazine.com/haiyan-natural-disasters-human-trafficking/.

CdeBaca, Luis. 2010. *Keynote Remarks to the Harvard Kennedy School's Ash Center for Democratic Governance and Innovation*, Washington, DC, May 24, 2010, US. Department of State, Diplomacy in Action. https://2009-2017.state.gov/j/tip/rls/rm/2010/142160.htm.

DMA. 2005. Wikipedia. https://en.wikipedia.org/wiki/Disaster_Management_Act_2005.

Dutta, M. 2001. *Evaluation of the Devadasi Rehabilitation Project by MYRADA*, Gokak, Belgaum, Karnataka, India, sponsored by NOVIB, Netherlands, December 2001.

Dutta, M., et al. 2010. *Evaluation Study on the UNIFEM Regional Anti-Trafficking Programme in South Asia (2000–2009)*. UNIFEM South Asia Regional Office, New Delhi, February 2010. http://www.unwomensouthasia.org/2012/evaluation-of-regional-anti-trafficking-programme-2000-2009-2/.

Dutta, M. 2011. *Situation of Human Trafficking in the Maldives—A Rapid Assessment* sponsored by UN Women and Human Rights Commission, Maldives, May 2011.

Dutta, M. 2015. '*Understanding Maldives in the Context of Trafficking*' in Development and Regional Cooperation in Central and South Asia: Euro-Asian Perspectives, Edited By Henrik Berglund, Mondira Dutta & Per Hilding, Pentagon Press, Oct 2015, New Delhi. ISBN: 978-81-8274-864-4, 9788182748644.

ECPAT International. 2006. *Global Monitoring Report on the Status of Action against Commercial Sexual Exploitation of Children—India*. Bangkok, Thailand.

Finn, Joshua. 2016. Human trafficking and natural disasters exploiting misery. *Humanitarian Aid and Natural Disaster, International Affairs Review XXIV*.

Goldenberg, Suzanne. 2014. Natural Disasters Displaced More People Than War in 2013 in *The Guardian*, September 17, 2014. http://www.theguardian.com/world/2014/sep/17/natural-disasters-refugee-people-war-2013-study.

Ghose, Dipankar. 2020. NCRB Data: 7% Rise in Crimes Against Women. *The Indian Express*, Sept 20, 2020. https://indianexpress.com/article/india/ncrb-data-7-rise-in-crimes-against-women-6636529/.

Goździak Elżbieta, M., Alissa Walter. 2014. *Misconceptions about human trafficking in a time of crisis. Forced Migration Review 45* (2014).

IFRC. 2003. *World Disasters Report—Focus on Ethics in Aid, 2003*. https://www.ifrc.org/Global/Publications/disasters/WDR/43800-WDR2003_En.pdf.

ILO. *21 Million People Are Now Victims of Forced Labour*. June 1, 2012. http://www.ilo.org/global/about-the-ilo/newsroom/news/WCMS_181961/lang–it/index.htm.

ILO & IOM. 2015. *Impact of Livelihood Recovery Initiatives on Reducing Vulnerability to Human Trafficking and Illegal Recruitment: Lessons from Typhoon Haiyan*. https://publications.iom.int/system/files/impacts_of_livelihood.pdf.

IOM. 2019. https://www.iom.int/counter-trafficking.

Kolbe Athena, R., et al. 2010. Mortality, crime and access to basic needs before and after the Haiti earthquake: A random survey of Port-au-Prince households. *Journal of Medicine, Conflict and Survival 26* (4). https://www.tandfonline.com/doi/abs/10.1080/13623699.2010.535279.

Luis, CdeBaca, 2010, *Best Practices: Human Trafficking in Disaster Zones*. U.S. Department of State, May 24, 2010. http://www.state.gov/j/tip/rls/rm/2010/142160.htm.

Miko, Francis, 2007: International Human Trafficking. In *Transnational Threats*, ed. Kimberly Thachuk, p. 40. Westport, CT: Praeger Security International.

NCRB. http://ncrb.nic.in/index.htm.

NDMA. https://ndma.gov.in/en/about-ndma/evolution-of-ndma.html.

Nellemann, C., R. Verma, and L. Hislop, (eds.). 2001. Women at the frontline of climate change: Gender risks and hopes: A rapid response assessment. *United Nations Environment Programme, GRID-Arendal*.

Samuels, A. 2015. Narratives of Uncertainty: The Affective Force of Child-Trafficking Rumors in Post disaster Aceh, Indonesia. *American Anthropologist*.

Singh, David. 2012. Child Traffickers Thrive on Disasters. *UNISDR News*, March 26, 2012. http://www.unisdr.org/archive/25934.

Sur, Priyali. 2015. Climate Change and Human Trafficking: A Deadly Combination. *The Diplomat*. http://thediplomat.com/2015/02/climate-change-and-human-trafficking-a-deadly-combination/.

The Guardian. 2013. https://www.theguardian.com/world/2014/sep/17/natural-disasters-refugee-people-war-2013-study.

The Guardian. 2014. *Indian Workers Awarded Millions After US Firm Found Guilty of Trafficking*. https://www.theguardian.com/world/2015/feb/19/indian-workers-awarded-millions-after-us-firm-found-guilty-of-trafficking.

The Age, 2005. *UN Confirms Tsunami Child Trafficking Case*. January 8, 2005. https://www.theage.com.au/world/asia/un-confirms-tsunami-child-trafficking-case-20050108-gdzbu2.html.

UNICEF. 2011. *Children's Charter: An Action Plan for Disaster Risk Reduction for Children by Children*. May 2011. http://www.unicef.org/mozambique/children_charter-May2011.pdf.

UN Women. 2020. *Socio Economic Impact of COVID 19: Gender Perspectives*, in collaboration with NITI Aayog, Dec, 2020 (Yet to be published).

US Department of State. 2019. https://rs.usembassy.gov/wp-content/uploads/sites/235/2019-Trafficking-in-Persons-Report.pdf.

US State Department. 2004. *Global Survey of Human Trafficking*. https://www.ifrc.org/ar/news-and-media/news-stories/international/the-new-slave-trade/.
U.S. Department of State. 2010. *Best Practices: Human Trafficking in Disaster Zones*. May 24, 2010. http://www.state.gov/j/tip/rls/rm/2010/142160.htm.
USAID. http://pdf.usaid.gov/pdf_docs/PNADK469.pdf.
WHO. 2005. *Department of Injuries and Violence Protection, Violence and Disasters*. http://www.who.int/violence_injury_prevention/publications/violence/violence_disasters.pdf.

Chapter 3
Civil Society Organizations and Community Participation

Significance of CSOs and NGOs

The present chapter is an attempt to collate and consolidate some of the significant contribution of the civil society organization in collaboration with the community. It brings forward the various community-based preventive measures that have been taken from time to time in curbing human trafficking. These are based on several field studies undertaken over the period. This chapter enables the documentation of various strategic preventive measures that have been and are being implemented over time. This will be handy for dissemination and make readily available experiences for policy recommendations. It would facilitate knowledge sharing of emerging models/best practices and other community-based preventive measures. The chapter examines how simple innovative preventive measures can contribute to awareness generation and efficacy of handling situations by trafficked victims in the vulnerable areas. Exploring comparative experiences as envisaged in different field situations will be interesting. The focus of these community-based preventive measures will be to overcome challenges that are faced while linking the impact of their activities during a disaster within the multilateral platforms. Thus, disaster mitigation will usher in sustainability within the programme besides deepening the understanding and identification of perceptions, knowledge and attitudes among the community members. Sharing of these preventive measures in the already identified vulnerable areas of disaster and human trafficking is of crucial significance for any future development strategy by the concerned stakeholders, especially the roles and opportunities that are permitted for women to perform, the need and benefits of migration to seek

Disclaimer: The presentation of material and details in maps used in this book does not imply the expression of any opinion whatsoever on the part of the Publisher or Author concerning the legal status of any country, area or territory or of its authorities, or concerning the delimitation of its borders. The depiction and use of boundaries, geographic names and related data shown on maps and included in lists, tables, documents, and databases in this book are not warranted to be error free nor do they necessarily imply official endorsement or acceptance by the Publisher, Editor(s) or Author(s).

M. Dutta, *Disaster and Human Trafficking*,
https://doi.org/10.1007/978-981-16-1630-3_3

work and the awareness about existence of trafficking. Participants for such an exercise had mainly focused on the victims and their families, the main watchdogs and decision-makers at the community level.

Identifying a successful preventive measure to trafficking of women and girls needs to be studied from the perspective of its relevance, effectiveness, sustainability and replicability. With a close monitoring and frequent supervision, proper budget allocation and adequate management information systems in place, reporting of the progress to the management does get ensured. The effectiveness of the activity needs to be measured in terms of continuity of staff and consultants. Further, the activity should be designed in such a way that it can be modified to adjust to changing conditions or demands. Its methods and services must be simple and appropriate to the context. It is also important that the activity needs to be implemented as an opportunity rather than charity suggesting its orientation towards capacity building and self-support leading to its sustenance. Preventive measures to human trafficking should not be considered as a one-time charity having bleak future prospects. An assessment and evaluation of the activity thus become of crucial significance for a possible replication of the intervention in other areas with similar conditions.

In this connection, some studies become of relevance based on secondary sources of information. Besides relevant documents from the various ministries in the Government of India, UN Women, UNODC, UNICEF, UNDP, regional organizations like SAARC, anti-trafficking network coalitions, police, media clippings, Panchayati Raj Institutions (PRIs), reporting by the law enforcing agencies, civil vigilance committees, community-based organizations, professionals and NGOs have been taken into consideration. In addition, Internet-based preventive measures that were based on education, communication and technology were also consulted. Studies (Nair and Sen 2007; Dutta et al. 2010) of crucial importance also provided an insight into the increasing trend in the trafficking of women and children in South Asia and an alarming decrease in the age of the trafficked victims. The research study led to the understanding that human trafficking is ‘a process consisting of four stages: pre-movement, movement, exploitation and post-exploitation at the source, route and destination areas and established its linkages with other crimes including those that perpetuate violence against women’ (Dutta et al. 2010). The study was instrumental in chalking out the goals and strategies required at source/supply, route/borders and transit areas and destination/demand areas for the implementation of the anti-trafficking programme. The present chapter relies on experiences based on previous studies undertaken and sponsored by UN Women. An evaluation study of the UNIFEM (now known as UN Women) was undertaken over the South Asia where almost 89 NGOS were involved. The widespread activities and interventions have been studied carefully, and some of the excellent strategies adopted have been discussed in this chapter.

The evaluation study undertaken under the UN Women had a series of initiatives mainly at the source and destination countries of South Asia during 2000–2009. Its anti-trafficking programme was primarily intended for countries such as Sri Lanka, Nepal, Bangladesh and India—the latter three often being referred to as the ‘Golden

Triangle'. It clearly shows how the border areas are fuzzy and porous for the traffickers to exploit the situation well. Most of the activities therefore tend to focus on the Indo-Bangladesh and Indo-Nepal borders. The study highlighted the rights-based approach, targeting the vulnerability of women and children in particular through preventive measures, protective measures and rehabilitation and repatriation. Some of these measures led to development of good practices for human rights-based interventions that defend against pushing the victims out of their present vulnerable exploitative situation into getting trafficked. The evaluation study also highlighted the community-based models of preventive measures that were successfully implemented in the source areas. The UN Women's programme adopted a multi-pronged strategy to address trafficking in women and girls, including sex tourism, paedophilia, commercial sexual exploitation and forced labour in the South Asian region. The anti-trafficking measures addressed the political, social, economic and severe human rights violation challenges. The study delved into some critical dimensions of the work, reflecting upon its relevance, effectiveness, efficiency, impact/outcome and sustainability. It was with this as the base, rich experiences from the field have been shared and the challenges highlighted.

The study clearly reveals how certain preventive measures have been most effective when implemented in the field at the grassroot level ('Panchayat'—the local governance). Unfortunately, these have been hardly disseminated among the target group or even among the concerned stakeholders. Keeping the nature of preventive measures implemented in the field, documentation of the various community-based models and the best practices of preventive measures to trafficking of women and girls in particular becomes imperative and provides a ready backup for their replication efficiently and effectively under similar situation. Without having to reinvent the wheel all over again, among other recommendations, it is recommended to build on the excellent community-based models. In addition, other best practices and materials developed such as films, posters, toolkits, action guides and publicity material on safe migration procedures need to be executed for a comprehensive awareness of ushering in a behavioural changed strategy in the region. It clearly emphasized upon the enormous significance of preventive measures in combating trafficking of men, women and children and the urgent need for dissemination of such processes.

Studies have attested the fact that a majority of the trafficked victims belong to socially deprived sections of society, including the Scheduled Castes, the Scheduled Tribes, etc. Children from drought-prone areas and places affected by natural or human-made disasters are particularly more likely to fall prey to traffickers (NHRC 2005). The NHRC estimated that almost half of the children trafficked within India are between the ages of 11 and 14, are subjected to physical and sexual abuse and are kept in conditions similar to slavery and bondage (Nair and Sen 2007). Debt bondage is one of the many strategies used by exploiters to keep children in constant servitude.

Another important study (Dutta 2011) carried out in 2010 carved out the most vulnerable districts to trafficking of women and girls in India with selected indicators of vulnerability having a formative component of field validation. The important deprivation indicators based on secondary sources of information relate to social, economic, environmental and cultural dimensions. The study had demarcated six states as the most vulnerable ones in the country. These were Andhra Pradesh, Bihar, Jharkhand, Orissa, Rajasthan and West Bengal. Several innovative strategies and community-based models in the prevention of human trafficking have been adopted with the much desired results. A considerable willingness on the part of the key partners had been noticeable. In addition, the prosecutors, judges and the police did try to usher in a shift in their approach from conventional crime prevention to focusing more on the prevention and protection of the potentially trafficked/trafficked persons seeking ways and means to decriminalize the victims. Some of the important non-governmental organizations who were interviewed include Bhoomika Vihar, Prajwala, Stop, Impulse, Lawyers Collective, Manav Seva Sansthan, Saanlap, Shakti Vahini, ATSEC India, ATSEC Bihar and many others. Other important stakeholders such as NGOs, members of the CBATN, community-based organizations, Border Security Forces, members of the civil vigilance committee, women's groups, police, media, AHTU, law enforcing professionals and other academic professionals also participated in the focused group discussions.

These activities however need to be viewed from the perspective that several of these activities may overlap with each other resulting in common and multiple outcomes. For example, a training programme may help in the capacity building for livelihood options and at the same time create awareness and sensitization. Similarly, IEC materials will also generate awareness and sensitization while contributing to training and capacity building. It is difficult to segregate these from each other and will be studied as such. However, the fundamental goal is to review the community-based preventive strategies that have been initiated and implemented at the grass roots with outcomes of consequence. The study also considered NGOS located at the source and their concentration of activities in the most vulnerable areas lying at the international borders like the Indo-Nepal border and the Indo-Bangladesh border and organizations that have had previous experience in developing and implementing community-based preventive measures to human trafficking. Focus was particularly on those community-based preventive measures that were successful and those that are still ongoing.

It has often been observed that the community-based preventive measures to trafficking of men, women and children may be classified into two major categories, first those that adopt a top-down approach with welfare orientation perspective and those that have a bottom-up approach, essentially remaining community-based encompassing an empowerment orientation. Most of the top-down/welfare-oriented programmes tend to be a one-time activity mainly focusing upon raising awareness and sensitization programme. As such, these programmes have minimal follow-up with hardly any sustainable community-level support. Their existence is sudden and short-lived. They tend to be prescriptive (telling people what to do) rather than facilitating an institutionalization process of informed decision-making. A bottom-up empowerment-oriented programme on the other hand tends to be ingrained among the communities that target anti-trafficking initiatives among women and children, in the context of other needs and priorities with empowerment as the ultimate goal. These activities help in establishing a community for developing a group support system for helping those under difficult circumstances and address trafficking issues with the synergy of collective strength.

Some of the most popular and effective community-based preventive measures in terms of 'Awareness and Sensitization' include activities like rallies/campaigns/camps, undertaking research activities such as seminars/workshops, organizing street plays/puppet shows/films and documentaries, forming groups of adolescents/women/young girls (*Kishori*) and preventing the second-generation victims and 'at-risk' population. Based on all previous experiences gathered from the field, the community-based preventive measures that have been most effective and impactful have been thematically classified under five heads:

- Awareness and Sensitization
- Networking, Advocacy and Media
- Training and Capacity Building
- Vigilance, Prosecution and Conviction
- Information, Education and Communication (IEC) Materials.

Awareness and Sensitization

Awareness and Sensitization programme for anti-human trafficking covers a wide range of activities which have proved to be immensely successful in the areas of implementation. The range of activities includes information campaigns through publications, poster making, advertisements and pamphlets in electronic and print media, airing of radio and television programme, videos and creation of anti-trafficking websites, screening of films and documentaries, plays, exhibitions, street play, puppet shows besides holding of seminars on human trafficking, workshops and lectures, border vigilance lifeguards, organizing camps, formation of pressure groups consisting of adolescents, women and young girls and other programme that target the second-generation victims and the 'at-risk' population. Each of these has contributed effectively towards combating trafficking of human beings. It has also been found that notes and write-ups in vernacular languages, in collaboration with partner NGOs, international and regional organizations, national human rights institutions, media and also with the business sectors have been extremely effective. Sometimes, popular bazaars to launch public rallies against trafficking are an instant success. Massive campaigns are undertaken utilizing marketing techniques to deliver messages via posters, billboards, leaflets, magazines, on T-shirts and even on train and airline tickets. Such campaigns reach messages beyond the potential abusers and have been instrumental in raising public awareness of the criminal behaviour of the exploiters (Boonpala and Kane 2001). However, the ground reality is that there are very few authentic reported instances of demand-oriented awareness activities in the major destination areas of the country. The ultimate aim of such campaigns is to bring about a reduction in the number of trafficked victims. Unfortunately, most of the programme does not have an effective monitoring policy in place to follow up and evaluate the effectiveness of such programme.

Awareness and Sensitization programme not only targets stakeholders such as NGOs, Cross-Border Anti-Trafficking Network (CBATN), community-based organizations, Border Security Forces, members of the civil vigilance committees, local leaders, police, district/village officials, teachers and schools but also simultaneously addresses the marginalized population such as the women and girls belonging to India's most disadvantaged socio-economic strata that are vulnerable to trafficking for commercial sexual exploitation. All community-based preventive measures that generate awareness and sensitization have been subdivided into the following categories:

(a) Rallies, campaigns and camps
(b) Research, seminars and workshops
(c) Street plays, puppet shows, films and documentaries
(d) Formation of groups (adolescents, women, Kishori)
(e) Second-generation victims and 'at-risk' population.

(a) Rallies, Campaigns and Camps

There has been a massive drive in organizing marches, rallies, campaigns, prevention camps, poster making, lifeguards at check points in the vulnerable areas and a whole range of other such activities that have been implemented by NGOs and community-based organizations. There have been wall writing, hoardings and exposure of traffickers by publishing their photographs on the wall in the villages/Panchayats, and public places have been initiated by network coalitions. Posters on trains and railway stations have been introduced for a greater coverage. The vehicle campaign through painting of public vehicles about human trafficking and who to contact if human trafficking is suspected is another popular method among the community-based preventive measure that seems to be very effective. Posters and pamphlets in English and local languages and printing on caps, T-shirts, walls and post card campaigns are the other initiatives that have been found to be most effective according to the NGO impulse located in the north-east.

Some important initiatives include the Mukti Caravan (Campaign on Wheels) primarily for awareness generation and sensitization of the community and the Beti Bachao Sammelan (Save the Daughters)—a social movement with civil society organizations, local bodies, social workers and media sends the message across the society to protect the girl child by creating awareness among the community at large about the dangers of sending off children to unknown destinations. Information is disseminated by painting messages on rickshaw/vehicles and high way walls. This is mostly implemented in the Indo-Nepal and the Indo-Bhutan border. Yatra or travel is a popular method adopted by NGOs for the community-based organizations located in the remote and far-flung areas. The Yatra includes anti-trafficking rally through the adjoining vulnerable border districts, boat rally on unsafe migration, car rally and other road rallies. Vulnerable routes are selected for undertaking the rally. A sensitization programme had identified ten such routes where 40 buses were plied with posters on them campaigning against trafficking of women and girls. The time selected is usually during the festival period when a large number of people can be gathered. Some of the areas that were covered include the south and north Parganas, districts of Darjeeling, Siliguri and Jalpaiguri.

Exhibit No 1

Bus Rally being organised by Sanlaap to create awareness among the community, 2012

Some of the areas where rallies and campaigns have been actively implemented are found in Araria, Supaul, East Champaran, West Champaran, some of the areas in the Nepal–Bihar border such as Madhubani, Sitamarhi, Sheohar and Kishanganj, and the Nawada area near Jharkhand border. Such initiatives have also been implemented in Delhi, Mumbai, Kolkata, Ranchi, Bhiwandi of Maharashtra, the Petrapole area in North 24 Parganas, Panitanki in Darjeeling, South 24 Parganas, Nadia, Murshidabad, Malda, Uttar Dinajpur, Jalpaiguri, Cooch Behar and Darjeeling along the West Bengal–Bangladesh border, the Jogbani area of Bihar and Shillong. A massive anti-trafficking awareness and sensitization generation through rallies and campaigns were also seen in Goa. Other areas include the Nepal–UP border districts of Maharajganj, Basti, Bahraich, Siddharthnagar, Shrawasti, Balrampur, Lakhimpur Kheri and Gorakhpur.

(b) Research, Seminars and Workshops

Organizing seminars and workshops are accepted as some of the best methods for disseminating information. Undertaking research activities followed by the dissemination process of holding seminars and workshops is thus a frequently witnessed activity among the concerned stakeholders. Workshops on legal issues related to trafficking and right-based options, protection and advocacy of rights for the vulnerable groups are some of the important workshops of relevance. National- and state-level workshops/seminars and research activities on the causes and consequences of trafficking in women and children seem to have been an ongoing activity with community participation. Workshops and awareness camps with women college students, local government staffs and BDO at the block level are witnessed on issues such as violation and abuse of gender, child rights as in human trafficking and sex tourism, child abuse and violence against women. Forum for workshops and interaction among media personals, faith based organizations, Rights Based Media Reporting and public interaction at the grassroots ushers in effective initiatives to combat trafficking by sharing their experiences of working together. Legal information and assistance to victims through awareness programme and community initiatives in the slum and marginalized communities of Delhi metropolitan centre have been provided in order to focus on legal rights. Meetings with community key influential persons and holding discussions on the process, mode and preventive methods of trafficking have been a constant process. Other community outreach and awareness/sensitization programmes are held frequently at the grass-roots level.

Many pioneering research publications have been brought about based on field research and secondary sources of information. There is no dearth of research publications brought out by NGOs, government and other stakeholders; however, disseminating these with stakeholders concerned has been lagging behind. Publications from various NGOs in the local vernacular languages are worth mentioning. Many of these publications touch upon sensitive issues such as about 'Traditional Prostitution in India' and assessing a situational analysis of cross-border trafficking (Sanlaap 2012). There has been several youth consultation, public hearing and other counselling where multi-stakeholders have been involved. Some of these have been on cross-border trafficking particularly the Indo–Bangladesh and Indo–Nepal consisting of GO/NGO actors and decision-makers of India and Bangladesh.

Exhibit No 2

Study material by NGOs and CSOs for dissemination [books, pamphlets and posters]

Some of the places where meetings, talks and dialogues have been undertaken include Gaya, Patna, Muzaffarpur in the central parts of Bihar, Kishanganj, Motihari on the Nepal–Bihar border, Nawada located in Jharkhand border, Kolkata, Ranchi, Delhi, Goa, Maharashtra, the Petrapole area in North 24 Paragnas, Panitanki in Darjeeling and Jogbani in Bihar, Shillong and Damanjodi area of Orissa which largely consists of tribal population. Such grass-roots-level workshops were also held in Nalbari on the Bhutan border, Kamrup and Guwahati in Assam, Gorakkhpur,

South 24 Parganas, North 24 Parganas, Nadia, Murshidabad, Malda, Uttar Dinajpur, Jalpaiguri, Cooch Behar and Darjeeling along the West Bengal–Bangladesh border.

(c) Street Plays, Puppet Shows, Films and Documentaries

Awareness generation and sensitization has been best depicted through street plays, drama, theatre and ventriloquism (puppet shows). This has attracted immediate attention and draws a crowd even in the most remote parts of the country such as the border areas of Indo-Bangladesh. It has been found to have a tremendous impact in sensitizing and mobilizing community-led actions. Film-making and video shows are some of the other methods of attracting attention especially in the rural areas. Important issues such as trafficking of women and girls, sexual exploitation, HIV/AIDS and violence against women are some of the issues that have been covered through such awareness programme. Fostering artistic and cultural activity such as dances and street performances performed by the victims not only help in relieving the trauma of the victim but also help in spreading awareness and generally sensitize the local people. Many such performances are regularly held in the tea gardens and in the local markets on 'Haat' (local market) days. There have been instances on such occasions when local persons have come forward stating that their daughter has been gone missing. Some of the tourist package includes in-flight films, advertorials that focused on case studies of victims and child rights. Community radio programme has also been undertaken to ensure community involvement in the anti-trafficking efforts.

Areas that have been covered under such initiatives are largely the vulnerable rural areas along the Indo-Nepal border such as Madhubani, Sitamarhi, Sheohar and Kishanganj in addition to the Raxaul area, Balmikinagar and Bettiah of Bihar. Areas along Indo-Bangladesh border like South 24 Parganas, North 24 Parganas, Nadia, Murshidabad, Malda, Uttar Dinajpur, Jalpaiguri, Cooch Behar and Darjeeling besides Shillong, Nalbari near Bhutan border, Kamrup and Guwahati have also shown a display of such activities. It also includes areas in and around Delhi, Mumbai, Kolkata and Ranchi.

Exhibit No 3

Puppet Show organised by Bhoruka Public Welfare Trust, at Petropole, India Bangladesh border, North 24 Parganas, West Bengal (2010)

(d) Formation of Groups

Formation of groups essentially viewed as a pre-emptive measure concentrates largely around the source areas. It addresses mainly the individuals including women from at-risk groups, communities, especially those with at-risk females, and even the local and national state officials. Such an activity essentially involves high-school students (adolescents), as volunteers who are imparted with awareness training programme on the dangers of trafficking. They also campaign against trafficking among the high-risk communities. Often such a group has more impact on the adolescents and youths as compared to a generalized awareness-raising effort. Mobilizing potential victims under Adolescent Girls Forums (AGFs) and Self-Help Groups (SHGs) has often been adopted by the organizations for creating awareness. Formation of a migrant resource centre to council potential migrants/vulnerable group is a frequently adopted strategy by the NGOs. Creation of women's groups in villages along the Indo-Bangladesh border has also been found to be effective. The creation of Kishori Shiksha Kendras (education centres for adolescent girls) has often been undertaken to spread awareness among the local community, women, youth, adolescent girls and ICDS workers.

Some of the areas where such a programme has been implemented include the Jogbani, Araria, Kishanganj area in the Nepal–Bihar border, Katihar between West Bengal and Bihar, Purnia in eastern Bihar and Muzaffarpur in Central Bihar. Such groups have also been found actively participating in Petrapole in North 24 Parganas, Panitanki in Darjeeling, Hyderabad, Goa, Maharashtra and Shillong. The areas along Indo-Bangladesh border like South 24 Parganas, North 24 Parganas, Nadia, Murshidabad, Malda, Uttar Dinajpur, Jalpaiguri, Cooch Behar and Darjeeling also found the participation of such groups in various forms.

Exhibit No 4

A 'Kishori' Group Meeting among the youths being held in Rajshahi, Bangladesh, 2010

(e) Second-Generation Victims and 'At-Risk' Population

Integrating awareness raising among communities and 'at-risk' groups through improved education options for women and girls, as well as enhanced legal literacy, offers a potentially sustainable strategy towards empowerment. This contributes in prevention of second-generation trafficking of women and children in addition to providing care and support services to the trafficked victims. There are trained volunteers, who are familiar with the villages and the local dialects. They are encouraged to develop specific awareness-raising methods that are suitable for different parts of the country.

Prajwala in Hyderabad has contributed significantly towards this regard starting from 5 children in 1996–7000 in 2012 through transition centres and drop in centres (Prajwala). Prajwala in 2012 ran over 17 transition centres in Andhra Pradesh for the sex workers' children. Education has rehabilitated thousands of vulnerable children and the second-generation victims. There is a wide range of educational activities through non-formal education, bridge schools, drop in centres and transit schools which assists a child victim and children of prostitutes for being mainstreamed.

Exhibit No 5

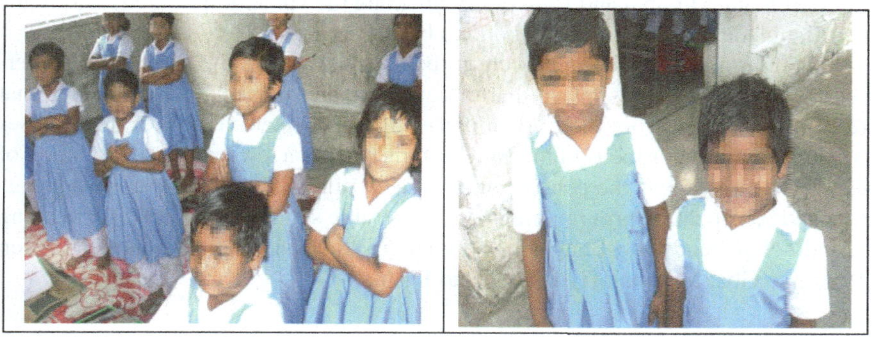

Rescued child victims under the protection of Prajwala, Hyderabad in their Transition Centres 2009

The red light areas of Kolkata and its suburbs similarly have an ongoing programme on mainstreaming children through preschool support and school admission for the children residing in the area in collaboration with the ICDS programme for Prevention of Second-Generation Prostitution. There are about 700 children per year that is catered to. Coaching support to prevent school dropouts is also provided for the community since 2003. According to Late Mrs Indrani Sinha of Sanlaap, a total of 100 children were being taken care of since 2010 onwards. An equal number of women in prostitution (WIP) were also being taken care of for generation of awareness on Child and Women Rights and Child Protection since 2010. Identification of vulnerable children and sensitizing them and their parents have been accomplished in the 9 vulnerable districts of West Bengal (South 24 Parganas, North 24 Parganas, Nadia, Murshidabad, Malda, Uttar Dinajpur, Jalpaiguri, Cooch Behar and Darjeeling) in collaboration with the district-based NGOs and CBOs.

Exhibit No 6

ICDS programme for 2nd generation victims and 'at-risk' population run by NGOs in the red light areas of Sonagachi. Kolkata, 2010

Some of the areas where such centres are operating include Goa, Maharashtra, Delhi, Kolkata, Mumbai and Hyderabad, all along the vulnerable source areas in the Indo-Bangladesh and Indo-Nepal borders besides others.

Although most interventions seem to be concentrated in the rural areas, nevertheless NGO experiences reveal that there is an increasing number of women that are being trafficked from their urban places of employment. However, these cases have not been a major focus of the NGO efforts barring a few exceptions. A study of Map 3.1 clearly shows the concentration of activities in terms of awareness generation and sensitization programme in the vulnerable source areas particularly along the Indo-Nepal and Indo-Bangladesh borders in addition to some other destination places like Goa, Mumbai, Hyderabad and Delhi.

Networking, Advocacy and Media

An effective networking can achieve those shared goals which are difficult to achieve independently. NGO networking has grown immensely over the past couple of decades. A network organization essentially shares a common vision and provides a platform to share and debate ideas that can collectively bring about a wider impact. Networking has been found to be extremely effective tool in addressing cross-border trafficking of women and girls. It contributes significantly to all the measures that are adopted for prevention, protection, rescue and repatriation. Networking has been considered as one of the best means of effective advocacy. A networking initiative is usually considered as a strong representation and one which enjoys the support from the communities they work with. This ushers in urgency among the concerned governments to attend to the issues raised. Donor agencies have the advantage of working with a wider base of NGOs bringing about a stronger impact. A network organization ensures greater effectiveness and efficiency in the use of resources and also in reaching out to the masses. The present section has been studied under three subsections:

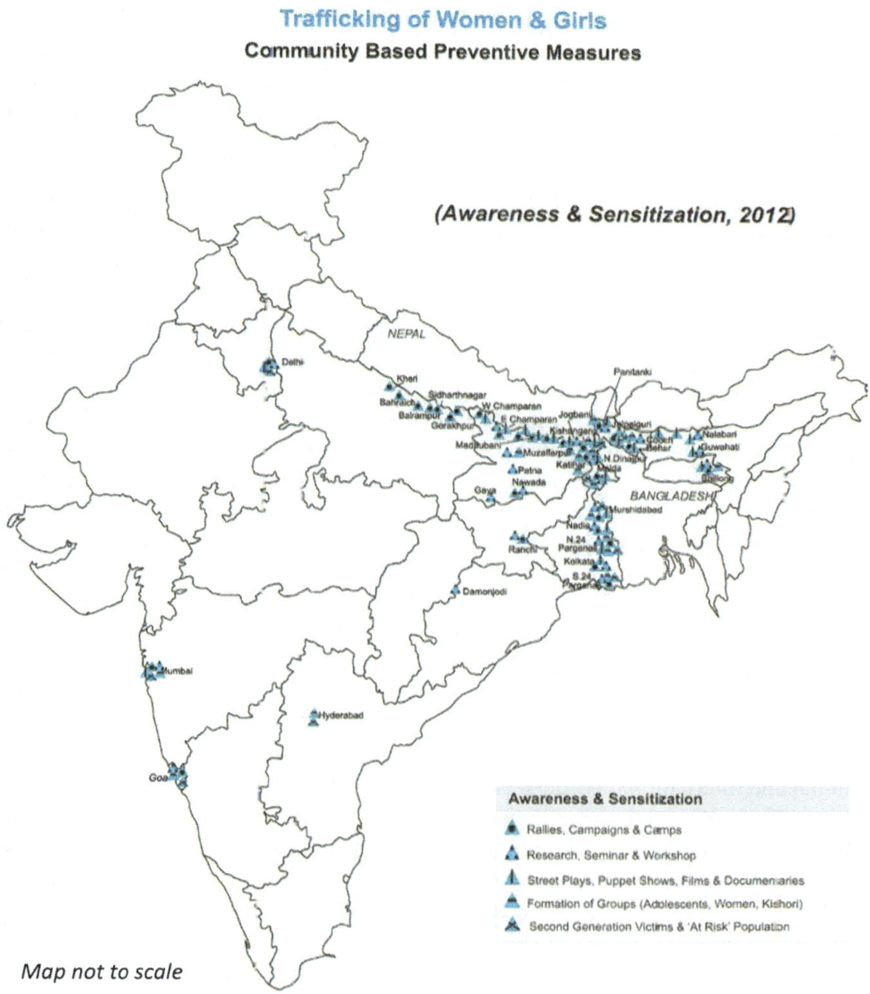

Map 3.1 Awareness and sensitization, 2012

(a) Networking
(b) Advocacy
(c) Media.

(a) Networking

Partner organizations have been working towards developing a better networking among the primary, secondary and tertiary stakeholders. Simultaneously, attempts are also made to develop anti-trafficking interstate networking among the CBOs, NGOs and the local representatives. In the north-east, the government provided opportunities of financial sustenance. Networking has strengthened the cross-border mechanism for interaction among government and NGOs of both countries to streamline anti-trafficking interventions along the borders. On the other hand, there has been active liaison with the local police for increased cooperation between the police and the NGOs for effective prosecution of traffickers and in the rescue and repatriation of the victims. A strong and stable NGO coalition is considered of utmost importance for developing the community-based prevention strategy for addressing trafficking issues within specific geographic regions. Community networking initiatives enhance and build the capacity for being more knowledgeable in understanding the referral mechanisms. It activates the NGOs to be quick and alert in addressing cases of varied nature. 'Action against Trafficking and Sexual Exploitation of Children' (ATSEC) India is a network coalition that facilitates advocacy and creates awareness and social mobilization. It helps in providing technical support, initiating research to support the grass roots for fighting exploitative sexual crime and trafficking in women and children. It also helps in establishing contacts and facilitates networking and linkage among individuals as well as organizations concerned in the issue of children and women trafficking and sexual exploitation. ATSEC initiatives have been designed to build up the capacity of community networks for implementation of their own monitoring and surveillance strategies. ATSEC India has initiated several awareness campaigns through its NGO partners in the various source areas of the country. Partner organization, with support from ATSEC Bihar, has been working in partnership with government, judiciary, police, PRI representatives, decision-makers and community members.

ATSEC Bihar focuses to monitor and curb the illicit movement of persons across national and international borders. A project entitled 'Combating Cross Border Trafficking (2003–06)' is being implemented in East Champaran (Motihari), West Champaran, Sitamarhi, Sheohar, Madhubani, Supaul, Araria and Kishanganj areas which are some of the most vulnerable areas to trafficking. With UN Women's support, ATSEC Bihar established an 'Inter-Religious Priest Forum (IRPF)', in 2005. ATSEC Bihar is one of the members of state-level Anti-Human Trafficking Committee and also is a member of the district-level Anti-Human Trafficking Cell in Patna. The Bihar Chief Secretary and the district collector of Patna, Government of Bihar, is the Chairman, respectively. In addition, there are other initiatives being undertaken such as the Campaign Against Child Trafficking (CACT) in raising public awareness and strengthening preventive measures against trafficking in collaboration with other state partners such as Jharkhand, Bihar, West Bengal, Assam, Orissa and other north-east states. The CACT Bihar has 42 collaborating partners involving NGOs, CBOs, youth clubs, academia, media, women leaders, PRI members, students, social activist hailing from Katihar, Araria, Kishanganj, Purnia, Saharsa, Khagaria, Muzaffarpur, Madhubani, Vaishali, Nawada, Gaya, Buxar, Bettiah, Darbhanga and Jahanabad. Similarly, the 'Beti Bachao Andolan' (Protect the Daughter Movement) works for the promotion and protection of the rights and dignity of daughters. This is being implemented jointly by partner organizations in Bihar, Jharkhand, West Bengal and other surrounding areas. One measure that the network coalitions have been able to implement vigorously is the imparting of exclusive training programme for professionals involved in relevant fields to trafficking. The faith-based organizations, teachers, journalists, social workers, security guards, Juvenile Welfare Officers, law enforcing officers, police, PRIs and government officials are often offered training through workshops, networking events and other initiatives designed to reach at-risk individuals and communities. Undoubtedly, there is an increase in awareness along the Indo-Bangladesh and Indo-Nepal border areas due to organized campaigns for awareness generation by network coalitions and their partner NGOs.

Other joint efforts towards building national NGO network and coalition capacity are the formation of the Cross-Border Anti-Trafficking Network (CBATN), a South Asian regional coalition of NGOs established in 2004 to act as an instrument for coordination to encourage and strengthen cooperation among the countries of South Asia in order to streamline and accelerate existing efforts to combat human trafficking in the region.

CBATN is registered under Indian society's registration act 186054. CBATN chapters are currently operational in India, Nepal and Bangladesh with a total membership of over 300 NGOs from these SAARC countries. It has been instrumental in addressing issues such as unsafe migration and registering cases against traffickers under ITPA and IPC through their CBATN Partner NGOs55. The most important fact about CBATN is that it forms a link with the government to improve protection and prosecution efforts while creating the desired professional referral mechanisms for improving border monitoring. In India, CBATN is active along the Indo-Nepal and Indo-Bangladesh borders covering the areas of Araria, Kishanganj, Madhubani, East Champaran (Motihari), West Champaran (Bettiah), Sitamarhi, Sheohar, Supaul, in the Indo-Nepal Border and Katihar, Purnia, Saharsa, Khagaria, Muzaffarpur, Vaishali, Darbhanga, Buxar, Jahanabad, Nawada, Gaya and Ranchi. It also covers Maharajganj, Basti, Bahraich, Siddharthnagar, Shrawasti, Balrampur, Lakhimpur Kheri and Gorakhpur in UP along the Indo-Nepal border. CBATN is active in the north-east in Nalbari along the Bhutan border, Kamrup and Guwahati. On the Bangladesh border, it covers the South 24 Parganas, North 24 Parganas, Nadia, Murshidabad, Malda, Uttar Dinajpur, Jalpaiguri, Cooch Behar and Darjeeling.

(b) Advocacy

Although the SAARC convention has limited scope in view of the restricted definition of 'trafficking', yet it was a major transnational instrument indicating joint action against sexual exploitation of women and children in South Asia. Unfortunately, more needs to be done in expanding its scope to make it fully effective. As mentioned earlier, the definition of trafficking also needs a review to make it in line with the Palermo Convention. Governments from the SAARC countries have taken some steps to strengthen the collaboration but continue to face difficult challenges. The SAARC regional convention calls for prevention of use of women and children in international prostitution networks, particularly where countries of the region are the countries of origin, transit and destination. Although slow, progress has been made in developing anti-trafficking tracking indicators as part of UN Women—SAARC gender data Infobase: Mapping Progress of Women in the South Asia Region. Parallel to this official-level pursuit, political-level consultations have also been held to advance the cause of women. Several ministerial conferences have been convened to address the specific concerns of women.

NGOs and network coalitions have been advocating for forming regional parliamentarian platforms for a better bilateral coordination and collaboration to address human trafficking as well as migration rights. Regional parliamentarian/legislative forums have been lobbied to integrate voice of migrants/victims into their agenda. Sensitization of MPs and MLAs on trafficking of women and girls and on inter- and intra-country migration rights has also been implemented through lobbying and advocacy attempts. There have been core groups formed of key regional parliamentarians for policy advocacy and lobbying at the national level. Some of the activities include formation of SAARC core advocacy group, coordination, training of prosecutors/judiciary on existing laws and policies, involvement of lawyers and judiciaries, creation of legal forums, involvement of CBATN in national-level forums, advocacy for implementation of existing laws and treaties.

At the state level, partner organizations and network coalitions have lobbied for developing linkages with cross-border organizations, advocating with personnel from Border Security Force (BSF), Sashastra Seema Bal (SSB), media, involvement of lawyers and judiciaries, legal forums for public interest litigation (PIL) and efforts to support national advocacy programme. At the same time, there have been district-level efforts in mapping the source area and data collection and need assessment studies, linking with cross-border organizations, identifying the agents and pimps, awareness generation for community people, establishing vigilance cells for monitoring of human trafficking, training of local partners, community mobilization to prosecute the culprit/trafficker or others involved in trafficking of women and girls.

Impact of some of the post-advocacy and networking emerged in the development of state plans for Goa, Maharastra, Andhra Pradesh and Bihar. Post-ratification of Goa Children's Act, 2003, along with its amendments in 2005, several NGOs including Child Rights of Goa and the UN Women partner—Salgaocar College of Law—were consulted by Goa government to frame the operating procedures for operationalizing the Goa Children's Act. The plan envisaged duties and responsibilities of government departments, especially women and child, education, tourism, transport, home, prosecution, etc. Likewise, Maharashtra government was sensitized by Prerna, Apne Aap and Save the Children India (partner organizations of the UN Women) to develop the state action plan for combating commercial exploitation of women and girls. Rules of the ratified ITP Act, 1986, were framed in Maharashtra in 2009. Fast-track courts were operationalized in Mumbai to bring traffickers and other trafficking nets under the purview of existing laws of the state especially the Bombay Police Act and the ITP Act. Police were trained not to invoke ITP Sections 8 and 20, which criminalized victims (Refer Annexure I). Activities of ATSEC Bihar especially the awareness of interfaith leaders in collaboration with partner organizations sensitized the government to prepare a state action plan—'ASTITVA' in 2008. The plan is an integrated programme of action particularly against interstate trafficking from Bihar particularly due to forced labour and fraudulent marriages. Partner organizations have provided legal aid and community-level advocacy for trafficking victims and assistance to prosecution of traffickers through the local governance bodies such as the 'Panchayats'. Issues such as extensive human rights abuse and gender inequalities in the community and homes, leading to pronounced vulnerability of being trafficked, were addressed. Similarly, the village-level and district-level advocacy programmes have been initiated along the Indo-Nepal border with 'Panchayats', local administrators, NGOs and media.

(c) Media

Media is an important pillar in the crusade against trafficking of women and girls for commercial sexual exploitation. The media network coalition works jointly in creating mass awareness about trafficking of women and children. The UN Women has supported building of networks and coalitions at various levels, such as the Cross-Border Anti-Trafficking Network (CBATN), South Asia Professionals against Trafficking (SAPAT) and South Asia Forum against Human Trafficking (SAFAHT) which provides a platform for a wide range of stakeholders and strengthens the voice against human trafficking. As a result of media, there is a much greater awareness as to what trafficking is today. Media has been instrumental in provoking sensitivity and improving the 'response systems' among the law enforcement agencies. It has helped in 'breaking the "culture of silence" and in generating positive community activism' (Nair and Sen 2007). Some of the partner organizations expressed concern over the fact that media can only be reached through personal contacts.

Partner organizations have engaged themselves in coming out with media handbooks, training programme and sensitizing the media personnel. According to 'Meghalaya Times', Shillong, the CSO has been found supporting a culprit. A 14-year-old girl was raped by a 27-year-old man, but he is out on bail. 'Such instances of society's reaction can be very shocking' (Interview with Mr. Thomas Lim, Editor, Meghalaya Times, Shillong, August 2012). He explained that even though Meghalaya was a matrilineal society and women are the custodians of inheriting property, the region remains essentially male dominated. The Impulse Media Info Centre is a data bank created by Impulse NGO Network where information is disseminated to all the journalists.

In a meeting held with media personnel and Television News channel, stakeholders expressed that there is a lot more coverage now and it is only after their coverage that the police and government officials get to know about an incident. Workshops and training programme have been organized by partner organizations. The CBATN/MSS in partnership with media has formed a Cross Border Media Forum against trafficking. Its workshop in 2006 was attended by several journalists representing various media from within and across the border. There were several media awareness and sensitization programmes held from time to time in all the eight states of the north-east of India. Additionally regional media editors consultation meetings were held in Shillong as well. Sanlaap organizes training of youths for media advocacy among the nine vulnerable districts of West Bengal (South 24 Parganas, North 24 Parganas, Nadia, Murshidabad, Malda, Uttar Dinajpur, Jalpaiguri, Cooch Behar and Darjeeling).

A study of the map (Refer Map 3.2) does suggest that most of the activities in terms of network coalitions, advocacy and media are mainly concentrated in the vulnerable source areas of Indo-Bangladesh and Indo-Nepal borders in addition to Goa, Jaipur, Mumbai, Bhopal and Bhubaneswar.

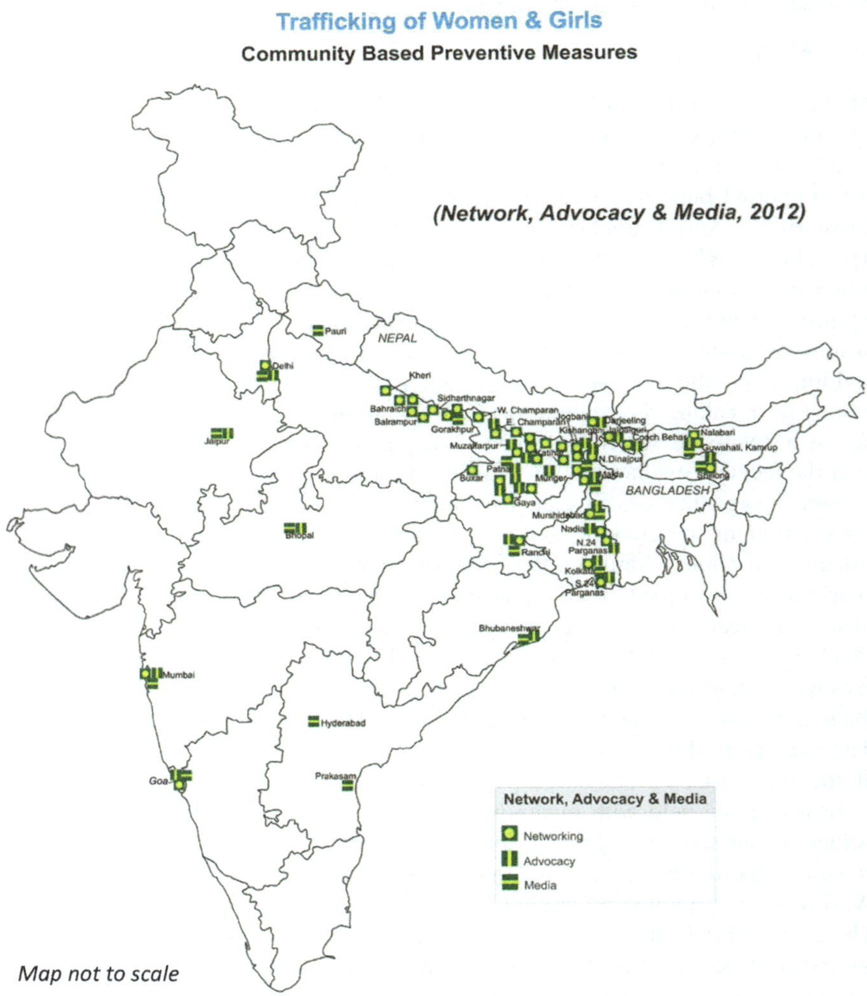

Map 3.2 Network, advocacy and media

Training and Capacity Building

This is one of the major areas of focus, where many NGOs take a lead in working with concerned stakeholders in the various vulnerable areas. The vast nature of activities imparted under training and capacity building involves nearly all major concerned stakeholders ranging from the grass roots to officials that belong to the decision-making bodies and strategy implementers. Activities include vocational training, skills building, micro-credit and support for formal or non-formal education. It also includes training for awareness generation among the law enforcement and security personnel, parliamentarians, PRIs, bureaucrats and other officials. While such initiatives have a significant deterrent effect, they are no substitute to formal prosecution and conviction at the end of the day. Typically commonly identified groups who received training include the down trodden, the marginalized low-caste women and girls, out-of-school youth, impoverished women and girls, unmarried young girls and those who migrate in search of livelihood options. It becomes pertinent to have a proper identification of the vulnerable groups who are in need of such training programme rather than broadly classifying the grass roots based on common sense and intuition. Studying their socio-economic background is essential for determining the level of vulnerability. It is important to know the difficult family circumstances like alcoholism, physical abuse and violence that may be inflicted on the women. Hence, a detailed research is a prerequisite for identifying the determinants of vulnerability and thus would help in identifying the most appropriate focus for targeted interventions. A study was conducted by UN Women in collaboration with the National Commission for Women in 2010 which undertook a mapping exercise to study the vulnerability of women and girls to trafficking in India based on district-wise data. Such studies help in deciding where the interventions should begin and what kind of interventions need to be implemented.

Anti-trafficking training and capacity building operates at two levels: first, at the grass roots to build the capability of the different segments of the local communities who would prevent trafficking at the source, and second, to strengthen the capacity of law enforcement, border control and immigration authorities in apprehending traffickers and rescuing victims of sex trafficking. The present section has therefore been divided into two categories:

(a) Training for capacity building, skill development and livelihood opportunity
(b) Training for policy strategy implementers.

(a) Training for Capacity Building and Livelihood Opportunity

The training programme is an attempt to develop the capacity building measures for enhancing community-level monitoring of the trafficking activity, encourage private-sector responses, build the capacity for better-informed referral mechanisms and initiate NGO responses. It also attempts to utilize the government's income generation schemes, utilize the micro-credit mechanism and promote vocational training for girls and women especially the 'at-risk' population with a rights-based approach. Due to the stigma of sex work that gets attached to the rescued trafficked victims, it becomes difficult for the survival victims to return to other work. Many are encouraged by their pimps or traffickers to become involved in recruiting new women, creating employment opportunities for the formerly trafficked women. Hence, it becomes even more pertinent to provide livelihood options to the rescued victims so that they do not get trafficked another time. These technical assistance and capacity building efforts are increasingly participatory, facilitating the NGOs and other sections of the communities for an enhanced knowledge on existing government schemes and livelihood options. The trained volunteers, who are familiar with the villages and the local dialects, are encouraged to develop specific awareness-raising methods that are suitable for each region. It also sensitizes the faith-based groups on the issue of violence against women, gender and trafficking of women and girls.

A hoard of activities has been implemented by partner organizations and network coalitions with funding from host governments and international donor agencies. Among noted successful efforts is empowerment-oriented skills instruction implemented by several partner organizations in source, destination and transit areas of India. Such efforts are through partnership between the Indian government, CBOs and NGOS. Workshops for utilizing government schemes such as the Mahatma Gandhi National Rural Employment Guarantee Act (MGNREGA), the Indira Awas Yojana, the Below Poverty Level (BPL) card, SMART Card/Rashtriya Swasthya Bima Yojana (RSBY), Ladli Scheme and Kishori Shakti Yojana (KSY) were organized by partner organizations. In addition, other initiatives of the Government of India have been utilized for providing education to the 'at-risk' and second-generation potential victims. Prajwala has utilized government schemes for the rescued women and trained them with livelihood options. These women are trained as masons, welders, paper making and so on.

Exhibit No 7

Rescued victims being imparted skill training in welding and paper-making at Prajwala, Hyderabad

There have been capacity building programmes to enable local NGOs and training the civil society organizations to apply learned knowledge to access the government schemes. In the Indo-Nepal border, a community called the 'Musahars' are located in a village called Nichloli. The Musahars belong to one of the most underprivileged and marginalised groups of the society. They had been trained by the NGO partner organization, Manav Seva Sansthan (MSS), how to access government social welfare schemes like the 'Indira Awas Yojana' (IAY) and the 'Mahatma Gandhi National Rural Employment Guarantee Act' (MGNREGA).

More than 150 men and women had availed of this scheme. This community-based organization (CBO) met regularly to discuss the various problems and action that needs to be taken as a follow-up and whom to contact for their rights-based demands. The group consisted of a large number of women who looked after various components such as education, health, child welfare and so on. They were receptive and quick to voice their opinion on how to access their rights and handle situations when their children are lured into being trafficked. It was a marvel to see them speak up altogether and ready to challenge anyone who would try to lure their young ones into the world of trafficking.

Exhibit No 8

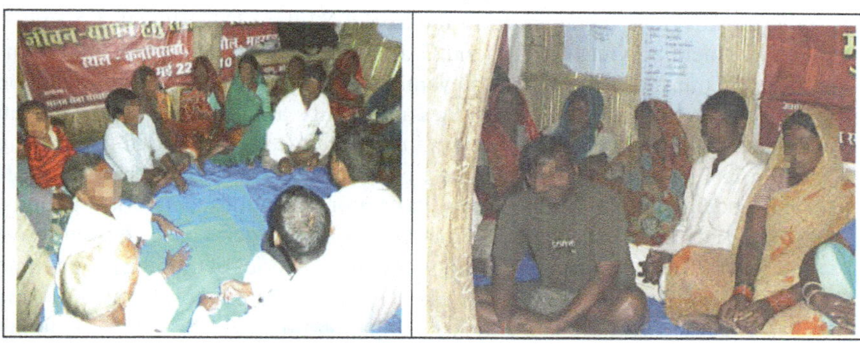

Meeting with the 'Musahars' - the most marginalised community in Nichloli, Maharajganj District, Indo Nepal border, 23 August 2012

Manav Seva Sansthan (MSS) has helped in addressing unsafe migration and human trafficking through training to trainers from NGOs from India, Nepal and Bangladesh along the Indo-Nepal and Indo-Bangladesh border areas. In addition, they have offered training to police and officials of Sashastra Seema Bal (SSB) for sensitizing issues on trafficking of women and girls. Sanlaap imparted training programme to CBOs/NGOs, SHGs, police officers and constables, BSF Officers, doctors and medical student, members of CWC/JJB, youth members, lawyers and public prosecutors and social workers all over West Bengal including the Indo-Bangladesh borders in order to address issues related to unsafe migration, trafficking, life skill education, law and legal issues, child rights and protection, trafficking-related laws and dealing of cases by doctors of violence against women and youth leadership. Partner organization 'Impulse' has been involved in training many concerned stakeholders such as police, judicial like judges and lawyers, administrative officials including divisional magistrates, in addition to local governance—the Panchayat members for capacity building and enhanced sensitization. The NGO

'Apne Aap' created a girl's hostel (Kasturba Gandhi Balika Vidyalaya) in partnership with the Indian government's 'Education for All' initiative to prevent the trafficking of Nat girls that were growing up in home-based brothels in Forbesgunge, Bihar. Other partner organizations like Bhoomika Vihar, ATSEC Bihar, Prajwala and many others have been involved in such training programme in collaboration with the local governments.

(b) Training for Policy Strategy Implementers

While imparting training to the grass roots, it is important to strengthen the capacity and sensitize the implementers of policy strategies. Sensitization programmes targetting the police, Border Security Forces, in addition to undertaking workshops for enhancing coordination between police and prosecutors, improve police understanding and use of anti-trafficking laws all contributes to bringing about an attitudinal change for taking an effective action in preventing crime, undertaking rescue operations and protecting the victims.

Training and capacity building of state governments, judiciary, police, immigration authorities, NGOs, members from the Social Welfare Department, Integrated Child Development Services (ICDS) and Gram Panchayat (local governance) eventually results in transforming them as preventive agents against trafficking of women and girls. They in turn develop committees and groups at the village level who can fall back upon a ready referral mechanism in times of need. Consultation involving political parties, NGOs, legislative bodies, etc., is important in apprehending traffickers and rescuing the trafficked victims. Partner organizations, network coalitions, local and state governments and the international donor agencies have all been active participants in such endeavours. Sanlaap has organized a series of training programme for police officers in collaboration with UNODC. Their training programme for the police has become institutionalized. They impart training to the Police Training School in Kolkata in addition to others like officers from the Crime Investigation Department (CID). If the police encounter any problem, they call the NGO 'Sanlaap' to assist them. They also have offered training for law enforcement, judicial and government transport employees. 'Impulse' from Meghalaya has implemented training programme to all the seven states of north-east. Impulse has implemented training programme for the law enforcement agencies, the police and the journalists in all the eight districts of the north-east. The north-east police academy appreciated the problem of human trafficking especially that of women and children. A 'Handbook for Law Enforcement on Trafficking in Persons', 2006, was developed for the law enforcement officers and is used in each police training school in the north-east. Impulse has also offered training of border guards to recognize trafficking, rescue potential victims and arrest traffickers at seven border areas.

The Manav Seva Sansthan (MSS) in Gorakhpur similarly has undertaken capacity building of personnel from the Sashastra Seema Bal (SSB) on migration and human trafficking. It has held workshops for sensitization of MPs and MLAs on inter- and intra-country migration, human trafficking and migrant rights. Life Guards from the SSB in coordination with the state police (Uttar Pradesh, Uttarakhand, Bihar and West Bengal Police) located at major transit locations along the Indo-Nepal border are instrumental in nabbing the culprits. These cells counsel the cross-border migrants and hand them over to Government of Nepal, who comes under any suspicion during the counselling. Regional parliamentarian platforms have been formed for better bilateral coordination and collaboration to address migration, migrant rights and human trafficking. Core group of key regional parliamentarians have been formed for policy advocacy and lobbying at the national level.

'Shakti Vahini' on the other hand has been organizing judicial colloquiums in collaboration with the Ministry of Home Affairs in Rajasthan, Jharkhand and other vulnerable areas of the country. They are assisting in collating and compiling the number of missing children that are reported in the police station and have been training the police and law enforcing officers for a better understanding and a quicker implementation of the laws. Besides, there are several other training and sensitization sessions organized by partner organization for the NGOs, ATSEC partners, police, border police, Railway Protection Force, professionals and other concerned government bodies dealing with survivors of human trafficking. Many of the training and capacity building initiatives have been depicted in Map 3.3. It clearly displays the concentration is along the border areas and the surrounding areas. Additionally, there are a few other destination places such as Delhi, Jaipur, Bhopal, Mumbai, Goa and Hyderabad where these training programmes are implemented. The map shows that the training programmes for the grass roots are mostly in the border areas and their surroundings and not in the metropolitan areas excepting for Goa and Delhi, they mainly being the demand areas. Map no 3.3 shows the concentration of training and Capacity Building at the relevant areas.

Vigilance, Prosecution and Conviction

The most understandable preventive measures are in the apprehension and prosecution of recruiters/traffickers and brothel owners. Strengthening the national criminal justice systems has been a major goal for the regional governments and to see that a greater number of convictions are achieved globally. This is also largely the purview of the state, since the enactment of the law, training of border and law enforcement personnel, and apprehension and prosecution by criminal justice authorities are viewed as the state's responsibility. They are also expected to act as deterrents to trafficking. So networking with the Border Security Force (BSF), the Sashastra Seema Bal (SSB) and police personnel is expected to translate into active prosecution and conviction rates.

An earlier study by the non-governmental organization 'Lawyers Collective' had indicated excessive usage of Sections 8 and 20 of the ITP Act, by police during pre-2002. An interview with Lawyers Collective in September 2012 expressed that cases under prosecution and conviction have a 'ballooning effect' with an end result of zero-sum game. Arrests under Section 8 of the ITPA may have reduced as a result of the advisories issued by the Ministry of Home Affairs, Government of India, and also as a result of the sensitization and training programme being imparted at the source areas.

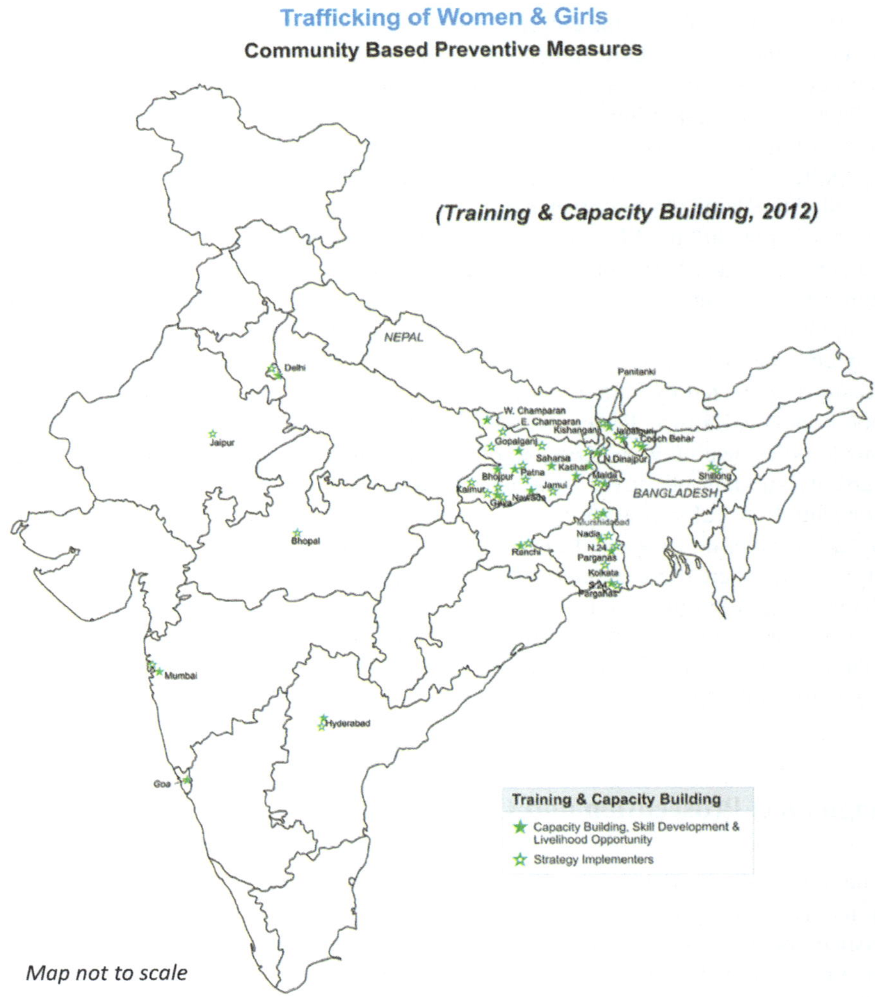

Map 3.3 Training and capacity building, 2012

This was mainly to check women getting arrested on some or the other pretext—a trespasser or an illegal migrant, etc. Ever since the extent of women arrested and engaged in prostitution under Section 8, have actually decreased. However this needs to be scrutinized and looked further into as formal procedures were not in place for most of the law enforcement authorities. Identifying trafficked victims among the arrested women for prostitution was questionable. It is possible that some victims may have been arrested and got doubly punished for acts committed as a result of being trafficked through fraud and cheat. The evaluation study (Dutta et al. 2010) undertaken by UN Women on the anti-trafficking measures suggests that the Goa

Convention did provide a platform for dialogue between policy-/decision-makers and victims/survivors of human trafficking building upon gender-sensitive and rights-based approaches. Goa has its own laws prohibiting child trafficking and prescribed penalties under the 2003 Goa Children's Act which included imprisonment and/or fine.

Field data collected from Sanauli border (from Nepal Police Post at Sanauli) during the months (March–October 2009) indicates that 'Manav Sewa Sansthan' in close partnership with Nepal's partner organization and Nepal Border Police intercepted 314 suspicious persons at Sanauli border. An in-depth analysis of the data indicates that significant proportions of girls were from ages 18 to 25 (Fig. 3.1a and b).

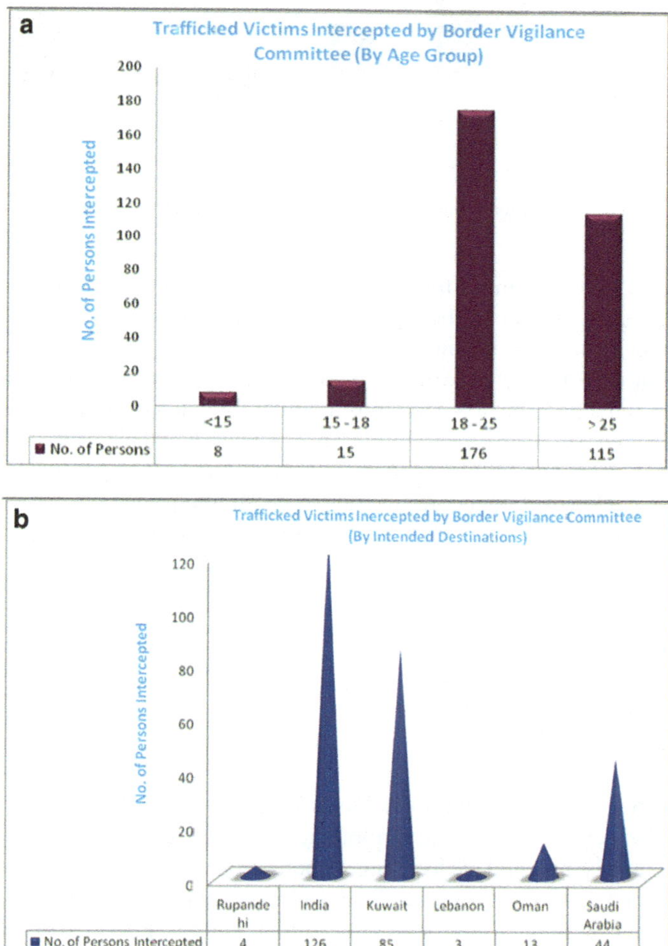

Fig. 3.1 **a** Trafficked victims intercepted by age (Border Vigilance Committee). **b** Trafficked victims intercepted by intended destination (Border Vigilance Committee)

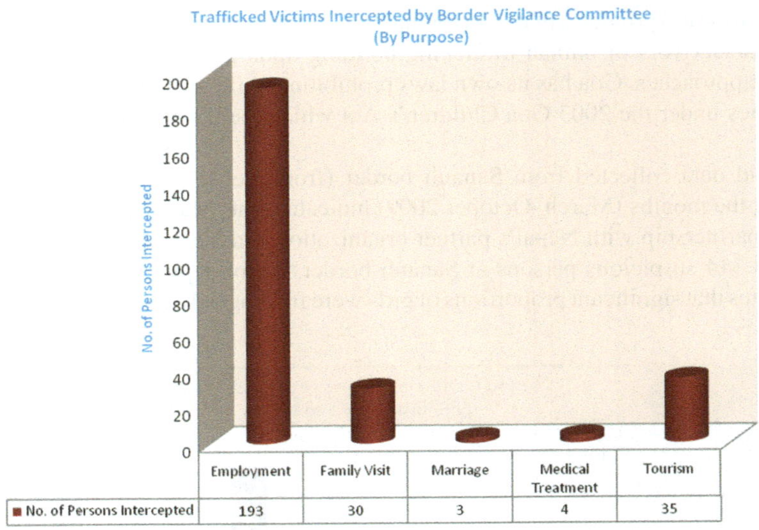

Fig. 3.2 Trafficked victims intercepted by purpose (Border Vigilance Committee)

Majority of them got lured for being providing with better job opportunities in India and the gulf countries. The figures indicate that human trafficking continues unabated from the inaccessible mountainous areas of Nepal. But the surveillance and border vigilance committee have been effective in making strong networks for sharing information. India happens to be the most popular intended destination followed by Kuwait and Saudi Arabia in order of preferences. Other intended places of destination include Oman, Lebanon and Rupandehi (a remote place in Nepal located close to Indian border). However, there are several which go unreported.

The most common reason for the migration has been reported as 'employment' (Refer Fig No 3.2). The present section may be studied under the four subheads:

(a) Prosecution
(b) Conviction
(c) AHTU
(d) Community surveillance.

(a) Prosecution

The Government of India's 'Immoral Trafficking Prevention Act (ITPA)' prohibits trafficking for commercial sexual exploitation with penalties ranging from seven years to life imprisonment. Due to a long arduous process, in many occasions victims have been reluctant to testify against their traffickers and also because of a lurching fear of the vengeance that the traffickers may inflict. The data provided by the National Crime Record Bureau (NCRB) in terms of prosecution has been depicted in Fig. 3.3.

The graph shows the cumulative frequency of cases under prosecution from 2003 to 2010. The NCRB data indicates that persons prosecuted have increased from

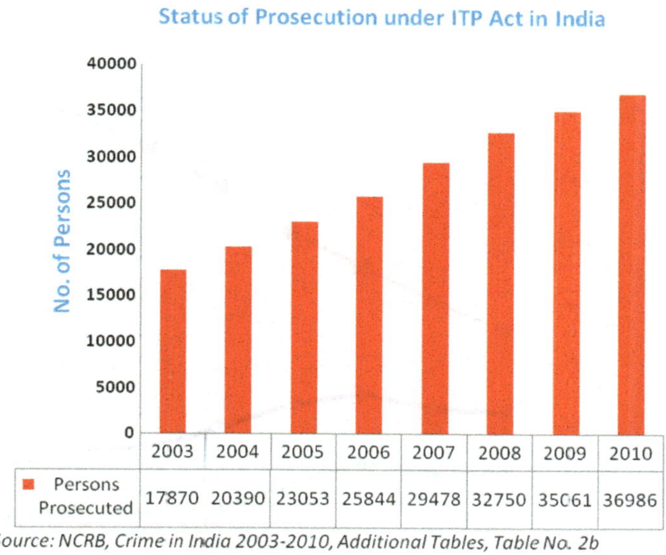

Fig. 3.3 Status of prosecution under ITP Act of India

17,870 in 2003 to 36,986 in 2010. The trend has been a steady increase. However behind the increasing trend, a careful observation reveals that there has actually been a decline in the number of cases under prosecution year-wise over the last three years (2008–2010). In terms of absolute numbers, the total prosecution in 2010, 2009 and 2008 has been 1925, 2311 and 3272, respectively. This may possibly be attributed to the observance of restricted use of Section 8 of the ITPA. However, this cannot be determined in the absence of proper data.

(b) Conviction

There has been an active attempt to develop capacities of law enforcement machinery and prosecution, through training programme and workshops so that appropriate legal actions are taken to book culprits and decriminalize the victims. In this direction, partner organizations in Goa and Mumbai had conducted training programme. Training and orientation workshops were also conducted for judiciary and prosecutors in Goa and Mumbai. Judges and police were made aware about the factual circumstances leading to the victims being trafficked (such as fraudulent tactics and allurements adopted in source areas) so that victim-friendly judgments could be pronounced. In Maharashtra, 120 voluntary organizations formed a network (NASCET) to train police officials. The post-training did help the police to understand the legal provisions better and to avoid the usage of Section 8 of ITP Act that had been most frequently utilized by the police force earlier. There was a change in their perception about customers who can also be booked and adults who can get trafficked. However, translation of these learnings by the police does not reflect any

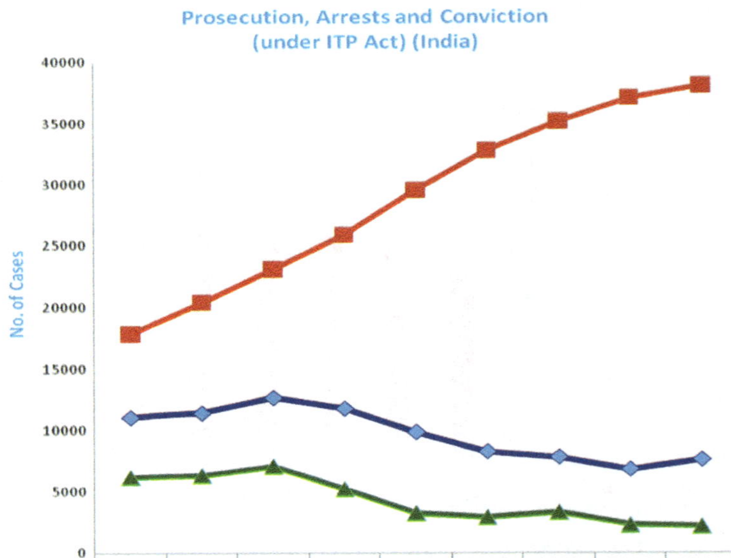

	2003	2004	2005	2006	2007	2008	2009	2010	2011
Persons Arrested	11101	11428	12665	11783	9861	8250	7802	6775	7581
Persons Prosecuted	17870	20390	23053	25844	29478	32750	35061	36986	37973
Persons Convicted	6202	6341	7075	5201	3220	2884	3288	2242	2133

Source: National Crime Records Bureau, 2003-2011

Fig. 3.4 Prosecution, arrests and conviction

significant change as per the records of the National Crime Records Bureau (NCBR) under incidences of crime for women and children under ITP Act, 1956.

Figure 3.4 displays the trend in terms of number of prosecution, arrests and conviction from 2003 to 2011 as per the data obtained from NCRB. The number of arrests under ITP Act, 1956, shows a decline 11,101 in 2003 to 7581 in 2011. In terms of convictions, a steady decline was observed from 6202 in the year 2003 to 2133 in the year 2011. It was also observed as discussed earlier that there has been a decrease in the number of cases prosecuted as well. So, the trend lines from 2003 to 2011 all show that there has actually been a decline in the number of cases registered for prosecution, arrests and conviction.

However, the fact needs to be acknowledged that India's efforts to protect victims of trafficking vary from state to state. It is worth mentioning that some of the states such as Goa, Maharashtra and Andhra Pradesh convicted a significant number of sex trafficking offenders, while in many others there have been only a few cases of conviction among the sex trafficking offenders. The state of Goa showed that the conviction rates of persons under the ITP Act, 1956, and Goa Children's Act, 2003, had improved. A study of Fig. 3.5 shows a total number of registered cases in Goa for the period 2004–2009 as 205. A total of 119 cases were disposed out of this, while 28 cases were convicted. This is almost 14 per cent of the total registered cases.

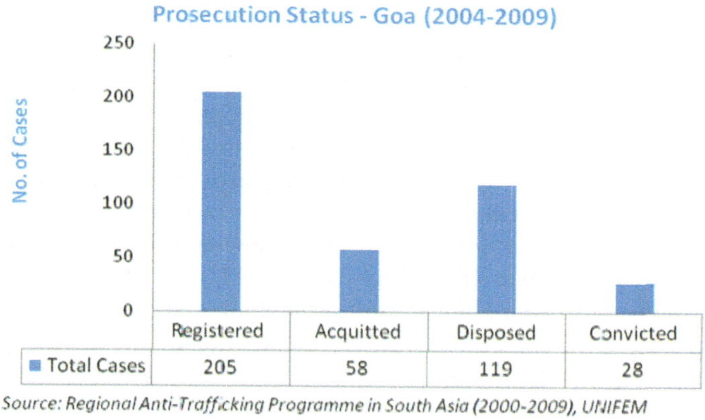

Fig. 3.5 Prosecution status, Goa (2004–2009)

Records state that in Mumbai, the special anti-trafficking court recorded convictions in at least 81 cases under the ITPA, many of which had multiple defendants. Some of these 81 cases included convictions of 'clients' as well as sex trafficking victims. Sentences ranged from $2 fines under the solicitation provision of the ITPA to three-year prison terms for traffickers and clients. Mumbai police, working with an NGO, helped secure the convictions of eight sex traffickers in the Mumbai Sessions Court under the ITPA and the IPC in 2009. One sex trafficker received a sentence of three-year imprisonment, four received sentences of five-year imprisonment, and three received a one-year sentence each. The Andhra Pradesh court convicted 55 convicted sex traffickers and 'clients' and sentenced them to four to 14 years' imprisonment during the period October 2008 to February 2010. All these convictions were under Penal Code 366A, 372, 273 and 376(2)71. The Team Leader, Ms. Hasina Kharbhih, from Impulse NGO Network, Shillong, had filed a FIR on 6 July 2005 to arrest a trafficker named Rafiquddin alias Manual Haque for trafficking two women (Case No: ATSEC/INGON/2001-05/38). After several rounds of court appearance and witness disposition in 2012, the court finally convicted him after a long period of almost 7 years had lapsed. This is justice delayed indeed!

(c) AHTU

A special Task Force named the 'Integrated Anti-Human Trafficking Unit' (IAHTU) was set up involving the primary responders, who need to work together in addressing the issues of human trafficking. The IAHTUs have a comprehensive mandate for attending to the 3 P's that is prevention, prosecution and protection. Through the ITPA, which provides a wide-ranging involvement of NGOs in the implementation of the Act, it envisions a synergy of efforts among the judiciary, executive magistrate, police, other government departments and NGOs, thereby ensuring a comprehensive and rights-based approach towards victims of human trafficking (UNODC and GOI 2007). The role of NGOs is crucial and can facilitate all activities of AHTUs starting with intelligence collection up to conviction of the trafficker. They also have a major role in prevention of trafficking and re-trafficking of victim—survivors. In the absence of IAHTUs, most of the response agencies and stakeholders have been working independently to the extent that at times duplicating efforts and at times, even being counterproductive. The few combined efforts that started were unfortunately ad hoc in nature and were far off from being institutionalized. The creation of IAHTUs facilitates in strengthening such efforts and would help in translating visions into reality. The Ministry of Home Affairs, Government of India, had started establishing the 115 Anti-Human Trafficking Units (AHTUs) scheduled for the period 2010–11. Another 110 Anti-Human Trafficking Units (AHTUs) were to be set up during the period 2011–2012 (AHTU 2011). At present, the AHTUs that are mainly functional are only in 146 districts of the country which is far below the requirement considering the mass scale trafficking that takes place. However in one of the Rajya Sabha, unstarred question number 251, dated 12 December 2018, gives the following distribution of AHTUs in various states (Refer Table No 3.1).

Although no reliable study has been completed yet, the magnitude of trafficking in terms of forced and bonded labour has been estimated to be affecting 20–65 million Indians according to the NGOs. Men, women and children get trafficked in India for diverse reasons.

A state-wise analysis suggests that the 'Anti-Human Trafficking Units (AHTUs)' in the state of Andhra Pradesh work in close liaison with partner organizations (such as Prajwala, HELP, Stree, Ankuram and REDS) in the districts of Hyderabad, Eluru and Anantapur, which are extremely vulnerable to trafficking of women and girls. Shakti Vahini has been closely involved with AHTUs and the prosecution of the accused/traffickers. They assist the AHTUs, police and the Border Security Personal to file First Information Report (FIR) and help the entire process of prosecution and conviction. Several other NGOs have been associated with AHTU for prevention, protection and prosecution. Such of these NGOS have been acknowledged for their best practice initiatives (UNODC and GOI 2008). These include the National Inter-Religious Priest Forum (IRPF), Action against Trafficking and Sexual Exploitation of Children (ATSEC India and its state chapters of Bihar, Jharkhand), Vimochana, Sakhi, Contact Base, i-Land Informatics Limited, Apne Aap, Manav Seva Sansthan, Bhoomika Vihar, Jabala, Nedan, MV Foundation, Prayas Juvenile Aid Center, STOP, Centre for Child Rights, Just Trust, Bachpan Bachao Andolan (BBA) and the Rescue Foundation.

According to the then nodal officer in Shillong (Mr Anurag Kumar, IPS, Nodal Officer, Anti-Human Trafficking Unit, Shillong, Impulse, August 2012), there were around 20 infiltration centres in the north-east and four girls had been rescued from Silchar. There are two AHTUs established in the north-east, and two more are likely to be established. With cases from remote areas such as Khasi and Garo hills, the AHTU looks after all the preventive and rehabilitative measures of the north-east.

Table 3.1 Funds released for Anti-Human Trafficking Units (MHA), 2018

State	Number of AHTUs for which funds were released by MHA
Andhra Pradesh	7
Arunachal Pradesh	8
Assam	10
Bihar	14
Chhattisgarh	8
Goa	2
Gujarat	15
Haryana	10
Himachal Pradesh	4
Jammu and Kashmir	7
Jharkhand	8
Karnataka	9
Kerala	9
Madhya Pradesh	24
Maharashtra	12
Manipur	5
Meghalaya	3
Mizoram	4
Nagaland	6
Orissa	17
Punjab	8
Rajasthan	12
Sikkim	2
Tamil Nadu	12
Tripura	2
Telangana	3
Uttar Pradesh	35
Uttarakhand	7
West Bengal	7
Total	270

Before the AHTUs were established, CID office used to look after the anti-trafficking issues. Now, AHTU looks after the entire training of the state and district level, and TOT for awareness generation and sensitization among the police. He acknowledged that Shillong 'does have any organized trafficking, no brothels and no red light areas nevertheless with the regions international borders it is a source, transit and destination'. The AHTU has training programme three times a year. It will produce specialized officers who will deal with all cases of crime. With a common border with

Bangladesh, the AHTU adopts a multi-pronged approach strategy with the Border Security Force (BSF), the Bangladesh Rifles (BDR) and the Meghalaya Police.

(d) Community Surveillance

Community surveillance is a popular initiative among the community-based interventions. This provides a platform where communities can take substantial action. Several NGOs find surveillance effective and cite numerous examples where groups have been successful in intercepting traffickers with accompanying potential victims and girls. They also claim that they could monitor and keep a tag as to whether any girls have gone missing from a community. Nevertheless for want of authentic documentation, such initiatives have not been that effective. Community surveillance nonetheless has increasingly being recognized as an important model of preventive measure especially in the border areas. The border-based rescue has been a best practice initiative implemented by partner organizations. Members of the group that assist the partner organizations are trained and work as members of the civil vigilance committee. These members are ordinary people like a barber who has a saloon close to the border, a tea shop owner or a teacher from the Madrasa nearby. They assist NGOs by being the watch dog and monitor any suspicious looking migrants. Members of such group often proudly reveal to the number of trafficked victims they have intercepted single handed. Once anyone behaving suspicious is intercepted, the member of the vigilance committee immediately informs the volunteer of the partner organization who arrives on the spot and handles the rest of the process. The border-based rescue is usually in collaboration with the police. Trafficking is normally assumed only when the suspected victim gives hesitant or conflicting answers upon questioning. However, this strategy does not assure a hundred per cent surety of intercepting the right cases. There are instances of women and girls who have been prevented from crossing the border of Nepal despite their vehement protestations that they are travelling of their own free will. Moreover, attempts to intercept trafficked persons at the border cannot really cover all the border points. There are more than 26 Indo-Nepal border points, another dozen along Indo-Bangladesh border in West Bengal and another 20 in the north-east. Thus, it seems but natural that the traffickers would simply shift their operations to the border crossings that are unmanned and unmonitored. Without proper documentation, it is not feasible to predict the success of such initiatives. Nevertheless, such an initiative cannot be brushed away as it does monitor and create awareness among the people.

Exhibit No 9

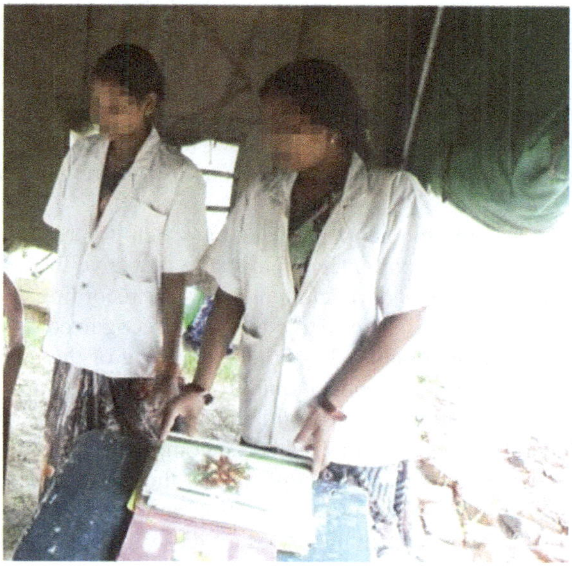

Life Guards being trained by Sahastra Seema Bal and Manav Seva Sansthan, at the Indo Nepal Border areas, Gorakhpur, UP, Aug, 2012

Partner organization such as the Manav Seva Sansthan (MSS) implemented the strategy of the 'Seva Satarkta Prakosht', also referred to as the 'Life Guard Centers' in collaboration with the Sashastra Seema Bal (SSB). The SSB is assisting MSS at four border outposts of Sanauli, Thoothibari, Aligadawa and Badhni with counselling of cross-border migrants and rescue, rehabilitation and repatriation of apparent victims of human trafficking. The centres are essentially units from which volunteers identify and apprehend traffickers and counsel victims as well. It involves a close collaboration with the police. The corresponding units run by partner organizations across the border keep vigil on that side. Upon finding anything suspicious and someone who may be getting trafficked, the lifeguard volunteers keep a vigil on all such antisocial elements and the traffickers. Care is taken to ensure that the rights of migrants are not violated. Sometimes, the trafficking survivors themselves are posted at border stations to intercept any potential victim. Whenever there is any doubt about their position even after being questioned by the police, they are held in a transit home until some guardian comes. At times, they do not wish to return home, in which case they are referred to shelter homes run by NGO partner organization. Persons who look vulnerable to trafficking are subsequently invited to the centre, and the volunteers engage them in conversation. The victims are informed about their rights, their privileges under the constitution and the law. The Life Guard Centers operated by MSS were identified as 'Good Practice' to counter human trafficking by UNHABITAT in 2010 and received many awards for its services to prevent child trafficking and rescuing trafficked victims. One such centre at Sanauli on the Indo-Nepal border, two Nepali women were engaged as lifeguards by Manav Seva Sansthan in collaboration with SSB. They continued to work despite the fact that funds had long stopped for the purpose. The partner organization provides them with a minimum salary so that the initiative does not die a natural death. Their knowing of local language is an added advantage for dialogue with girls and women who are hesitant to talk in the first place.

The volunteers are only too happy to extend any help to prevent trafficking and offer safe migration tips. The volunteers make sure they give them handy numbers to call in case of any trouble and maintain registers for recording and documenting the details of the case. Such an initiative has been recognized as a best practice by the UNODC. While the monitoring and documenting of the number of women and girls that leave a village is a good attempt for studying the impact, nevertheless distinguishing between trafficking and legitimate migration can be tricky and therefore does not accurately measure the desired outcome of reduction in trafficking at the village level. One needs to clearly understand the two processes and develop indicators that can distinguish between migration and trafficking. Map 3.5 shows the spatial distribution of such activities. Most of these concentrate along the Indian border areas besides some slum areas of the metropolitan centres (refer Map 3.4).

The fight against human trafficking is difficult, and there are few indicators that can be used to identify success. The indicators that are available suggest that, to date, 'the number of victims prosecuted and the number of victims helped have been low'. In recent years, attention has started to get diverted to the linkage between human trafficking and natural disasters. It is now amply clear based on micro-level qualitative studies. Scholars have started to concentrate on this important aspect. Nevertheless, there is agreement that the root causes that lead human trafficking to flourish, including instability and poverty, are often exacerbated in the aftermath of a disaster. With a greater exposure of people and their assets, disasters are bound to exacerbate those that are poor and vulnerable. While the focus on immediate needs in the immediate aftermath of a disaster is and should continue to be important, the needs of the vulnerable population—whether to find a safe space for children or to make efforts to resume as close to a normal routine as possible—must be just as important. The follow-up to the Hyogo Framework for Action provides an excellent opportunity to ensure that the needs of vulnerable populations, and mitigating the potential for trafficking, are also at the top of the list when dealing with an emergency situation.

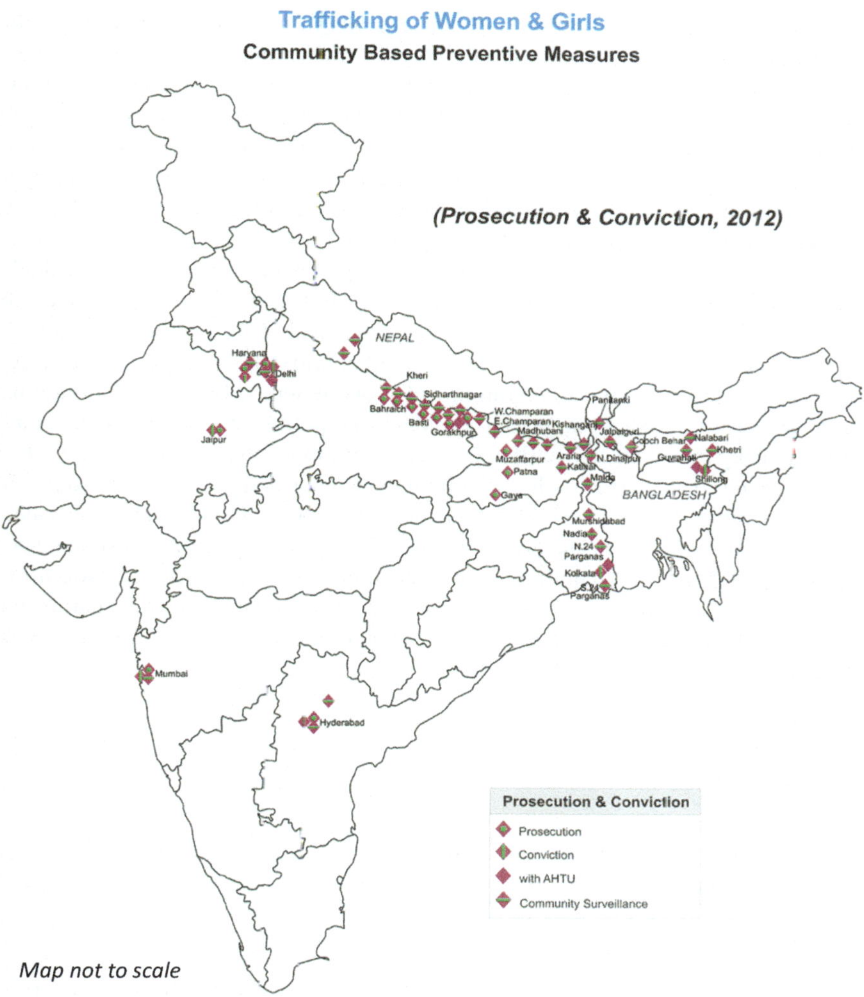

Map 3.4 Prosecution and conviction, 2012

Information, Education, Technology and Communication (IETC)

In addition to community-based preventive measures that are operating in the field for raising awareness and sensitization of the concerned stakeholders, there also exists a plethora of Information, Education and Communication (IEC) materials which are of immense significance. As stated earlier, there are overlapping areas of the various community-based preventive measures. This section may seem to overlap with some of measures discussed under 'Awareness and Sensitization'; however, the perspective is much different and hence needs to be revisited. Several useful knowledge products and resources in the form of films, interactive materials, calendars, puppet shows, *nukkad nataks*, handbooks, CDs, resource materials, ready reckoners, marches, posters, films, training manuals and standard operating procedures for creating effective awareness, investigation and rescue as well as care and attention post-rescue of the victims have been developed. IEC materials have been developed for religious leaders, media sensitization for the print and electronic media. The IEC materials have been distributed at the village level.

The IEC strategies have frequently been implemented, targeting individuals, communities and other stakeholders. It engulfs a whole sea of information in easily and readily available handbooks for all concerned stakeholders. There are extremely practical and functional training modules and other booklets designed and produced by partner organizations in collaboration with Government of India and international donor agencies in order to target stakeholders like police, law enforcing agencies, border security personnel and parliamentarians. Simultaneously, there is no dearth of resource material available for the communities, women and girls, at-risk and potentially vulnerable, NGOs/CBOs, 'Panchayats' (members of the local governance) and other stakeholders. These are available in the form of pictorial displays such as posters, banners, wall paintings, music, cassettes, TV/radio talks, cartoon films, dance and so many other displays which are educating and provide information and awareness to the community and the most vulnerable. The entire material may be further categorized under the following:

(a) Print
(b) Audio
(c) Audio-visual
(d) Internet.

Almost all partner organizations are involved in producing one or several of these resource materials.

(a) Print

The print material includes posters, wall writings, banners, handbills, leaflets, booklets, periodicals, books, training manuals and other pictorial representations. In areas of destination, the print material has been displayed in ticket folders, luggage tags, brochures and pamphlets, knob hangers and lobby poster. Print displays are exhibited in terms of comic books, as car and bike stickers and also as a mobile public notice. Some of the metropolitan centres have developed community package including press ads, hoardings and kiosks, danglers in photo shops, popular local music and helpline numbers. Reaching out to communities through letters and postcards is also been a popular way of disseminating messages. Making a banner with signatures of local communities in support against trafficking and related abuse, and getting film stars and celebrities to sign on anti-trafficking slogans are all successful and popular ways of attracting attention. Newsletter, resource directory, periodical and books are also some of the beneficial production that captures volumes of experiences. To name a few of the books, it includes 'Mothers for Sale' and 'Guilty without Trial' and the list is unending.

(b) Audio

The audio cassettes are an instant hit in the rural areas. This not only includes music but also holds regular poetry recitation competition involving some of the stake-holders to be the judge. These are held at opportune moments such as the Durga Puja (an ideal time for attracting public attention in Kolkata) to prevent trafficking during festive season. Partner organizations from the concerned region are quick to grab such opportunities. Radio programme has been found to be useful especially where an ensuing discussion is held with some of the well-known people in the community. Other ways include announcements

(c) Audio-visual

Some of the skits and street plays, puppet shows and nukkad nataks have been well appreciated by the local community members and the youths. During festival period or on a Sunday, it attracts a large number of people to watch, enjoy and learn. Documentary films, cartoon shows, short films, dance, drama (theatre), puppet shows and cartoon shows are some of the other methods adopted. These are also produced in vernacular language. Television programme and TV soap operas often invite crowds from the vulnerable lot especially if they are produced in their vernacular language. Short film/documentaries have been most favoured where concerned stakeholders have found it to be most captivating. Some of these include 'The Day my God Died', 'Sold' and so on.

(d) Internet

Presently, there are blogs and Web portals created which are essentially interactive. Emails, websites and creation of electronic material are a regular feature that is used by partner organization. There are website development at the regional, national and the international level. There are excellent community-based IEC materials available to execute a comprehensive awareness for ushering in a behavioural change strategy in the region. However, what seem to be lacking is a mechanism to share evidence, knowledge and information on prevention of trafficking at a regional, national, the local government and civil society stakeholders for ensuring a greater awareness and a cohesive approach of the programme and their implementation in prevention of trafficking among women and girls.

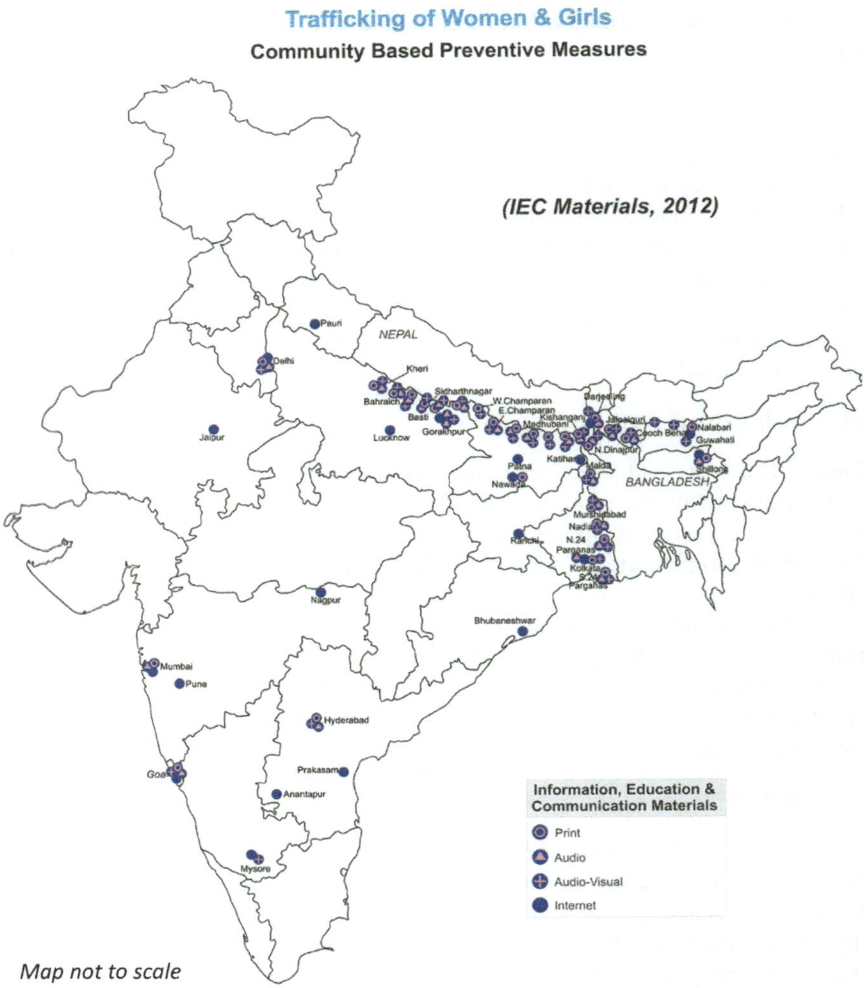

Map 3.5 IEC material, 2012

Community-Based Preventive Measures—A Composite Picture

An overall picture of all the five categories of community-based preventive measures has been depicted in Map 3.6. It clearly depicts a massive concentration in the border areas with a few at the destination places such as Hyderabad, Mumbai and Delhi. On several occasions, it has been observed that in a particular source area the preventive measures are been duplicated by several NGOs/CBOs. Instead of being duplicated and supplemented, these preventive measures should rather complement each other.

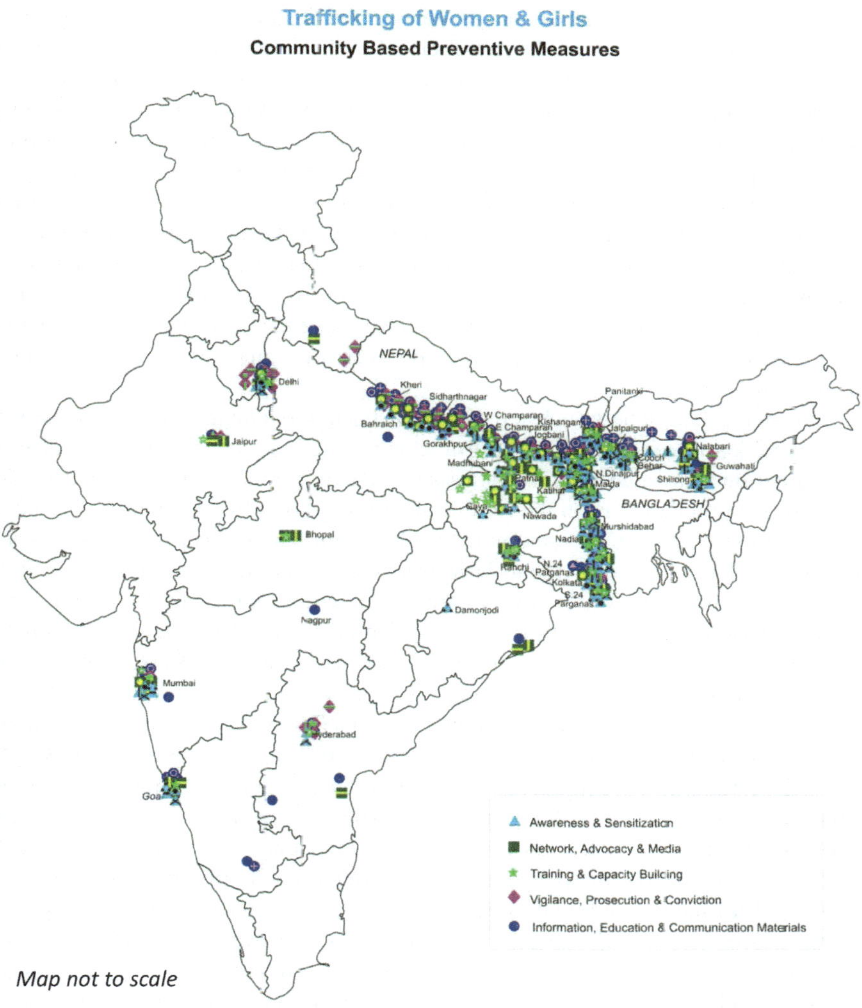

Map 3.6 Community-based preventive measures—the composite picture, 2012

This is necessary more so due to the non-availability of funds and budget constraint. Many of these measures are of immense significance which can be replicated in other areas rather than inventing the wheel again. The training programme needs to be an ongoing process. The officials and BSF staff either retire or get transferred, and without a regular training, the process gets slowed down. It is important to maintain the continuity.

Over the last couple of decades, NGOs have come forward on a war footing to implement a multiple number of interventions for preventing human trafficking. Many of the preventive measures are also area focused in the migration process such as the point of origin or transit, or a border or a destination. However, a majority of the preventive measures are largely focused in the source areas involving target groups such as community members, women, girls, adolescents, members of the local 'Panchayat', faith-based organizations and the NGOs/CBOs. The local women's NGOs have often been preferred over others as they seem to be better equipped to implement preventive strategies at the grass-roots level. It is not uncommon to come across a successful community-based preventive measure going unnoticed for want of a proper dissemination process. Documentation of the rich experiences gained in the field and the lessons learned, at source, destination and the transit areas, is of extreme importance for replication and efficacy in the implementation of the preventive measures. This has been a well-attested fact that information sharing and data collection on aspects of trafficking especially for women and girls remains an under-documented area.

Some of the areas where such activities have been implemented are not only along the vulnerable source areas in the Indo-Bangladesh and Indo-Nepal borders but also in the destination areas such as Goa, Maharashtra, Delhi, Kolkata, Mumbai, Hyderabad and so on. Despite a focus on the rural to urban migration trend, NGO experiences reveal that there are an increasing number of women that are being trafficked from their urban places of employment. However, such of these cases have not been a major focus among the NGO efforts barring a few exceptions. In the presence of so many networks, there is clearly some potential for overlap and duplication of activities. This has implications both in terms of efficient use of resources and in terms of the effectiveness of the activities.

Networking, Advocacy and Media interventions as a preventive tool are some of the initiatives which are of extreme significance. Network coalitions such as CBATN and ATSEC have been found to be extremely effective in addressing cross-border trafficking of women and girls. In fact, networking is considered as one of the best means of effective advocacy. Most of their activity tends to be centred on organizing workshops and conferences to raise awareness and engage in advocacy on the issue of trafficking. While these networks have a broad-based membership and engage in a wide range of anti-trafficking activities, however their effectiveness in addressing trafficking of women and children still remains to be proven. Obstacles such as ideological conflicts regarding the definition of trafficking could pose hurdles in networking and coalition building among NGOs engaged in preventive anti-trafficking initiatives. In addition to weakening the network coalitions, such an impact could create further hurdles in building regional cooperation programme.

The community-based preventive measures in terms of training and capacity building necessarily operate at two levels—at the grass roots to build the capability of the different segments of the local communities and secondly, to strengthen the capacity of law enforcement, border control and immigration authorities, parliamentarians and the police in apprehending traffickers and rescuing victims of sex trafficking. While the training for capacity building, skill development and livelihood opportunities concentrate along the borders of Indo-Nepal and Indo-Bangladesh and its surrounding areas, the training for Policy Strategy Implementers are mostly in the metropolitan centres.

Some of the awareness and advocacy activities are case sensitive, and the target groups such as parliamentarians, police or the law enforcement officials may comprehend conflicting messages and contradictory advice. There are no evaluations or assessment on the effectiveness of such intervention models, activities and approaches in place. The current trafficking interventions also lack the comprehensive and systematic monitoring and documentation. There is no standard documentation available for meaningful comparison. Hence, assessing the degree of effectiveness of such programme is difficult.

The very existence of anti-trafficking activities implemented by NGOs depends upon a steady flow of donor funding, but the organizations also often have to compete with each other to secure a share of the funds that is available. It is important that the NGOs build solidarity networks and coalition partnerships to pool in resources. With a resource crunch and serious threat to the ever-shrinking budget, it can be hard to achieve the long-term sustainability that is required in achieving the effectiveness of a preventive measure. For example, the lifeguards at the Indo-Nepal border exist on dwindling funds, while the initiative is an extremely important anti-trafficking preventive measure for women and girls. Most local NGOs depend on foreign donors and have only limited resources, and the programme is generally of short- to medium-term duration. Few of the NGOs working on community-based preventive measures are equipped to sustain a programme over a long period of time. Without a regular source of funding for the purpose, it is likely that such an initiative may not remain active and agile in due course of time. Nevertheless while monitoring and documenting the number of women and girls that leave a village, care needs to be taken to distinguish between trafficking and legitimate migration so that such documentation can throw light on the real impact and can accurately measure the desired outcome of reduction in trafficking of women and girls at the village level.

Given their limited financial resources, NGOs are seldom able to undertake follow-up studies or to monitor the situation after the completion of the project. While most donor agencies require NGOs to develop specific indicators to measure the success of the initiatives that they have funded, these indicators are mostly about reporting on actual numbers covered rather than on the medium- to long-term effectiveness of the initiative. Examples include records of the number of rallies held by women's groups, the number of times that women's groups discuss trafficking, the number of participants in prevention activities, the number of IETC materials produced and distributed, and the number of women and girls intercepted through border rescue or community surveillance strategies.

Consequently post-submission of the final report to the donor agencies, the implementing NGO seldom involves in independent evaluations of the efficiency of the community-based preventive measures that they implement. An assessment of community-based preventive measures to trafficking of women and girls undertaken particularly in the source areas suggests that those efforts that integrate awareness rising with some form of participatory activity are more likely to be sustainable and effective. Developing innovative forms of community leadership, empowering the young, challenging the intensely rooted habits and perspectives about gender and the life options for women and men all usher in the real change. It is thus recommended to essentially support local-level strategies designed to nurture grass-roots responses that tend to become self-generating over a period of time.

Community surveillance is found to be a most appropriate and effective tool of community--based preventive measure to trafficking of women and girls involving the community in collaboration with outside support. It assists communities to develop strong networking that eventually establish systems for taking action in the event of suspected trafficking. It is recommended that funding of such initiatives needs to be a long-term initiative. The funding needs to taper gradually rather than ending abruptly. Working with children and young people through schools, teachers or young girls (*Kishori* groups) is another innovative anti-trafficking strategy. The peer group support/influence helps in the formation of such groups and also provides answers especially to those children who may face family problems and require assistance. Field experiences have shown that people are more likely to identify with peer-led education rather than that given by social workers. It is recommended that creation of groups particularly the women's group and the adolescent group be formed for gathering such information for prompt action.

There is a lack of programme monitoring and evaluation mechanisms for a vast number of the community-based preventive measures to trafficking of women and girls. Most of the strategies' success is usually measured in terms of its short-sightedness based on the number game, for example, the number of people that had been reached in awareness campaigns and capacity building, the number of law enforcement officers and border guards who received training, the number of participants in skill-training schemes or other programme, and even the number of laws that have been passed in source and destination areas to prevent female sex trafficking. However, monitoring and follow-up of other responses and evaluating the effectiveness of such programmes are of immense significance rather than estimating the number of people reached. It is hence recommended that a wider and more qualitative evaluation and monitoring of anti-trafficking initiatives be inbuilt within each initiative.

Whether it is to sharpen awareness and alert people to the potential plight of innocent victims among a particular community, portray the cunning methods used by recruiters and demonstrate the illegality of the operations, the ultimate success of a campaign lies in the fact in bringing down the number of trafficked victims. There remains a big gap between the prosecution, arrests and conviction. It is recommended to initiate fast-track courts to settle the huge number of pending cases and punish the guilty which would in turn act as a deterrent to the traffickers. The military institutions and peacekeeping forces are encouraged to implement formal pre-emptive measures to discourage sexual exploitation of girls and women in their spheres of influence, and to incorporate education about trafficking, child prostitution and different views of masculinity in their training of young men and in their contact with local communities in the areas where they are posted.

References

AHTU. 2011. http://pib.nic.in/newsite/erelease.aspx?relid=82967.

Boonpala, Panudda, and June Kane. 2001. *Trafficking in Children: The Problem and Response Worldwide*. Geneva: ILO.

CBATN. http://www.cbatnsouthasia.net/CBATN_%20Membership_Brochure.pdf).

Dutta, M., et al. 2010. *UNIFEM, 2010: Evaluation Report on UNIFEM's Anti-trafficking Programme in South Asia, (2000–2009)*. [http://www.unwomensouthasia.org/assets/final_evaluation.pdf.

Dutta, M. 2011. *Mapping Vulnerability to Trafficking of Women and Children in India*, sponsored by UN Women and the National Commission for Women, March 2011, New Delhi.

Nair, P.M., and Sankar Sen. 2007. *Trafficking in Women and Children in India*, 2007. Orient Longman: New Delhi.

NHRC. 2005. *National Human Rights Commission (NHRC), 2005: Action Research Study, 2005.*

Prajwala. http://www.prajwalaindia.com/preventhruedu.html.

Sanlaap. 2012. *Withering Flowers—Traditional Prostitution in India, Kolkata, 2012.*

UNIFEM. 2010. *Evaluation Report on UNIFEM's Anti-trafficking Programme in South Asia (2000–2009)*. http://www.unwomensouthasia.org/assets/final_evaluation.pdf.

United Nations Office of Drugs and Crime (UNODC), and Government of India. 2007. *Synergy in Action, Protocol on the Structure and Function of the Integrated Anti-Human Trafficking Unit (IAHTU) in India.*

Chapter 4
Laws, Policies and Protocols

The Legal Framework

Today, the world has started to recognize the perils of vulnerability. Vulnerability of any kind leaves one completely unprotected and open for exploitation. Vulnerability becomes even more dangerous when there are more factors that combine together to target an already declared victim. There is hardly any place in the world which is hazard free, and life is full of risks. The present chapter draws the attention to the twin evils of both the atrocities of human trafficking and the devastation of natural disasters that befall a victim and the existing policies. These events leave human pain and suffering at outstanding levels.

The importance of effective legal frameworks for disaster risk reduction and early warning has been well recognised. The role of local authorities in early warning has been stressed repeatedly, and the importance of imbibing disaster risk reduction into development and poverty reduction strategies has been reiterated. Coordination of international systems, such as the proposed global early warning system, and national systems is of significance. Within the perspective of a disaster, when human and animal losses are in abundance, property destroyed in billions of dollars, infrastructure uprooted, it becomes even more pertinent that an effort be created at the international level to usher in transnational standards of law.

There has been a consistent effort in this regard for constructing and mitigating to respond to these calamities. Nevertheless, there have been shortcomings not only in terms of understanding the connection and correlation between the two but also in achieving a situation where the synergy of all stakeholders comes to a meeting point. The international law has no doubt made commendable strides towards achieving globally cooperative solutions in the respective areas of human trafficking and natural disasters, but the necessary legal action has been in deficit for overcoming the gap between these two. Despite the several case studies that go to show how human trafficking gets activated during as well as in the post-disaster scenario, scholars are reluctant to appreciate the grave nature of this problem due to a lack of data. Therefore, research at depth has been meagre. It was only in the post-2004 tsunami that

M. Dutta, *Disaster and Human Trafficking*,
https://doi.org/10.1007/978-981-16-1630-3_4

researchers began to realize and acknowledge the vulnerability that natural disasters create for human trafficking to get enhanced manifold. It is in this connection that international law becomes of even more relevance and must be further crystalized to battle this ever-increasing cross section of human suffering.

Human trafficking is a 150-billion-dollar industry that reaches every corner of the world and impacts every country (Human Rights First 2017). It is now a well-known fact that human traffickers prey on the most vulnerable and desperate, specifically targeting the defenceless young men, women and children.

Figure 4.1 characterises three elements—*Act, Means* and *Purpose.* It is basically the ability to execute the act of human trafficking essentially influenced through a series of factors at the individual, state, trafficker and international level (UNODC 2017). The individual factors relate to the absence of economic or social security that force the people into poverty, and eventually, they start trusting the traffickers as a last straw of hope. In contrast, the remaining deals with the opportunity for trafficking at the trafficker, state and international levels sometimes making the exploited as exploiters. Natural disasters thus always exacerbate the factors at every level. Particularly when the victim is ignorant of its own potential risk, or there is a deficit of social safety nets, lack of law enforcement machinery, less risk of prosecution and conviction, border regulations are fuzzy and a lack of international coordination (Brülisauer Manuel 2015).

Natural disasters further marginalize and perpetuate the vulnerability of the most at-risk groups. For example, if food production in the source country is low with high unemployment, traffickers generally respond by promising victims of a rosy scenario with jobs in a country where the demand for cheap labour force is high. The economic destruction caused by natural disasters will no doubt lead more people

Execution of Human Trafficking

Act +	**Means +**	**Purpose**	
Recruitment	**Threat or Use of Force**	**Exploitation Including**	
Transport	**Coercion**	**Prostitution of Others**	
Transfer	**Abduction**	**Sexual Exploitation**	**= TRAFFICKING**
Harbouring	**Fraud**	**Forced Labour**	
Receipt of Persons	**Deception**	**Slavery or Similar Practices**	
	Abuse of Power/ Vulnerability	**Removal of Organs**	
	Giving Payments /benefits	**Other Types of Exploitation**	

Source: https://www.unodc.org/unodc/en/human-trafficking/what-is-human-trafficking.html

Fig. 4.1 Execution of human trafficking

to even accepting the risks for exchange of a better economic opportunity, even though it may lead to their getting trafficked. However, the most detrimental impact of natural disasters occurs due to the crumbling infrastructure. During the Nepal earthquake, studies show how traffickers purposefully enter disaster zones, impersonate themselves as relief workers and lure an outstanding number of vulnerable people to a lifetime of slavery. Human traffickers capitalize the lack of coordination, breakdown of the government infrastructure and general communication by posing as relief workers, from well-known organizations, in order to lure victims and sell them as slaves. Thus, international protocols signed by the countries and regional laws become of crucial significance.

Children separated from their families due to natural disasters are the worst hit and are 'at risk' to the lure of predators. According to UN officials, it has been confirmed that 'some people exploit the chaotic environment that follows a natural disaster to engage in criminal activities, like selling children for the purpose of illegal adoption, organ trade, forced labour or sexual exploitation' (Singh 2012). Undoubtedly, the more the chaotic situation following a natural disaster, greater is the opportunity to lure and fraud vulnerable survivors in the already impoverished economic state. Although poverty and lack of economic opportunities pose as the major factors for human trafficking, but its more the disorder and lack of communication caused by natural disasters that create the opportunities for traffickers to build up their supply of free labour.

The present chapter highlights some of the international protocols and conventions that are related to human trafficking and natural disaster. It will study the various regional policies and domestic laws created in the country that are compatible with the international law.

International Protocols

There has been an extensive research on international law which has been created in the United Nations to prevent human trafficking. Accordingly, several countries have generated their corresponding domestic law. A cooperative relief effort post-natural disaster has also been a tremendous contribution, especially given the fact that countries incur huge losses in terms of their GDP during a disaster. It is estimated that India loses a 2 percent GDP or more during disasters every year. Though these efforts are noteworthy, but they remain inadequate in addressing the issue. Neither of the problems can get resolved until the prevalence of the other is recognized. It is the synergy of both that generates the 'push' it needs. International law surrounding human trafficking is based on the *Universal Declaration of Human Rights* (1948) which establishes the basic freedoms and rights of human beings, regardless of race, nationality, gender, political preference or any other self-identifying category (Pashcke 2019). This was followed by the *Universal Declaration of Human Rights* of the United Nations. The resolution, documented the '*Convention for the Suppression of the Traffic in Persons and of the Exploitation of the Prostitution of Others*' that precisely termed the end of human trafficking (Cherry et al. 2011). A couple of decades later, the UN ratified yet another international standard, the *International Covenant on Civil and Political Rights*. This promoted the rights of all individuals throughout the world. This reflected a secure affirmation of the international communities' to eradicate 'slave-trade' in all its forms. The UN always considers that slavery and human trafficking are offenses that cannot be tolerated in any form. Thus, the twentieth century encouraged a battle against trafficking and set a standard of freedom for every citizen of the world.

Finally, the United Nations ratified the *protocol to prevent, suppress and punish Trafficking In Persons, especially women and children, in November 2000* supplementing *United Nations Convention against Transnational Organized Crime*. This protocol called every nation to criminalize human trafficking, protect human trafficking victims and coordinate to prevent future cases of human trafficking (Gilligan 2018). Further, a resolution supplemented this protocol called '*The United Nations Protocol against the Smuggling of Migrants by Land, Sea, and Air*'. This was in order to emphasize the measures adopted by countries to stop the actual smuggling of people into their borders. Subsequently, another major international law came into existence, called the '*Optional Protocol to the Convention on the Rights of the Child on the sale of Children, Child Prostitution and Child Pornography*'. It was amply clear that such gruesome crimes on children did exist and disasters undoubtedly aggravate the gravity of the situation and promote child trafficking. This law thus further criminalizes the sale of children and warrants the coming together by all nations to synergise their work in order to stop the expansion of child slavery.

Though these laws are great efforts by the international community, there are many gaps when trying to actually solve the devastating problems. The main problem of these laws is that they contain gaps in enforceability issues. Every state defers in creating their own law, based on the guidelines of the resolution (Federal Ministry of Labour and Social Affairs). Eventually, it is these international laws that act as a high standard, encouraging countries to try their best to meet the goals. However, for want of a compatible law between the states, the international law falls weak and allows space for traffickers to operate from within. This is just the tip of the iceberg, while the larger failure of the laws is because of the lack of awareness about natural disasters and other related crisis that play in the operations of human trafficking.

The United Nations Office on Drugs and Crime (UNODC), as guardian of the United Nations Convention against Transnational Organized Crime (UNTOC) and the protocols thereto, assists states in their efforts to implement the 'Protocol to Prevent, Suppress and Punish Trafficking in Persons'. This is referred to as 'Trafficking in Persons Protocol'. The protocol was adopted by the United Nations General Assembly in 2000 and entered into force on 25 December 2003. As of February 2018, it has been ratified by 173 parties. It defines Trafficking in Persons as the '*recruitment, transportation, transfer, harbouring or receipt of persons, by means of the threat or use of force or other forms of coercion, of abduction, of fraud, of deception, of the abuse of power or of a position of vulnerability or of the giving or receiving of payments or benefits to achieve the consent of a person having control over another person, for the purpose of exploitation*'. Exploitation includes prostitution of others or other forms of sexual exploitation, forced labour or services, slavery or practices similar to slavery, servitude or the removal of organs besides many other form of exploitation.

This definition (UNODC) essentially implies criminalization in domestic legislation. Although domestic legislation does not mean following in strict precision, the language of the Trafficking in Persons Protocol but should be adapted in accordance with domestic legal systems to give effect to the concepts contained in the protocol both in letter and spirit. In addition to the criminalization of trafficking, the protocol also requires criminalization of the following:

- Any attempt to commit a trafficking offence
- Participation as an accomplice in such an offence
- Organizing or directing others to commit trafficking.

Thus, the national legislation is expected to be able to adopt the broad definition of trafficking prescribed in the protocol. The legislative definition should be dynamic and flexible enough to adapt and modify itself so as to empower the legislative framework to respond effectively to trafficking which,

- Occurs both across borders and within a country (not just cross-border)
- Is for a range of exploitative purposes (not just sexual exploitation)
- Victimizes children, women and men (not just women, or adults, but also men and children)
- Takes place with or without the involvement of organized crime groups

States receive practical help from time to time from UNODC. It offers help in drafting laws and creates comprehensive national anti-trafficking strategies but also assists with resources to implement them. States receive specialized assistance including the development of local capacity and expertise, as well as practical tools to encourage cross-border cooperation in investigations and prosecutions. The adoption by the United Nations General Assembly in 2000 the trafficking in Persons Protocol marked a significant landmark towards international efforts to stop the trade of people in bondage. The UNODC is the guardian of the protocol, addressing human trafficking issues through its global programme against Trafficking in Persons. A vast majority of states have now signed and ratified the protocol. But translating it into reality is still a distant dream. As stated earlier, very few criminals are convicted and most victims are probably never identified or assisted. That human cost is loud and clear. One can see the alarming numbers of people that are getting internally displaced every year by disasters, often losing their homes and their livelihoods, in extreme weather events and earthquakes. The trafficking protocol makes an easy target for attack. Its origins lie in an attempt to control a particularly exploitative form of migration that was challenging the ability of states to control their own borders. Its parent instrument is a framework agreement to address transnational organized crime. While paying fleeting attention to the rights of victims, the Protocol, with its emphasis on criminalisation and border protection is nowhere near being a human rights treaty. On top of all that, it does not even have a credible enforcement mechanism, allowing states parties wide latitude in interpreting and applying their obligations. Strangely, these seemingly insurmountable flaws have not stopped the protocol's emergence as perhaps the single most important development in the fight against human trafficking. Without the protocol, arguments around definitions would have continued to block the evolution of principles and rules. Without the protocol, it is likely that the human rights system would have continued its shameful tradition of side lining issues such as forced labour, forced sex, forced marriage and the ritual exploitation of migrant workers through debt. Most critically, the protocol provided the impetus and template for a series of legal and political developments that, over time, have served to upgrade some of its greatest weaknesses, including the lack of human rights protections and of a credible oversight mechanism.

Addressing issues on human trafficking as a solo problem will not yield the desired results. It is quite apparent that disasters do exacerbate the vulnerability differently to different persons and places which becomes a cool place for traffickers to 'make hay while the sun shines'. If the international community really wants to address these issues in preparation for response to natural disasters, they must take into consideration how vulnerability, chaos and crisis create huge opportunities for traffickers to easily perpetrate horrendous acts of slavery. International law and efforts in response to natural disasters will be incomplete and ineffective in achieving their own outlined goals until action is taken to include an understanding of the connection between human trafficking and natural disasters.

Disaster Risk Reduction (DRR)

It is found that disasters displace more people than conflict and violence put together. The growing magnitude of people that are being affected by natural hazards is being recognized by governments and organizations. Therefore, building resilient communities and reducing disaster risk have become a core initiative of the UN. In an effort to create effective relief, the UN created several initiatives. The main among them is being the United Nations Office of the Disaster Risk Reduction (UNDRR). The UNDRR [formerly referred to as the United Nations International Strategy from Disaster Reduction (UNISDR)] established in 1999, brings governments, partners and communities together to reduce disaster risk and losses, ensuring a safer, more sustainable future. DRR is a relatively a new concept in formal terms, but it embraces much earlier thinking and practice. It is getting widely popular and being embraced by international agencies, governments, disaster planners and civil society organisations. DRR is such an all-embracing concept that it has proved difficult to define or explain in detail, although the broad idea is clear enough. It is generally understood to mean the broad development and application of policies, strategies and practices to minimise vulnerabilities and disaster risks throughout society.

At present, the DRR has taken the shape of a broad-based global movement focused on sustainable development. Natural hazards are a regular feature, and by themselves, it does not pose a threat. But, it was the 2004 Indian Ocean tsunami that sent the world community into a shock. It cost the world more than 200,000 lives and billions of dollars in economic loss. The horrifying images of devastation shook the world to a new size and showed what the magnitude of risk can be like. The shocks further pushed the process of international agencies and national governments and did not remain limited to a mere rhetoric. The pressure resulted in developing most policy statements and setting of clear targets and commitments for DRR.

Post-2004 during the Indian Ocean tsunami, it was realised how the early warning system can make some communities fortunate. Some were fortunate to have received the warning that a wave was on its way and managed to seek shelter on a higher ground. While others perished. In the present global village, the world has shrunk through the interconnectivity brought about through globalization. Humans have pushed the planet beyond its boundaries. There are man-made and natural disasters. Man-made hazards, like financial system collapse or radiation are also bringing new risks. The impact of risk is multi-layered and deep rooted. It is both systemic and a cascading risk. It may begin with tsunami and end up with another like the nuclear station melt down during the huge Japan earthquake of 2011. Therefore, investing in resilience building is of prime importance. It is estimated that every one USD invested in risk reduction and prevention can save up to 15 USD in post-disaster recovery. Every 1 USD invested in making infrastructure disaster-resilient saves 4 USD in reconstruction (UNDRR). The DRR is wide-ranging with much broader and deeper than conventional emergency management. There is potential for DRR initiatives in just about every sector of development and humanitarian work. The UNDRR works globally towards the prevention of new, and the reduction of existing disaster risk. It supports the Sustainable Development Goals, the Paris Agreement on Climate Change and other global development goals. It promotes the strengthening resilience through successful multi-hazard disaster risk management.

The Yokohama Strategy

The Yokohama Strategy and Plan of Action for a Safer World were a major world conference on International Decade for Natural Disaster Reduction (IDNDR). This was held in Yokohama, Japan from 23 to 27 May 1994. This set out the guidelines for natural disaster prevention, preparedness and mitigation and its plan of action, endorsed by the UN General Assembly in 1994. It was the main outcome of the mid-term review of the International Decade of Natural Disaster Reduction (IDNDR) and established 10 principles for its strategy, a plan of action and a follow-up. Furthermore, it provides guidelines for natural disaster prevention, preparedness and mitigation. The ten principles of the Yokohama Strategy includes (Guidelines under Yokohama)

1. Risk assessment for successful implementation of disaster reduction policies and measures.
2. Disaster prevention and preparedness for reducing the need for disaster relief.

3. Disaster prevention and preparedness should be considered integral aspects of development policy and planning at all levels.
4. The development and strengthening of capacities to prevent, reduce and mitigate disasters was to be a top priority.
5. Early warnings of impending disasters and their effective dissemination.
6. Preventive measures are most effective when they involve participation at all levels, from the local community through the national government to the regional and international level.
7. Vulnerability can be reduced by appropriate education and training of the whole community.
8. The need to share the necessary technology to prevent, reduce and mitigate disaster, be made freely available and in a timely manner.
9. Environmental protection as a component of sustainable development consistent with poverty alleviation is imperative in the prevention and mitigation of natural disasters.
10. The international community should demonstrate strong political determination required to mobilize adequate and make efficient use of existing resources, including financial, scientific and technological means, in the field of natural disaster reduction, bearing in mind the needs of the developing countries, particularly the least developed countries.

Since natural disasters do not recognise borders and administrative boundaries, regional and international cooperation becomes important in order to synergize the global energy of real progress in mitigating disasters through technology transfer, information sharing and providing joint disaster prevention activities. Bilateral and multilateral assistance in addition to financial resources need to be organised and mobilised to support these efforts. The strategy mainly focused on improving the existing coping mechanisms in order to better manage the recovery processes from disasters' impact. Therefore, the strategy was extremely important as it valued the knowledge and experience that existed at the local level among the at-risk communities. The framework of action of the International Decade of Natural Disaster Reduction was to provide all vulnerable countries with the opportunity to achieve a safer world by the end of this century and beyond. T*he Yokohama Strategy was followed by significant World Conferences on Disaster Reduction* such as the *Hyogo Framework* and the *Sendai Framework of Action* (Florini 2003).

Five specific gaps were identified under the Yokohama Strategy. These were

(a) Governance: organizational, legal and policy frameworks
(b) Risk identification, assessment, monitoring and early warning
(c) Knowledge management and education
(d) Reducing underlying risk factors
(e) Preparedness for effective response and recovery.

Based on the above key areas, a relevant framework for action for the decade 2005–2015 was prepared under the Hyogo Framework for Action.

Hyogo and the Sendai Framework

The Hyogo Framework for Action 2005–2015 was aimed to build resilience of nations and communities to disasters in 2005 in quick succession to the Yokohama Strategy and plan of action for a safer world in 1994. It was the global blueprint for disaster risk reduction efforts between 2005 and 2015. The main aim being to substantially reduce disaster losses by 2015 both in terms of lives and in the social, economic and environmental assets of communities and countries. This was the Second World Conference on Disaster Reduction held in Kobe, Japan from 18 to 22 January 2005. It became of particular significance since it was almost 10 years from the day after the Great Hanshin earthquake hit Kobe and less than a month after the 2004 Indian Ocean tsunami occurred (World Conference on Disaster Risk Reduction 1994). The occurrence of December 26, Indian Ocean tsunami, gave a big push to the much necessary needed attention and attracted the international media for taking cognisance of the Hyugo conference. The emperor of Japan, Akihito, inaugurated the conference and welcomed more than 4000 participants from all over the world. This was a most opportune moment to introduce the concept of the International Early Warning Programme (IEWP). The IEWP was initially proposed at the Second International Conference on Early Warning in 2003 in Bonn, Germany.

As long as exact hazard predictions are and will remain difficult, curtailing disaster risk will be a tough proposition. Although natural hazards cannot be prevented, their human, socio-economic and environmental impacts can and should be minimized through appropriate measures, including risk and vulnerability reduction, early warning and preparedness. A strong focus is often given to these problems, during or in the immediate aftermath of a disaster. Disaster risk reduction measures require ongoing attention in order to effectively reduce the growing vulnerability of communities and assets. Hence, it emerges that a multi-hazard approach to early warning systems is the best way to move forward and at the same time recognizing that different hazards would require individual preparedness and response strategies.

The HFA was responsible for providing a detail work plan of all sectors and stakeholders concerned for reducing disaster losses. This was agreed upon by many partners such as governments, international agencies, disaster experts and others. The partners were brought together onto a common platform for a better coordination. The HFA (2005–2015) set out five specific priorities for action attempting to 'capture' the main areas of DRR intervention (World Conference on Disaster Reduction 2005). These include,

1. Making disaster risk reduction a priority
2. Improving risk information and early warning
3. Building a culture of safety and resilience
4. Reducing the risks in key sectors
5. Strengthening preparedness for response.

The Sendai Framework was the first major agreement of the post-2015 development agenda. This initiative is unique in character as it has perfect synchronization with all other 2030 Agenda Agreements, including

- The Paris Agreement on Climate Change
- The Addis Ababa Action Agenda on Financing for Development
- the New Urban Agenda and
- the Sustainable Development Goals.

The UNDRR has been given the responsibility to support the entire implementation, follow-up and review of the Sendai Framework. It coordinates all action within the UN system around disaster risk reduction. This is the third in the series of United Nations World Conferences on Disaster Risk Reduction. This was held in Sendai, Japan, from 14 to 18 March 2015 well attended by as many as 6500 delegates and another 50,000 people being associated with the public forum. Sendai was hit by the Great East Japan earthquake, 130 km from the epicentre in 2011. This was one of the most powerful earthquakes that killed 19,000 people. The earthquake triggered powerful tsunami waves estimated to have reached heights of up to 40.5 m (133 ft) which travelled at 700 km/h (435 mph) in the Sendai area for up to 10 km (6 mi) inland. Residents of Sendai had only eight to ten minutes of warning (Tōhoku Earthquake and Tsunami 2011). This was also the period when the Cyclone Pam hit Vanuatu in the South Pacific Ocean sending the people helter-skelter. This made many developed nations come forward to partner with smaller countries and prepare a map to face the future disaster relief operations. The Sendai Framework conference deliberated on the aftermath of the Japanese response to the 2011 disaster and how the country's early warning system saves lives when earthquakes and tsunamis strike. The conference declared an amount to the tune of 4 billion USD to prepare for disasters over four years. It was at this conference that the Sendai Framework for Disaster Risk Reduction 2015–2030 was adopted.

The Sendai Framework has seven targets and four priorities for action endorsed by the UN General assembly in 2015. This is a 15-year non-binding agreement, recognizing that the state has the primary role to reduce disaster risk but that responsibility must be shared with other stakeholders including local government and the private sector. This was the result of three years of deliberations with UNISDR being the coordinating authority bringing together UN member states, NGOs and other stakeholders onto a common platform. The discussion made calls for an improved version of the existing Hyogo Framework, with a set of common standards, a comprehensive framework with achievable targets, and a legally based instrument for disaster risk reduction.

The Sendai Framework has four specific priorities for action:

1. Understanding disaster risk
2. Strengthening disaster risk governance for better management
3. Investing in disaster risk reduction for resilience
4. Enhancing disaster preparedness to 'Build Back Better' in recovery, rehabilitation and reconstruction.

These priorities in turn pinpoints to seven global targets. These are,

1. Substantially reduce global disaster mortality by 2030, aiming to lower average per 100,000 global mortality between 2020–2030 compared to 2005–2015

2. Substantially reduce the number of affected people globally by 2030, aiming to lower the average global figure per 100,000 between 2020–2030 compared to 2005–2015
3. Reduce direct disaster economic loss in relation to global gross domestic product by 2030
4. Substantially reduce disaster damage to critical infrastructure and disruption of basic services, among them health and educational facilities, including through developing their resilience by 2030
5. Substantially increase the number of countries with national and local disaster risk reduction strategies by 2020
6. Substantially enhance international cooperation to developing countries through adequate and sustainable support to complement their national actions for implementation of the framework by 2030
7. Substantially increase the availability of and access to multi-hazard early warning systems and disaster risk information and assessments to the people by 2030.

Based on the letter and spirit of the Sendai Framework, the first meeting was held in New Delhi as part of the Asian ministerial conference for disaster risk reduction. Post-2004 Indian Ocean tsunami, India, was among the five countries that were very badly impacted. India happened to be among the few that had been most enthusiastic in endorsing the creation of new laws for disaster risk management. In fact although 87 countries expressed their commitment to the Sendai Framework, India is one among the few who displayed implementation plans showing its dedication to the cause.

Sustainable Development Goals (SDG)

This period also synchronized with the setting of Sustainable Development Goals (SDG). Members emphasized the need to tackle disaster risk reduction and climate change adaption for ushering in the SDGs, particularly due to the lack of focus during the Millennium Development Goals (MDG) on risk reduction and resilience building. The Sendai Framework for DRR is people centric, and hence, the SDGs are achievable through a reduction in disaster losses. This enabled a major paradigm shift from disaster management to disaster risk management. This warrants an integration of disaster risk reduction into private investment decision-making and public policy in urban, environmental, social and economic sectors.

UNISDR besides coordinating on making cities resilient, schools' were engaged with governments in developing national disaster loss databases. Collecting data has been a major drawback. Better record-keeping and standardized loss indicators help planners improve their management techniques. The technique of geo-referencing was introduced to reveal the relative vulnerabilities of the rich and the poor. This quantifies the actual human cost of disasters and displays the gradual increase of

Table 4.1 Loss incurred among different income groups in the disaster-affected areas

Income level of countries	Deaths per million living people	People affected	Population concentration
Low-income countries	130 (7 times higher)	7.8% (6 times more vulnerable)	Largest absolute numbers of people affected by disasters
High-income countries	18	1.3%	Lesser than low-income countries

Source CRED, UNISDR (2017)

disaster losses whenever the national income level tends to decline. It was found that since 2000, geo-referencing in disasters did provide some useful data.

Table 4.1 clearly shows that people exposed to natural hazards in the poorest nations were more than seven times more likely to die than equivalent populations in the richest nations. In terms of people affected (but not killed) by disasters, 7.8% were in the low-income countries, while 1.3% were in the high-income countries implying people in the poorest countries were on an average six times more likely than people in rich nations to be injured, to lose their home, be displaced or evacuated or require emergency assistance. (UNISDR 2017).

Such a data may suggest that while absolute economic losses may be concentrated in high income countries, but in terms of the human cost of disasters, it is overwhelmingly on the low- and lower middle-income countries. Thus, vulnerability to risk and degrees of suffering are determined by levels of economic development, rather than simple exposure to natural hazards. The CRED report highlights the ever widening 'protection gap' that exists between rich and poor. It is believed that those who suffer the most from climate change are those who contribute least to it. Disasters are no doubt a combination of hazard, exposure and vulnerability. The economic losses suffered by low- and lower middle-income countries have crippling consequences for their future development and undermine all the efforts to achieve the 17 Sustainable Development Goals, in particular the first goal which is eradication of poverty. Hence, the Sendai Framework of Action becomes of crucial importance and disaster risk reduction need to be achieved. The Sustainable Development Goals (SDG) were adopted by all United Nations member states in 2015, providing a shared map for ushering in peace and prosperity among the people and the entire world today and into the future. At its core lies the 17 Sustainable Development Goals (SDGs), which are an urgent call for action by all countries—developed and developing—in a global partnership. What is unique in these goals is the interconnection between them. Each goal involves addressing not only its own theme but issues that are more commonly associated with others. The inter-connecting link among the SDGs helps in building partnership and pragmatism to opt for the right choice towards improving life that would remain sustainable. Ending poverty and other deprivations have been recognized as a simultaneous process and needs to be addressed together with strategies that would impact an improvement in health and education, reduce inequality and spur economic growth, at the same time tackling climate change and working to preserve the oceans and forests. The SDGs are essentially an inclusive agenda with a commitment 'to leave no one behind'. Achieving any SDG goal essentially warrants developing the partnership of governments, private sector, civil society and taking along the citizens of the region. It has been planned in such a manner that a change in one of the goals does leave a corresponding change in the others. Eradicating poverty in all its forms and dimensions, including extreme poverty, is the greatest global challenge and an indispensable requirement for sustainable development. All countries and all stakeholders, acting in collaborative partnership, were expected to implement this plan. This was intended to be built on the lines of the Millennium Development Goals (MDG) and take on the job of completing the unfinished task of the MDG. Most importantly, the SDGs sought to address the human rights of all and achieve gender equality and empowerment of all women and girls. The goals and targets formulated under the SDGs were expected to stimulate action over the next fifteen years in areas of critical importance for mankind and the universe. Integrated monitoring and constant reporting on the Sendai Framework and disaster-related Sustainable Development Goals (SDGs) is a reality today!

In accordance to the 2030 Agenda, the member states agreed for a High-level Political Forum (HLPF) to be carried out through inclusive regular voluntary reviews of the 2030 Agenda for both developed and developing countries as well as relevant UN entities and other stakeholders. The reviews were to be state led involving ministerial and other relevant high-level participants. This would enable a platform to be created for partnerships, including participation of relevant stakeholders. The establishment of the United Nations High-level Political Forum on Sustainable Development (HLPF) was mandated in 2012. The forum meets annually for eight days. This includes a three-day ministerial segment on a four yearly basis. The HLPF is the main United Nations platform under the General Assembly on sustainable development, and it has a central role in the follow-up and review of the 2030 Agenda for Sustainable Development—the Sustainable Development Goals (SDGs) at the global level (UN, High-level Political Forum on Sustainable Development). The meeting of the High-level Political Forum on Sustainable Development was convened in July 2019. The theme was on *'empowering people and ensuring inclusiveness and equality'*. A set of six goals were reviewed at length. They were,

Goal Nos.	Goals
4	Ensure inclusive and equitable quality education and promote lifelong learning opportunities for all
8	Promote sustained, inclusive and sustainable economic growth, full and productive employment and decent work for all
10	Reduce inequality within and among countries
13	Take urgent action to combat climate change and its impacts
16	Promote peaceful and inclusive societies for sustainable development, provide access to justice for all and build effective, accountable and inclusive institutions at all levels

(continued)

(continued)

Goal Nos.	Goals
17	Strengthen the means of implementation and revitalize the global partnership for sustainable development

In July 2020, fifty-one countries were to present their national voluntary reviews to the HLPF. Such reviews do face a difficult task ahead in the absence of authentic data. The national statistical offices all geared up trying to build a framework for including disaster-related data within the domain of official statistics. Member states left no stone unturned for putting their best effort to collect data pertaining to economic losses for various income groups during the last five years. Unfortunately, none of the least-developed countries today have a complete set of national statistics of their country. It is observed that the poorer a country is, the spottier their data gets. Within this perspective, the 2030 Agenda for Sustainable Development got adopted in 2015. The 17 SDGs have 169 targets, all meant to guide and usher in a more sustainable, prosperous and equal future for all the countries.

There are dozens of different development agencies working in each country that assess the SDG progress based on models and various methodologies. Due to a lack of national statistics, or available fragmented data in bits and pieces, leads to their scope becoming limited. The picture displayed is not a complete one for analysing whether the project goals were being met with and whether the spending of donor funds were getting justified. There exist innumerous different datasets that may be overlapping or conflicting for each country, with no mechanism to collect or process them into a composite picture. Moreover, by focusing on project-based data and working in silos, it becomes like competing with the national statistical offices. With meagre financial resources and limited support, member states get restricted in utilizing their ability and resources within the prescribed framework. With constrained resources, the member states get focused in building a robust national statistic matching with the advance sustainable development rather than generating a micro-level need-based data bank for their state from their own perspective.

Presently more than one-third of the way towards 2030 has been reached. Progress made by several countries in assessing and reporting on whether they are on track to meet those goals is doubtful. But, this evaluation has to face the blatant truth that data is in deficit for many countries, especially the most vulnerable areas, thus evaluating the progress will not throw the correct picture. It is said that if 22 least-developed countries in sub-Saharan Africa are unable to measure their own poverty rates, it is difficult to expect them to report on, cross-tabulation such as disaggregated indicators like proportion of population that has convenient access to public transport, by sex, age and persons with disabilities and so on. There is a deeper understanding today than ever before of the underlying factors which drive up the likelihood of a future disaster event. Immediate and focused action is warranted to meet the 2020 deadline for national and local disaster risk reduction (DRR) strategies aligned with the HLPF of the Sendai Framework. Progress has been steady, but is insufficient given that such strategies are seen as the foundation for achievement of the 2030 targets.

Regional Policies and the Disaster Management Act

Understanding disaster risk is one of the important priorities under the Sendai Framework. The regional policies can play a very important role provided there is clarity in understanding of disaster risks in the country. Disaster management policies and practices should be based on an understanding of risks and not merely on an ideological level. Gap and key challenges need to be highlighted identifying areas of weak coordination, cooperation and linkages among the sectors related to DRR. A serious loss assessment and post-disaster needs, lack of strategic research agenda, absence of consensus regarding terminology and limited coordination between stakeholders all need to be spelt out.

As already stated, it is common to find more people living in areas that are vulnerable to natural disasters; nevertheless, scientists predict frequency and intensity of the disasters are likely to increase over the years, as a result of the effects of climate change. Some mega-disasters have already been witnessed that have been creating an awareness among the people. Today, there is a realisation, for capacity building of national governments, civil society organizations and international actors to gear up and prevent, respond to and recover from natural disasters. In this context, the disaster risk management (DRM) and the regional organizations become of crucial importance. This refers to all activities intended to reduce risk, prepare for disasters and associate with emergency relief and reconstruction. Although regional mechanisms play an increasingly important role in disasters, research in this context has been rather slender. There are few published studies about the relative strengths and weaknesses of regional bodies, much less comparisons of their range of activities or effectiveness in DRM.

A study undertaken under the Brookings Institution (The Brookings Institution 2013) talks about the gap by providing some basic information about the work of more than 30 regional organizations involved in disaster risk management and by drawing some comparisons and generalizations about the work of thirteen of these organizations through the use of 17 indicators of effectiveness. Scholars have speculated that regional cooperation can be a force for peace, security and economic progress. Many argue that there is a need for political commitment to a broad vision of regional identity, while others maintain that cooperation between countries on specific practical issues can lead to better cooperation on broader issues, which would reduce conflict and lead to regional identities. In today's globalizing world, regions can be seen as serving as an effective bridge between the international and national systems. Regional organizations play a leading role between migration and climate change. Regional processes to deal with labour migration have been increasing in importance over the past decade. In terms of disaster response, regional mechanisms not only are able to respond more quickly than international ones, but their interventions are usually more acceptable.

The South Asian region is particularly prone to multiple disasters due to geo-climatic conditions. As per the Centre for Research on Epidemiology of Disasters (CRED), more than 1625 major disasters have occurred in South Asian Association for Regional Cooperation (SAARC) region since 1990 causing life loss of more than 12 million, affecting 2.8 billion and causing damage more than 100 trillion US$. (SAARC Disaster Management Centre). Owing to its population density, hazard probability and existing vulnerabilities, South Asian region is one the most disaster-prone regions in the world. In last decade 2006–2016, the region has experienced more than 450 disaster events causing life loss of more than 56,000 affecting more than 570 million people. Interestingly, more than 60% of the losses were due to floods and cyclones.

In 2015, according to UNISDR, 54% of the total disaster-related deaths occurred in member states. More than one-third of the global disaster-related deaths occurred in the Nepal earthquakes of 25 April and 12 May 2015. Considering the regional dimensions of natural disasters, the 3rd SAARC Summit had commissioned a comprehensive regional study on the causes and consequences of natural disasters. More and more countries are moving to put in place national and local strategies for disaster risk reduction by 2020 in line with target number 5 of the Sendai Framework. India for example has committed to the world's largest rural roads programme with an investment of 500 million USD, and all contract bids has to be risk informed and take account of resilience. The need for involvement and empowerment of local communities or a 'bottom-up approach' has consistently emerged. Stress was on utilizing existing community structures and systems along with the need for active involvement of people most likely to be exposed to hazards in all aspects of the early warning chain.

The *Sendai Framework* was established to replace the *Hyogo Framework* and will remain the most unescapable and omnipresent international standard in response to disasters until 2030. It aims to 'guide the multi-hazard management of disaster risk' as a transnational cooperative effort to mitigate the damages of high mortality, economic loss, personal suffering, spread of disaster zone and international cost (Florini 2003). The International Federation of Red Cross Societies has attempted to supplement the UN framework, by providing more specific guidance for best practices in disaster relief in order to prevent the most suffering possible. The International Federation of Red Cross Societies (IFRCS) other than the UN is worth mentioning for their efforts to address the lack of binding international law or plan of action for disaster response. The IFRCS have created the *International Disaster Response Laws*, which has been ratified and adopted by thirty-eight nations.

Though these actions are admirable and it is important to continue the effort towards more effective disaster response, not a single document produced by the UN or Red Cross considers the impact of human trafficking on the victims of the disaster. If the goal of the international community is to prevent the suffering of innocent humans after a natural disaster, they must take into consideration the vulnerability to slavery these innocent humans will face. Modern slavery affects every category of suffering the UN *Sendai Framework* seeks to stop. High mortality, economic loss, personal suffering, spread of the suffering of disaster and international cost are all consistently effected by human trafficking.

The international community is exerting a remarkable effort to prevent human trafficking and to respond to the suffering of natural disasters, and yet both of these endeavours will continually be insufficient until the community fully understands the connection between the two. Furthermore, an analysis of the overlap must be included in international law, acting as a guideline for countries to create their own domestic policies that reflect the need to combat human trafficking and respond to natural disasters while acknowledging the other. An effective understanding of the connection between these inevitable atrocities of life is crucial to developing productive and successful policies. There is no doubt that the international community desires to uphold basic human rights and prevent unneeded suffering caused by human trafficking and natural disasters; however, currently, its actions to achieve these goals are incredibly insufficient.

Following close to the Hyugo Framework of Action, India enacted the Disaster Management Act in December 2005. NDMA was constituted on 30 May 2005 by an Executive Order of the Government of India. Subsequently, the Disaster Management Act, 2005 was enacted on 23 December 2005. NDMA was thus officially born on 27 September 2006 under the provisions of the Disaster Management Act, 2005. The act provides for an 'effective management of disasters and for matters connected there with or incidental thereto'.

This act envisaged a three-tier structure of disaster management at national, states and district levels. Under this act, the National Disaster Management Authority (NDMA) was established with the Prime Minister of India as the ex officio Chairperson. The NDMA is responsible for 'laying down the policies, plans and guidelines for disaster management' and ensure 'timely and effective response to disaster' (DMA 2005). Under Section 6 of the act, the responsibility for laying 'down guidelines to be followed by the state authorities in drawing up the state plans' lies with the NDMA. The act provides for constitution of a Disaster Response Fund and Disaster Mitigation Fund at National, state and district level. This act sets the tone for the State Disaster Management Authority (SDMA) and the District Disaster Management Authority (DDMA), the National Disaster Response Force (NDRF) and the National Executive Committee (NEC). The act contains provisions for imposing penalties for obstruction, false claims, misappropriation. There is no discrimination in providing compensation and relief irrespective of caste, colour, sex and community.

The Disaster Management Act, 2005 also set up the National Institute of Disaster Management (NIDM) which has been assigned the nodal responsibilities for human resource development, capacity building, training, research, documentation and policy advocacy in the field of disaster management. The NIDM provides capacity building support to various national- and state-level agencies in the field of disaster management and disaster risk reduction. The National Policy on Disaster Management approved by the Union Cabinet and released on 18 January 2010 portrays a paradigm shift from erstwhile 'response-centric' approach to the holistic management of disasters with emphasis on prevention, preparedness and mitigation. The government has brought about a change in the approach to disaster management from a relief-centric to a holistic and integrated approach covering the entire range of disaster management (prevention, mitigation, preparedness, response, relief, reconstruction and rehabilitation). The approach is based on the conviction that development cannot be sustainable unless disaster mitigation is built in the development process (NDMA, Annual Report 2018–2019).

In 2016, the DMA was modified and made in sync with the Sendai Framework for DRR and community resilience. The National Disaster Management Plan (NDMP) got released on 1 June 2016 by the Hon'ble Prime Minister. In order to revise the plan, a two-day consultative workshop of all the stakeholders was held on 12 and 13 April 2017 to obtain views/inputs/recommendations. Based on the inputs, the plan was modified. As per the annual report of the NDMA, 2018–2019, the implementation of the Sendai Framework for Disaster Risk Reduction has been approved by NDMA at a cost of Rs. 2010.6 lakh for implementation in all the states and UTs for three years from 2018 to 19. The scheme provides for financial support for hiring of Disaster Management (DM) professional at SDMA in all states/UTs. The DM professional will facilitate/support the State Administration in taking measures for implementation of Sendai Framework for disaster risk reduction. The school education system has started including teaching of disaster management in their curriculum. Several workshops and training programmes are being conducted by NDMA on a regular basis.

'The Government of India is one of the first in the world to come out publicly with a plan which seeks to implement the four priorities for action of the Sendai Framework, focused on spreading a greater understanding of disaster risk through education and public information, investing in disaster resilient infrastructure and committing to improved disaster preparedness and building back better in recovery, rehabilitation and reconstruction' (UNDRR, 2016).

Following the inauguration of India's National Platform for Disaster Risk Reduction in 2014, this plan became a boost to disaster risk governance in India. The country is constantly faced with challenging range of both man-made and natural hazards particularly the drought that has affected over 300 million people. India has been trying hard to project itself as a champion of climate change and sustainable development. In order to meet the DRR goals, India has earmarked more than $8 billions for disaster mitigation and relief work over a five-year period. India was appreciated by the UN at its current global platform for being the largest democracy and the only country in the world to have come up with a national plan and a local strategy for DRR (Thakur 2017).

Nevertheless, the implementation of the National Disaster Act is not free from criticisms. It has been criticized for being slow and slack. There have been instances in 2013 when the Indian Supreme Court had to issue notices to the state governments of Uttarakhand, Tamil Nadu, Odisha, Andhra Pradesh, Gujarat, Rajasthan, Maharashtra and the central government for alleged failure to implement the Disaster Management Act, 2005. The petitioner alleged that the non-implementation of the Disaster Management Act by the Government of Uttarakhand endangered the lives of citizens. In fact a 'reasonable ex-gratia assistance on account of loss of life, damage to houses and for restoration of means of livelihood to victims of flash floods in Uttarakhand under the Disaster Management Act' was sought (Times of India 2013).

The act has also been criticized for marginalizing the non-governmental organisations (NGOs), elected local representatives, local communities and civic group and for fostering a hierarchical, bureaucratic, command and control, 'top-down', approach that gives the central, state and district authorities unrelenting powers. It is also alleged that the 'act became a law almost at the will of the bureaucrats who framed it'. (Max 2007).

Moreover, the disaster/crisis management should be a primary responsibility of the state governments rather than the union government who should play only a supportive role. In addition, the act should provide a categorization of disasters into local, district, state or national levels. The classification and intensity of each type of disaster would be helpful in assessing the level of authority primarily responsible for dealing with the disasters as well as the scale of response and relief that is required while the NDMA could work out the necessary modalities.

In addition, the law should make provisions for severe punishment for misutilization of funds which was meant for crisis/disaster management. The role of the local government should be brought to the forefront without involving the NEC. This would save time and improve efficiency.

Excessive dependency on relief and rehabilitation packages creates a system where there are no incentives for adoption of risk reduction. Insurance is a potentially important mitigation measure in disaster-prone areas as it brings quality in the infrastructure and consciousness and a culture of safety and prevention. Disaster insurance mostly works under the premise of higher the risk higher the premium, thus creating awareness towards vulnerable areas and motivating people to settle in relatively safer areas.

Following the success of micro-credit for rural development, micro-insurance has also emerged as a tool for possible risk management. In fact, micro-credit and micro-insurance support each other. The tool of insurance should be made attractive enough through a set of policy measures and fiscal incentives. A typical insurance example is from Japan. The Seismic Hazard Maps were put to use and have been found appropriate for modelling financial risk, including time-dependent and time-independent rates of earthquake recurrence.

Anti-trafficking Measures

It was only after the world women's conference that the issues of trafficking came to limelight and the movement towards modern anti-trafficking procedure came into existence. It began with the adoption of the Palermo Protocol in 2000 and has been seriously followed among the world community. More legislation criminalizing all forms of human trafficking, collaboration efforts among the civil society and human trafficking survivors have been introduced to strengthen victim protections at the policy and grassroots levels. Despite the best efforts, traffickers around the world leave no stone unturned to exploit millions of victims in forced labour and sex trafficking. Governments continue to bear the primary responsibility for addressing human trafficking although support from civil society and international organizations has had a significant contribution towards evolving a more holistic and effective anti-trafficking solutions.

The Palermo Protocols are three protocols that were adopted by the United Nations to supplement the 2000 Convention against Transnational Organized Crime (the Palermo Convention). They were the protocol to prevent, suppress and punish Trafficking in Persons, especially women and children. The protocol provides an agreed upon definition of Trafficking in Persons. It aims at comprehensively addressing Trafficking in Persons through the so-called three P's—prosecution of perpetrators, protection of victims and prevention of trafficking. It is the first global legally binding instrument with an agreed definition on Trafficking in Persons. An additional objective of the protocol is to protect and assist the victims of Trafficking in Persons with full respect for their human rights.

In May 2011, the Indian government ratified the United Nations Convention against Transnational Organised Crime (UNTOC) and its three protocols. Having ratified both conventions, India became the fourth South Asian country after Afghanistan, Pakistan and Sri Lanka to ratify the UNTOC. It took more than 11 years for India to ratify the protocol. States that have ratified UNTOC commit themselves to taking a series of measures to prevent and control transnational organized crime, including (i) the criminalising of the participation in an organized criminal group, of money laundering, related corruption and obstruction of justice and (ii) the adoption of frameworks for extradition, mutual legal assistance and international cooperation.

In India, trafficking is primarily an offence under the Indian Penal Code, 1860. It defines trafficking as

(i) recruitment
(ii) transportation
(iii) harbouring
(iv) transfer or
(v) receipt of a person for exploitation by use of certain forceful means.

In addition, there are other laws which regulate trafficking for specific purposes. For instance, the Immoral Traffic (Prevention) Act, 1986 deals with trafficking for the purpose of sexual exploitation. Similarly, the Bonded Labour Regulation Act, 1986 and Child Labour Regulation Act, 1986 which deal with exploitation for bonded labour. Each of these laws operates independently, has their own enforcement machinery and prescribes penalties for offences related to trafficking. The National Crime Record Bureau of India has started recording the magnitude of trafficked victims and the missing women and children. It shows the alarmingly high number of missing women and children on a regular basis. Figure 4.2 shows the missing figures from 2016 to 2018, and this is only the tip of the iceberg. Not all cases get reported.

According to the National Crime Records Bureau, in terms of human trafficking, there was a total of 8,132 cases that were reported in India in 2016 under the Indian

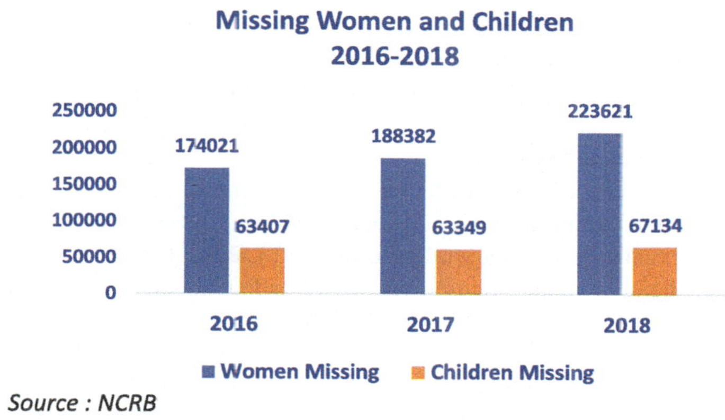

Fig. 4.2 Missing women and children, 2016–2018

Penal Code, 1860 (NCRB 2016). This is 15% increase from the number of cases reported in the previous year. In the same year, 23,117 trafficking victims were rescued. Of these, the highest number of persons was trafficked for forced labour (45.5%), followed by prostitution (21.5%). It is understandable that most of the trafficked victims for sexual exploitation go unreported, and hence, the figures are only a miniscule. Details of persons trafficked for various purposes in 2016 are depicted in Table 4.2.

In 2015, pursuant to an order of the Supreme Court, the Ministry of Women and Child Development constituted a committee to examine the feasibility of a comprehensive legislation on trafficking. The Trafficking of Persons (prevention, protection

Table 4.2 Victims rescued by purpose of trafficking

Purpose	2016	(as a %)
Forced labour	10,509	45.5
Prostitution	4980	21.5
Other forms of sexual exploitation	2590	11.5
Domestic servitude	412	1.8
Forced marriage	349	1.5
Petty crimes	212	0.9
Child pornography	162	0.7
Begging	71	0.3
Drug peddling	8	0
Removal of organs	2	0
Other reasons	3824	16.5
Total persons	23,117	100

Source Human Trafficking, Crime in India, 2016, National Crime Records Bureau and rehabilitation) Bill, 2018 was introduced in Lok Sabha by the Ministry of Women and Child Development. The bill was passed in Lok Sabha on 26 July 2018. The bill provides for the prevention, rescue and rehabilitation of trafficked persons. There was euphoria on the passing of the bill, but soon after the bill was not received well among the civil society organization.

It is a fact that there exists a plethora of laws which deal with specific forms of trafficking. The Immoral Traffic (Prevention) Act, 1986 covers trafficking for commercial sexual exploitation while the Bonded Labour System (Abolition) Act, 1976 deals with punishment for employment of bonded labour. These laws are bound by their own enforcement mechanism. Although the bill intends to serve as a comprehensive law to deal with all cases of trafficking, but it continues to retain all existing laws on trafficking and therefore these laws tend to overlap on each other. They tend to create a parallel legal framework and enforcement machinery of their own to deal with trafficking cases. Each one has their own different procedures to be followed, and hence, it creates confusion as to which procedure is to be applied for different trafficking cases.

For instance, under the Immoral Traffic (Prevention) Act, 1986, protective homes have been set up for rehabilitation of trafficked victims of sexual exploitation. The bill also contemplates setting up of protection homes. When a victim of sexual exploitation is rescued, it is unclear as to which of these homes she ought to be sent to. Moreover, each of these laws designates special courts to hear offences. The question then arises as to which of these courts will hear the case. Thus, the trafficking of persons bill has been criticised by many because the existing response seems to be scattered across different laws, which neither relates to each other nor do they have a common approach rather have varied inconsistent objectives.

The demand was, therefore, for a single legislation that would harmonise and integrate all the existing laws. This expectation was emboldened when, in the case of *Prajwala v Union of India* (2015), the MWCD told the Supreme Court that it had set up a committee to study existing laws, identify gaps and draft a comprehensive legislative framework covering all aspects of trafficking. However, the bill did not fulfil any of these promises. There were apprehensions that the bill will only end up complicating the existing legal framework on trafficking and its enforcement. It has been criticized that ‘the bill is founded on baseless claims and does nothing that it promises, except add yet another legislation to the already fragmented landscape of laws against human trafficking’ (Tandon 2018). The bill has been stated to replicate with fuzzy provisions that criminalise activities devoid of culpability or criminal intent. The bill introduces offences in relation to and authorises closure of premises, which are ‘to be used’ as a place of trafficking. Moreover, since the bill does not extend to citizens of India outside India (extraterritorial jurisdiction), the immunity clause gets restricted and does not protect trafficked victims who face the death sentence for crimes committed abroad, notwithstanding their vulnerability. The bill has thus been critically considered as not only flawed but merely another piece of legislation which hardly serves any purpose other than exposing vulnerable communities to a punitive overkill.

While the gender bias and social exclusion in the society start getting institutionalized and further crystalized, the role of the governance mechanism and civil society organization gets even more complex. Under such situations, the role of Institutions, law implementers and CSOs become so very relevant. The role of the civil society organization has been exemplary as was evidenced in the field visits. An absence of law and lack of governance add further to the deteriorating situation. The present environment, however, has set the tone for a growing international discourse in building resilient communities. It has been amply displayed at the international level that there is a gap between humanitarian assistance and development cooperation. This gap needs to be bridged in order to enable a more holistic approach towards achieving disaster risk reduction (DRR). Research on such aspects has been at a deficit, reiterating the fact that there is not only a dearth of empirical data on trafficking before a disaster and after the disaster, but also, there is hardly any studies that investigate the role of disasters in human trafficking mainly as a result of most cases going unreported!

Today, the world is gripped with issues of citizenship due to immigrants who have ventured out as a result of war, natural calamities and ethnic clashes. Such cases are amply displayed among the refugees from Afghanistan, Syria, the Rohingyas or the Bangladeshi immigrants. The borders are the most vulnerable areas where laws, policies and implementation of strategies become fuzzy and confusing. As stated earlier, South Asia is a frequent witness to disasters which, happen on a regular basis. With its porous borders one often comes across victims of trafficking in terms of men, women and children. However, India has been forthright in recognizing the gravity of the situation and has established a large number of anti-human trafficking units (AHTU) in such areas. But, without the help of CSOs and NGOs, it would be Impossible to contain the menace

Civil society organizations are indispensable. It occupies an important position in the development dialogue as it provides opportunities to bring together communities together for collection action, mobilising society to articulate demands and voice concerns at local, national, regional and international levels. Its commonly witnessed that they have often contributed towards development of laws and policies regarding human trafficking in an active, constructive and positive manner. With their vast experience, they should not merely be regarded as a group of specialized entities offering only technical support that too when permitted by the state. Often, it has been recognised that the primary responsibility for combating and preventing trafficking in human beings rests with participating states, but the link of this phenomenon to transnational organized crime requires cooperation not only at the international and regional level but even at the local level involving all the stakeholders including relevant NGOs, CSOs and the community.

The inclusion of civil society into an overall anti-trafficking response as reflected in the clusters of the four P's (prevention, protection, prosecution and partnership) is not always an easy endeavour. At times, civil society stakeholders challenge their role as mere technical providers without being included in political decision-making processes (OSCE 2018). In addition, given that the mission of civil society differs from that of governmental and intergovernmental institutions, its activities in the anti-trafficking sphere sometimes may be regarded as too critical towards governmental policies, thereby creating a mistrust between the two. Although defining the concept of civil society does pose certain challenges, but the engagement of civil society in victim support and counselling is always welcome. However when it comes to a critical response from the civil society towards state activities, authorities often get provoked with resentment. The state activities in terms of combating trafficking or protecting and assisting its victims, as well as those at risk of being trafficked, may not always be valued and tend to be ignored. Although state and non-state actors, including NGOs, have different interests and roles that may sometimes lead to tensions, but one thing is clear that there is a clear continuity in their efforts. Moreover, they have the same goal which is fighting the crime of human trafficking, assisting its victims and improving the overall situation. States often only allocate funding for assistance to officially identified victims of trafficking, while NGOs want to support all people in need as a result of exploitation and abuse (Van Doorninck 2017). A sustainable strategy for including civil society in the anti-trafficking response needs to reflect the many contributions that civil society can provide, while at the same time taking into consideration the potential tensions of a governmental/non-governmental partnership. It is being acknowledged that the inclusion of civil society is a pre-requisite for any viable anti-trafficking strategy. Despite the fact that existing legal and political instruments are explicit about the importance of cooperation between state actors and civil society organizations in ensuring a coherent and meaningful anti-trafficking response, our ongoing dialogue with civil society partners reveals that the such a cooperative approach is not always reflected on the ground. Nevertheless, their activities do address human rights, democratization, social justice, education and labour rights although sometimes they tend to be ad hoc in nature. It is a concern that both European and international organizations have raised concerns about the increasing restrictions on agency and activism among the civil society. Studies undertaken by the European Parliament have observed a significant decrease since 2004 in the number of NGOs and their activities. It has also observed that more than 120 restrictive laws were adopted in 60 countries, including EU members (European Parliament 2017).

The discussion above, points to only one thing. Although all the laws call nations to work together in order to prevent the spread of trafficking, outlining the important factors of trafficking to be weary of but unfortunately not a single one mentions how natural disasters play into the expansion of human supply. It is like trying to rid a house of termites without attempting to target the termite nest itself rather than killing the termites as and when seen. This is like having a ballooning impact. When air is compressed in one part of the balloon, the air simply rushes to other parts where the pressure is less. So, practically the impact becomes redundant with a zero-sum game.

If the international community wants to truly address the issue of modern slavery, at bare minimum, they must consider one of the greatest sources of supply of vulnerable people. Until the international community sets a standard of law for each nation to base their domestic policies addressing the connection between natural disasters and human trafficking, modern slavery will continue unabated. In fact, human trafficking needs to be imbibed into every segment of the development policies both at the international level and domestic policies, so that this menace can be cornered from every possible angle. Similarly, the international effort to mitigate the suffering from natural disasters will never be effective, until the coordinated effort acknowledges the prevalence of human trafficking in disaster zones.

References

Brülisauer Manuel. 2015. *Human Trafficking in Post-Earthquake Nepal*. https://ethz.ch/content/dam/ethz/special-interest/gess/nadel-dam/documents/mas/mas-essays/MAS%20Cycle%202014%20-%202016/Essay_Manuela%20Bruelisauer.pdf.

Cherry Miriam, A., and Judd F. Sneirson. 2011. Deep trouble: Legal ramifications of the deepwater horizon oil spill. *Tulane Law Review* 85: 983, 1010-14.

DMA. 2005. https://en.wikipedia.org/wiki/Disaster_Management_Act_2005.

European Parliament. 2017. *Directorate-General for External Policies, Policy Department, Shrinking Space for Civil Society: The EU Response*, p. 9. https://www.europarl.europa.eu/RegData/etudes/STUD/2017/578039/EXPO_STU(2017)578039_EN.pdf.

Federal Ministry of Labour and Social Affairs. *National Corporate Social Responsibility Forum*. Federal Ministry of Labour and Social Affairs. https://www.csr-in-deutschland.de/EN/Policies/CSR-national/National-CSR-Forum/national-csr-forum.html.

Florini, Ann. 2003. *Business and Global Governance: The Growing Role of Corporate Codes of Conduct*. Brookings, 1 March 2003. https://www.brookings.edu/articles/business-and-global-governance-the-growing-role-of-corporate-codes-of-conduct/.

Gilligan, Jonathan M. 2018. Carrots and sticks in private climate governance. *Texas A&M Law Review* 6: 179–180.

Guidelines Under Yokohama. *Yokohama Strategy and Plan of Action for a Safer World: Guidelines for Natural Disaster Prevention, Preparedness and Mitigation*. https://www.preventionweb.net/publications/view/8241.

Human Rights First. 2017. *Human Trafficking by the Numbers*, 7 January 2017. http://www.humanrightsfirst.org/resource/human-trafficking-numbers.

Max, Martin. 2007. *Disaster Management Act Farce Follows Disaster*. 8 February 2007; Retrieved 30 July 2013. http://www.indiatogether.org/disaster-relief.

NCRB. 2016. *Crime in India' 2016*. National Crime Records Bureau.

NDMA. Annual Report, 2018–2019. https://ndma.gov.in/images/annreport/NDMA-Annual-Report-2018-19-English.pdf.

OSCE. 2018. *Organization for Security and Cooperation in Europe, Office of the Special Representative and Co-ordinator for Combating Trafficking in Human Beings, Occasional Paper No. 8: The Critical Role of Civil Society in Combating Trafficking in Human Beings*. https://www.osce.org/secretariat/405197?download=true.

Palermo Protocol. https://www.ohchr.org/en/professionalinterest/pages/protocoltraffickinginpersons.aspx.

Pashcke, Megan. 2019. *Corporate Responsibility in International Law, Executive Editor of the Denver Journal of International Law and Policy*. http://djilp.org/corporate-responsibility-in-international-law/#post-9692-footnote-ref-11.

SAARC DMC. http://saarc-sdmc.org/.

Singh, David. 2012. *Child Traffickers Thrive on Disasters*. U.N. Office for Disaster Risk Reduction, 26 March 2012. https://www.undrr.org/news/child-traffickers-thrive-disasters.

Tandon, Tripti. 2018. India's Trafficking Bill 2018 is Neither Clear Nor Comprehensive. *Lawyers Collective*, vol. 53, Issue 28, 14 July 2018. https://www.epw.in/engage/article/trafficking-of-persons-prevention-protection-and-rehabilitation-bill-2018-is-neither-clear-nor-comprehensive.

Thakur, Pradip. 2017. Disaster mitigation: India working to build up a global coalition. *The Economic Times*, May 2017. https://economictimes.indiatimes.com/news/environment/the-good-earth/disaster-mitigation-india-working-to-build-up-a-global-coalition/articleshow/58864360.cms?utm_source=contentofinterest&utm_medium=text&utm_campaign=cppst.

The Brookings Institution. 2013. *In the Neighborhood: The Growing Role of Regional Organizations in Disaster Risk Management*. London School of Economics, Project on Internal Displacement, February 2013. https://www.brookings.edu/wp-content/uploads/2016/06/REGIONAL_DISASTER_MECHANISMS_2013.pdf.

Times of India. 2013. *Natural Calamity Prone States have No Disaster Management Mechanism: PIL.*

Tōhoku Earthquake and Tsunami. 2011. https://en.wikipedia.org/wiki/2011_T%C5%8Dhoku_earthquake_and_tsunami.

UN. *High Level Political Forum on Sustainable Development*. https://sustainabledevelopment.un.org/hlpf.

UNDRR. https://www.undrr.org/about-undrr/our-impact.

UNDRR. 2016. *India Puts Sendai Framework Into Operation*. June 2016. https://www.undrr.org/news/india-puts-sendai-framework-operation.

UNISDR. 2017. *Economic Losses, Poverty and Disasters, 1998–2017*. Centre for Epidemiology of Disasters (CRED), UNISDR. https://www.unisdr.org/2016/iddr/IDDR2018_Economic%20Losses.pdf.

UNODC. https://www.unodc.org/unodc/en/human-trafficking/what-is-human-trafficking.html.

UNODC. 2017. *Human Trafficking*. U.N. Office on Drugs and Crime. https://www.unodc.org/unodc/en/human-trafficking/what-is-human-trafficking.html. Last visited 12 Feb 2020.

Van Doorninck, Marieke. 2017. Changing the system from within, the role of NGOs in the flawed anti-trafficking System. In *Routledge Handbook of Human Trafficking*, ed. R. Piotrowicz, C. Rijken, and B. Uhl, pp. 419–426.

World Conference on Disaster Reduction 18–22 January 2005, Kobe, Hyogo, Japan, Hyogo Framework for Action 2005–2015: I S D R International Strategy for Disaster Reduction www.unisdr.org/wcdr. Building the Resilience of Nations and Communities to Disasters https://www.unisdr.org/2005/wcdr/intergover/official-doc/L-docs/Hyogo-framework-for-action-english.pdf.

World Conference on Disaster Risk Reduction. 1994. Wikipedia. https://en.wikipedia.org/wiki/World_Conference_on_Disaster_Risk_Reduction.

Chapter 5
Bridging the Gaps between Institutions and Civil Society Organization

Institutional Mechanisms

As observed, disasters can play havoc on the downtrodden and socio-economically weak people. The United Nations has held several conventions targeting at understanding the damage caused by past disasters and trying to promote in creating more effective future disaster responses. The UN started addressing the issue of international disaster relief in the late twentieth century with the *International Decade for Disaster Risk Reduction with* more and more nations gradually coming forward to coordinate disaster relief. This resolution places natural disaster response as a central issue for the UN to address (Lester 2004). The international community has no doubt dramatically increased its effort in the recent years, to help nations recover from unpredictable natural disasters. It has been observed that wealthy nations do provide aid and support to developing states towards stabilizing their societies and lessening the suffering of their citizens. However, such efforts may be in futile unless the horizontal and vertical mechanisms are systemized and are in place. The vertical linkages would create the smooth operations of institutions from the international, the national and local levels. While the horizontal linkages need to develop a smooth functioning among the stakeholders concerned at a particular level. Although national political commitment and leadership matters, it is the responsibility of local institutions for actual implementation within the perspective of the governance structures of most countries. A lack of institutional clarity, roles and responsibilities among governmental agencies engaged may challenge its implementation. Such challenges are not new and have been faced by many countries. For instance, in some countries, while reducing human trafficking was a broad unambiguously stated national priority, but the budget allocation at local levels sometimes did not follow the same prioritization. To achieve the milestones amidst the new areas and various cross-cutting issues, it is warranted that institutional collaboration, innovation and incentive systems that facilitate action and accountability across sectors as well as across government levels are fulfilled. Some of the major target groups are the policymakers at the national level including stakeholders from the government like heads of state's offices, finance,

M. Dutta, *Disaster and Human Trafficking*,
https://doi.org/10.1007/978-981-16-1630-3_5

planning, subnational bodies, sectoral ministries, national statistics offices and so on. Other experts and practitioners that matter are from multilateral and bilateral agencies, NGOs and civil society which are equally important in developing plans to implement and monitor the achievements while supporting government partners.

The present section attempts to assess the gaps between the institutions and the civil society organizations that operate at the grass root level. Most of the discourse in this section are based on the field visit undertaken in 2018 and the responses obtained from the government institutions and NGOs. The area of field visit was in Kolkata, West Bengal. Based on the detailed feedback that was received from the field, the existing gaps and challenges have been highlighted in the context of implementation of institutional support mechanisms. Such a gap becomes even more wider as the nature of the issue gets more and more complex. No one institution can tackle the global development challenges of the present day. Governments, CSOs, the private sector and international institutions all have a role to play. Their ability to work in coherence can usher in the desired results. The complementary and supplementary roles can only be able to address some of the most pressing development challenges in the field of human trafficking and disaster risk reduction.

When community and lives are lost in a natural disaster, it leaves a huge sense of a feeling of uncertainty as regards where and how to proceed with life. In a post-disaster scenario, with situations deteriorating towards worse, such feelings only get magnified. The Sendai Framework for Disaster Risk Reduction, a 15-year voluntary agreement, adopted by United Nations Member States in March 2015 is today in place. However, unless and until it has a linkage with the grass root realities, much of the achievements will be lost. In 2018, a field visit was undertaken to understand the actual working of the NGOs vis-a-vis the government's perspective. The field visit to West Bengal showed the vast gaps in terms of understanding, conceptualizing the implementation strategies and communication between the government and the civil society organization. There is a huge deficit in this respect, and therefore, the implementation processes are like half-baked cakes with no ownership, no transparency with unclear roles and responsibilities. When it comes to analysing from a gender prism, the whole exercise of a need-based strategy gets diluted. The present COVID period has clearly shown how the gender perspectives knowingly or unknowingly have been completely ignored (UN Women 2020). It was found that this was a time when the crime against women increased manifold, child marriages and child abuse became rampant with women and children held at ransom during the lockdown period. Indeed this is the best time for traffickers to target! Whether its trafficking of women and children or the agriculture sector or the care sector, women have been systematically ignored. They are always considered as playing a supporting role. When disasters hit a region, it is the women who venture out in order to provide nourishment and food for her young ones and for the family. In the agriculture sector, women constitute 42% of India's agriculture labour force according to NCAER data, (Times of India 2021), nevertheless they seem to be invisible. The patriarchal laws and traditions simply do not let the women inherit the agricultural land. In the COVID times, the study makes it amply clear that men were always incharge of the sales and marketing of the products while the women would end up providing the finished products without being involved in the profit the products were fetching. It is important to recognize the two main load bearing pillars that take care of disaster mitigation and human trafficking. They are the governmental institutions and the non-governmental organizations. These are the two important functionaries for providing the need-based support to the distressed. Hence, it is important that the two complement and supplement each other as per the requirement.

The success of any state machinery is dependent to a large extent on a vibrant civil society organization. The experiences in terms of the government initiatives showed a mixed response. Some of the institutions interviewed include the West Bengal Task Force, Directorate of Child Rights, the West Bengal State Commission of Protection for Child Rights (WBSCPCR), Anti-Human Trafficking Units (AHTU, WB), Office of the District Magistrate, South 24 Parganas, Border Security Force (BSF), judiciary, parliamentarians, the non-governmental organizations besides others. The role of the state machinery has been both good and bad according to the non-government organizations. Simultaneously, the governmental institutions have their reservation on the roles that the NGOs have played. However, it is important to recognize the role played by the two. For example, the Justice Juvenile Act (JJ Act) can only get activated if there is a vibrant NGO community present in the area. Otherwise, the Act becomes a sleeping act. Therefore, a convergence plan is a must. A 'One Stop Crisis' needs to be created especially for the victims across the borders. The 'West Bengal Task Force' on the other hand despite putting their best efforts to help the victims, have often faced confusions regarding the repatriation process creating several hurdles. Victims often provide a wrong address, out of fear and stigmatization particularly the women victims. The address needs to be checked and verified several times in order to authenticate the addresses provided. This is an area where the CSO and the governmental organizations need to generate their combined synergy in handling the problem. At the grass root level, there are confusions regarding each other's role. This leads to the victim getting doubly penalized for want of clarity on several occasions. Based on the field visit, the following is an assessment of how the functionaries worked at the field level based on the understanding of their roles and responsibilities.

The West Bengal Task Force, Directorate of Child Rights

The West Bengal Task Force was created with the objective of prevention, rescue, safe return and ensuring speedy repatriation of inter and intrastate trafficked victims and also to repatriate the Bangladeshi children lodged in shelter homes within the state. This was an initiative by the Government of West Bengal to combat human trafficking. Some were repatriated by the state itself, while some others were repatriated with the help of NGOs. However, there are evidences where many of these children were pushed back into Bangladesh across the border without any formalities or safety precautions. This naturally involved several risks for children such as disassociation with family, re-exploitation by several touts and pimps forcing the kids to land from the frying pan to the fire!

The 'Task Force' leads a Central Level Advisory Committee on Human Trafficking, under which all the states have a State Advisory Committee. The Minister from the Department of Women and Child and Social Welfare is the head. This committee consists of stakeholders from the police, health, judiciary, Panchayat, etc. All Principal Secretaries are members. The state of West Bengal also has a MOU with the state of Maharashtra since 2014. West Bengal is the only state where a separate directory in trafficking was constituted in 2015.

The West Bengal Task Force and Directorate of Child Rights have the following main activities:

(a) The State Action Plan: Discussions are held from time to time to discuss policy decisions with the MWCD. These meetings are held on a regular basis. All laws and legal decisions are discussed threadbare, and the flaws are highlighted.
(b) Although the WB Task Force came into existence since 2008, a separate Directorate in Trafficking in West Bengal got created from 2015. Over the last decade, changes have been incorporated within the framework. The Task Force meet every quarterly and discuss the operational issues while scrutinizing the rescue operations. The target groups are mainly women and girls. At least 1000 cases have been repatriated so far over the last ten years. SALSA is also now included into the Task Force. They are the ones who meet out compensation to the victims. Most of the victims are from Bangladesh, some are from Nepal, and one was also from Bhutan. A few Rohingyas were also existing, but their cases were not taken up on a war footing due to political crisis.

According to the Director, the Child Care Institutions are mainly contacted when a victim is interjected along the borders. They collect and collate the lists, inform the concerned ministry who in turn contact the Deputy Chief of Mission (DCM) of Bangladesh and eventually the repatriation order is issued. Finally, a date of repatriation is stipulated. However, the Child Care Institutions house all types of victims and not only the trafficked victims. Boys and girls are kept separately. As observed from the field visit, the SP provides the vehicle to transport the girls and women to the Child Care Institutions. Every district is provided money by the government to spend on the victims' expenses of food, lodging, transport, etc. This is provided from 2015 for rescue, rehabilitation and repatriation. From 2016, an order was passed that stated that NGOs will be involved for all repatriation. Earlier the multiple communication created a lot of confusion when a missing child was reported to various agencies. So, a decision was taken that each trafficked victim found was to be reported to the West Bengal Task Force, so that the confusion and duplication could be avoided. Prior to this, the repatriation order was not necessary. One could repatriate with or without a travel permit. Later, it was considered that the government needs to be kept in the loop especially, for children. It was felt that the repatriation should not only be merely on the basis of travel permits but a proper order. This was particularly taken up for children from Bangladesh and Nepal.

However, it is most unfortunate that the government has not been in a position to keep a tag of the children post their repatriation. The Director acknowledged that the NGOs were the best for such work. At the micro-level, it is difficult to coordinate with the repatriated victims. In Bangladesh, the Bangladesh National Woman Lawyers' Association (BNWLA) is the best to monitor and supervise the repatriated victims. The NGOs are in a position to supervise and keep a tag of the nine districts along the Indo-Bangladesh border areas among their NGO partners, but it is difficult for the government to do the same as protocol needs to be maintained. Moreover, the cases pending in the court get attention faster with help from the NGOs. Despite the presence of a fast-track justice system, the government agencies are handicapped to speed up the cases of trafficking. This is one area where the Civil Society Organizations can come to the rescue of the victim. Once the nationality of the victim has been authenticated, the governmental procedure tends to be sluggish in comparison with the NGOs. There have been occasions where the institutions have accused of accepting bribes. The police simply look the other way and do not proceed to conduct the raids for days.

For example, a case study was stated about a young girl from Bangladesh. She had to be rescued with enormous efforts from NGO Sanlaap and the BNWLA. It was found out that the police were actually involved in not being proactive. But luckily the informer was actually a client of the girl and helped in getting her rescued by constantly providing messages to the NGO and eventually to the Task Force. The other links are with the State Commission of Protection for Child Rights (SCPCR) and the United Nations International Children's Emergency Fund (UNICEF). There is an online portal called 'Track the Missing Child'. The district officials are incharge of monitoring these initiatives. Such cases never used to be registered or any FIR lodged earlier. In particular, during a disaster like the floods in North 24 Parganas, lots of children go missing. The scenario becomes worst post-disaster. Children are mostly hired for domestic labour in a post-disaster scenario as has been observed in many other countries. From domestic labourer, they get transformed into bonded labourers. While their parents back home do not hear from them for months and sometimes for years togeher. The recent COVID pandemic did witness a worst scenario for the state of Bihar (Dutta 2020). Thus, it was important to first register all the private placement agencies. A bill was also passed about it. A three-member committee was constituted. This bill was lying pending with the labour department during the time the field visit was being undertaken. The Director believed that NGOs were dependable for lobbying and advocating to get the bill passed. However, it was new to find that during a disaster, even strict and traditional Muslim girls have also got trafficked. For example, eight girls from Nadia district had been trafficked to Maharashtra. During the festival of Durga puja, several were intercepted while being trafficked from North 24 Parganas. Some of the major challenges were pointed out.

- Delay in repatriation has been the biggest challenge.
- Fund Crunch for rescue operation is another hurdle—for example, booking of railway tickets for the rescued victim becomes a serious hurdle. Booking reservations of train tickets for the rescued victims at the spur of the moment by the police becomes difficult. So, the police staff are usually reluctant to undertake such a task. There is an understanding with the railway department to find a via

media for these victims to be brought by train to the shelter homes, but actions are not prompt.

- Besides most of the people involved are untrained and lack education, skill and training, so the rehabilitation gets even more difficult.
- It has also been noticed that in the present times children are more eager to get rich 'quick'. Therefore, they are constantly comparing their incomes with others. Both in North and South 24 Parganas, the Director stated that '*sometimes a rescue seems to be giving birth to a trafficker*'.

The State Advisory Committee members emphasized that it is important to coordinate with all stakeholders concerned whenever a meeting is called by the Directorate. Coordination needs to be enhanced involving all concerned stakeholders like the police, SCPCR, Childline, Directorate of Child Rights, etc.

However, there has been a dispute and disagreement to the number of trafficking cases. The NCRB data has been challenged. The government gives a minimum amount of one lakh rupees to a trafficked victim to begin with even before the case starts. The Protection of Children from Sexual Offences Act (POCSO Act) 2012, was established to protect the children against offences like sexual abuse, sexual harassment and pornography. It was formed to provide a child-friendly system for trials to be undertaken so that the perpetrators could be punished. However, most of the cases under POSCO, the alleged victim turns hostile due to the long winding proceedings.

If one carefully observes the activities undertaken for creating awareness programme, it will be found that most of the awareness programmes are undertaken by the NGOs, but there is no follow-up on this. The Integrated Child Protection Scheme (ICPS) forms the Child Protection Committees at the grass root level. These committees are the same as the civil vigilance committee. Such committees are 341 at the block level. More such committees get formed in every constituency. But the mechanism to catch the feedback is completely missing. The same was also found in a study undertaken for Bihar (Dutta 2020) sponsored by the World Vision. The NGOs are mostly donor oriented and work accordingly. The state of West Bengal already has a MoU with the state of Maharashtra, since 2014 for trafficking. This is focused for the two states. Earlier all Bengali speaking victims used to be sent to Bengal, but it was realized that they are mostly from Bangladesh and not West Bengal. Since then, they are now not getting mechanically shifted to West Bengal but are initiated for direct repatriation procedures with Bangladesh.

West Bengal State Commission of Protection for Child Rights (WBSCPCR)

The Chairperson of the West Bengal 'State Commission of Protection for Child Rights' (WBSCPCR) stated during the field visit that one of their major activities was 'Creating Awareness'. However, this was possible only through NGOs like Sanlaap, Jabala, Kolkata Meri World and so on. Some of the major activities include

- Creating awareness through NGOs (mention was made of Sanlaap, Jabala, Kolkata Meri World, etc.). The awareness building programme is for all the 23 districts of West Bengal. All the 23 DMs are involved in this plus the CWCs and the Child Protection Units exist to safeguard and protect the child rights. As per the Government of India, no child below 14 years is allowed to work. However, it is difficult to establish whether the child is 14 years of age or more. Earlier according to 2015 rule, a test of the bones determined the age of the child. However, now, the rules have been changed. The CWC are authorized to take a look at the child and mutually decide if he/she is less than 14 years.
- Preventive measures through Panchayats such as introducing modules for TOT to sensitize child rights among boys and girls.

The West Bengal SCPCR has links with AHTU and the WB Task Force. Records state that West Bengal has the highest number of trafficked victims and also has the highest number of recoveries. According to the Chairperson, poverty and ignorance are some of the major challenges that the victims faced. Although Internet may have been a cause to lure the victims to fall prey to being trafficked, it has its advantages as well. It was believed that the situation had improved a lot with Internet facilities.

During the severe floods in North Bengal, several districts got badly affected. It is usually the SCPCR which immediately contacts the affected district's DMs, and proper measures are taken to curb trafficking. Not a single child was reported to have been trafficked during the recent floods that were in 2018. The major problem between the state machinery and CSO is that the CSOs work in independent pockets and without much coordination. Often, they tend to be repetitive in their approach, duplicating their work. They remain in competition with each other rather than complementing the activities. The SCPCR as a state machinery tries to coordinate and bring them together in a systematic manner. The role of the state is to harness the synergy and positivity of the various NGOs. During '*Aila*' and 'tsunami', the state machinery alerted the community and saved many orphans from getting trafficked.

A half-yearly report is usually prepared and submitted by the SCPCR to the NCPCR on a regular basis. The UNICEF is also a link with SCPCR. It guides and advises the SCPCR to build policy framework and also funds for various projects. Other links of SCPCR at the national level include the Kolkata Police, the CID, the law enforcement authorities, the administration, the MWCD, the health department and others. Meetings are held four times a year with the police. However, a joint meeting with all the partners is seldom held although independent meetings are held with various partners from time to time.

Both Bangladesh and Nepal are equally vulnerable. So, when the victims from these countries are rescued, the CWC authenticates their nationality before the process is completed. 'Shakti Vahini' also helps in the recovery. Clearly, it is now amply displayed that the children do not get tricked so easily anymore. They willingly accept the lures they get for a better life. They are willing to get married before 18 years, and they are willing to take up hazardous activities and other odd jobs.

However, if they are less than 18 years in age, their consent is not accepted. India too like the Scandinavian countries of Norway and Denmark has a law to criminalize the demand segment. The customers and the traffickers are criminalized and not the child.

Anti-Human Trafficking Units (AHTU, WB)

Strengthening the law enforcement response in India against Trafficking in Persons through training and capacity building under the Ministry of Home Affairs was taken up as a joint initiative by the Government of India and the United Nations Office on Drugs and Crime. A series of training programmes were initiated under this to raise awareness of law enforcement officers, such as the police and prosecutors, as a gesture towards addressing the issues of human trafficking. The main objective was to build their capacity so as to be able to better investigate and prosecute offenders perpetrating in this crime. Selected states were chosen initially for the training to address different types of trafficking such as trafficking of women and children for commercial sexual exploitation, child labour, bonded labour and so on. Such an initiative had very positive outcomes in most of the states, and the Anti-Human Trafficking Unit (AHTU) model seemed to be effective and hence got popular. The project has contributed towards developing of 12 very important resource books about protocols and Standard Operating Procedures (SOPs) and in setting up of Anti-Human Trafficking Units (AHTUs) under the police department of the project states. The project has shown positive outcomes in some of the states especially in raising awareness.

So far through the training programmes, more than 13,670 persons (police and prosecutors) have been trained. Besides, Anti-Human Trafficking Units involving government officials and NGOs have been set up in the states of Goa, West Bengal, Andhra Pradesh and Bihar, and they are all functional. In addition, the AHTUs were being set up by the state governments at the district headquarters level as well, with funds being provided under the scheme for infrastructure and equipment. The state governments were to provide the police personnel and officials from other departments for managing the AHTU. The police officials posted at the AHTU are required to directly report to the Superintendent of Police of the district. The state governments were also to identify the personnel who would be associated with the AHTU.

The beneficiaries of the project ultimately include,

- the vulnerable group of women and children, especially in the rural and tribal areas
- the law enforcing agencies in all the districts as they would substantially get strengthened in the effective discharge of their duties
- the prosecution agency will indeed be greatly benefitting because of the improved prosecution as a result of full proof cases supported by better quality evidence.

- the NGOs as expected would get better support from the police and prosecution in achieving their objectives.

The AHTU are to attend to all the three aspects of trafficking, viz. prevention, protection and prosecution. They will also develop databases on traffickers, network with all concerned agencies as and when required. The AHTU will thus be the field level functional unit to address human trafficking in a holistic manner. They are supposed to address the existing gaps in the law enforcement response to trafficking and serve as the institutional mechanisms for combating the crime, working across all the stakeholders, i.e. police, prosecution, rescue, NGOs and so on.

The presence of AHTUs is expected to ensure a victim-centric approach that would usher in the 'best interest of the victim/survivor' and prevent 'secondary victimization/re-victimization' of the victim as well as ensure a gender and child rights sensitive approach in dealing with the trafficked victims (Ministry of Home Affairs).

Figure 5.1 shows the distribution of the AHTUs state-wise with an expenditure to the tune of 2046 lakhs so far. However, both the governmental institutions and the non-governmental organizations feel that the AHTUs thrive best wherever the NGOs are. The West Bengal Task Force, for example, would never work without the NGOs. The two need to blend together to produce the best results. Nevertheless, according to the IPS officer at the Lal Bazar Police station, Kolkata, reservations were expressed, and it was stated that the NGOs alone cannot handle the cases if the police were not involved.

Fig. 5.1 State-wise No. of Anti-Human Trafficking Units, 2018. *Source* https://mha.gov.in/MHA1/Par2017/pdfs/par2018-pdfs/ls-02012018/2409.pdf

In the case of West Bengal, it shares international borders with Bangladesh, Bhutan and Nepal. The Anti-Human Trafficking Unit (AHTU) thus becomes the nodal agency for rescuing trafficked humans and creating awareness against trafficking in the state. Having started in 2011, AHTU has rescued a large number of trafficked girls and arrested many traffickers, international and interstate gangs. In one of the cases that has been much cited, the AHTU was able to arrange for deposition of two victim girls through videoconference who were earlier repatriated to Bangladesh. Such videoconference is first of its kind. During recent years, the High Court had entrusted AHTU particularly with eight *Habeas Corpus writs*, and this unit has successfully disposed of the same, according to the Special Superintendent. A *Habeas Corpus writ* allows individuals arrested and detained illegally to be brought before a judge in a court of law in order to ascertain whether the person was found legally or illegally detained and arrested. This becomes important because it protects peoples' individual freedom from the state when it acts lawlessly.

Besides, AHTU organizes sensitization programme at regular intervals. In another example, the AHTU has been able to submit charge sheet against a person within 15 days in relation to a case under POCSO in Nadia, according to the Officer incharge of AHTU. The Anti-Human Trafficking Unit (AHTU) of police in Delhi had reunited at least 130 missing children with their families in 2018 and 2019, according to the police. The AHTU of north-east district reunited 101 missing children with their families in 2018 and 37 in 2019. Most of the missing children hailed from various states like Bihar, Haryana, Uttar Pradesh, Madhya Pradesh and Delhi.

Office of the District Magistrate, South 24 Parganas

A meeting with the ADM along with the team members was held at Bhawani Bhavan on 16 November 2018. A new scheme called '*SWAYANG SIDDHA*' was introduced in schools which had a huge impact. *According to the ADM*, Swayang Siddha has been a unique initiative to prevent human trafficking and child marriages. This was spearheaded by the West Bengal Police with active support and participation of community and district administration. The main objectives of this initiative were to

- Form Swayang Siddha groups with school and college students in order to develop youth agency.
- Build awareness on ramifications of human trafficking, pitfalls of child marriage, healthy and hygienic practices and care and protection services.
- Map and sensitize vulnerable persons and families and to ensure access to entitlements, social security, livelihood and food security, in coordination with Panchayats and Child Protection Committees.

The vision was to build networks of aware, alert and proactive individuals and groups working together to build safe communities to prevent human trafficking and child marriage. Swayang Siddha groups were formed with students from Classes VIII onwards to colleges. Members of school-level groups like Kanyashree groups,

Swachha groups, Child Cabinets and college student bodies like Gender Equality Cell, Anti-Sexual Harassment Cell are part of Swayang Siddha groups. Survivors are also involved and helped to be empowered to lead a life of dignity. The partners include the district administration and Police, in partnership with UNICEF and Childline with technical support from Contact Base. They all work in collaboration to mobilize Swayang Siddha groups, educational institutions and Child Protection Committees to mentor and support the young agents of change. Self-awareness is of prime importance to reduce vulnerability. In this regard, the parents and families protect children from violence and abuse. Stakeholders mitigate push factors and ensure law enforcement to build safe communities. Till August 2018, over 90 schools in 12 blocks of South 24 Parganas had taken over 150 preventive actions. The various stakeholders had their roles to play. Some of the stakeholders were

- The Police: The Police were involved with
  - Outreach activities in the educational institutions for building awareness
  - Enhance accessibility and trust among the community.
- Educational Institutions: The educational institutions
  - Formed and mentored Swayang Siddha groups in schools and colleges
  - Built awareness on adolescence and sexuality
  - Facilitated awareness building among students and parents
  - Built grievance redressal mechanism through suggestion and complaints drop box in campuses.
- Women and Child Development was mainly to
  - Promote participation of adolescent group members in Child Protection Committees for strengthening coordination.
- Local Governance: The Panchayat on the other hand helped in
  - Building safe and child-friendly communities and public spaces
  - Involving adolescent groups in awareness programmes
  - Working with Block and Village Child Protection Committees and adolescent groups for fulfilment of rights and access to social protection schemes for survivors and vulnerable persons.
- NGOs
  - Involved the adolescent groups in awareness programmes
  - Shared and disseminated the available IEC materials with adolescents.
- Health
  - Facilitates access to counselling services
  - Provides referral linkages in special cases like sexual abuse.

The various stakeholders include the DM, ADM, Police, UNICEF, District Social Welfare Officer (DSWO), Differentiated Instruction (DI) of school education, the Block Development Officer (BDO), Child Development Project Officer (CDPOs), teachers, block officials, Shiksha Bandhu, Village level Child Protection Committees (VLCPC members), Anwesha Counsellors (which are Adolescent Friendly Health Clinics), Childline (Number 1098), Panchayati Raj Institution (PRI), local NGOs, District Legal Services Authority (DLSA) which renders free legal aid to under trial prisoners' cases that remain pending in Courts as well as the Para Legal Volunteers (PLVs) under the Delhi State Legal Services Authority. The PLVs are the first point of contact for inmates in need of legal aid or advice.

Some of the major outcomes of Swayam Siddha include

- The outreach programmes which had been conducted in over 400 schools from the 12 blocks in South 24 Parganas during 2017–18
- Over 50,000 students and 1600 teachers had been reached. The total reach had crossed 200,000 youths.
- Police reached out to schools in North 24 Parganas, Nadia, Murshidabad, Howrah and other districts of West Bengal.
- Teachers and police obtain regular information on attempts and cases of child marriages and human trafficking (reports suggested around 30–35 calls per month were received).
- Teachers were reported to have stopped at least more than 100 cases of child marriages and prevention of ten cases of attempted trafficking during 2017–18.
- A minimum total of 60 trafficking survivors had been main-streamed through community-based rehabilitation during 2017–18.

Border Security Force (BSF)

In terms of cross-border trafficking, the role of BSF becomes extreme significance. A civil vigilance committee that had been formed in the Indo-Bangladesh border areas helped in curbing human trafficking. These civil vigilance committees comprise mostly local people ranging from an adolescent, a barber, a tea stall owner or simply strangers who are located in the border areas. In the area of Indo-Bangladesh border in Nadia district and in North 24 Parganas, NGOs had created civil vigilance committee and developed 'Transit Centre Mode' as for example by the NGO Sanlaap. These were created with the idea to make it victim centric and house the victims who were found crossing the border during the night. They were to be kept in the 'transit center' until morning hours and returned back to their respective homes.

The BSF officials were introduced to this initiative and had been of great help. However, due to a problem in the modalities, transport expenses became a huge hurdle in shifting the victims to these centres. These transit centres are on either side of the Indo-Nepal borders. Due to the transport expenses involved in carrying the victims, they are reluctant to reach them to the transit centres. The BSF officials are given training periodically by the Seema Suraksha Bal (SSB). However, as per the

NGOs, the criteria fixed for selecting who can take part for the training are missing. Sometimes, the people who are most deserving are ignored. On other occasions, people who are closer to retirement are selected. Many lack the passion. On many occasions, people selected for the training are not given leave, and hence, they hardly attend the training programme. The senior women have other priorities towards their home and normally take up their duties only during the daytime. They are seldom seen to come for their training at night which is after their office hours. Hence, the BSF officials and the police do not participate in the training wholeheartedly. Rather the attitude and the environment prohibit them from participating enthusiastically. In front of the seniors, their work culture prohibits the juniors to open their mouth or participate in the discussions. They are too timid to dare to put forward their points. The new recruits are however smarter as compared to the old officials.

Judiciary

The judiciary is in urgent need to be more sensitive. The low level of conviction rate creates a big gap. A public prosecutor is engaged in multiple tasks. However, presently, the District Legal Services Authority (DLSA) provides a compensation to every trafficked victim immediately after it has been registered. This is under the provision of the 'Women Victims Compensation Fund from which the amount of compensation, as decided by the State Legal Services Authority or District Legal Services Authority. This is paid to the women victim or her dependent(s) who have suffered loss or injury as a result of an offence and who require rehabilitation' (NALSA 2018). They do not wait for the case to be over. According to a media report, (The Print 2020) India had 38,503 victims of trafficking between 2011 and 19. However, only 77 have got compensation. The number of trafficking victims that get compensation is a miniscule proportion. Many human trafficking victims in India either do not know that they can avail government compensation or are daunted by the sheer amount of proof it takes to claim it, according to the NGOs working in this field. Unfortunately, the prosecutors are handicapped for want of a proper charge sheet. Women magistrates are believed to be more sensitive in fastening such cases, but the long-drawn witnesses and documentation make the witnesses hostile. Even in the fast court tracks, there are a huge number of cases still pending. Out of more than 8000 human trafficking cases reported in 2016 as per NCRB, less than half were filed in court by the police, and the conviction rate in those that did go to trial was hardly 28% according to government data. Thus, the gap between prosecution and conviction is a widening gap that is gradually growing over time.

Parliamentarians

Unfortunately, NGOs expressed extreme disappointment where parliamentarians were concerned. They were convinced that 'it's better not to expect much from them. They come with their own set agenda' spoke one NGO during the field survey. The parliament and parliamentarians have the power to prevent human trafficking by raising awareness and curbing exploitative practices. They lack the basic understanding of the gravity of the situation. Many times they refuse to even acknowledge that there are any such cases in their own constituency. They could be useful in adopting the laws needed to prosecute the traffickers while at the same time, protecting the rights of the victims. The parliamentarians can play a huge role in the national legislation processes. It is important that the parliamentarians gain familiarity with and understand the definition of human trafficking in all its forms provided under the Trafficking in Persons protocol. They need to understand and address the three key elements of Trafficking in Persons—act, means and purpose for national legislation already mentioned earlier. A clear distinction needs to be made in the understanding between the crimes of human trafficking from other forms of organized immigration crime, including the smuggling of migrants.

Non-Governmental Organisation

As has been observed during the field visit, many of the state machinery have amply highlighted the importance of NGOs contribution in addressing the issues of human trafficking. Some of the feedback received from the NGOs during the field visit undertaken in 2018 have been extremely crucial and need to be discussed for a better understanding in removing the challenges faced.

There are two main approaches to a disaster. These are developing a 'Watch Dog' situation where the civil vigilance committee, the Kishori group, adolescents/youth group, have a regular interaction and frequent meetings exchanging notes among themselves as a preventive measure. Secondly, the provision of 'Relief Material', which had been initiated by several organizations, but the distribution remained disorganized. 'Sanlaap', for example, expressed their anguish while working in the border areas especially for deficit in documentation. Some of the highlights from the non-government organizations from the field are stated below:

- Lack of evidence has been a most crucial gap in addressing the issue: a place named Haldibari in the border areas near Cooch Behar district of West Bengal is extremely vulnerable in the present times. It is constantly hit by floods. People migrate in search of livelihood options and do get trafficked. It was found that several women of this area had been often trafficked by Kashmiri Shawl traders. But not much evidence was documented in this regard and hence goes unnoticed.
- In the current times, certain new trends have emerged. This pertains to online trafficking. Children often make friends over Internet/social media and get trafficked

without anyone suspecting anything. It has been often found that the trafficked victims are children who are not particularly happy in their home and tend to feel neglected by their parents. Although child marriages may have been on the decrease, online child trafficking leads to child marriages too. And before they know they are whisked away into the labour market, for prostitution, and willingly become bonded labourers. NGOs like 'Sanlaap' had initiated certain preventive measures in order to curb the menace such as (a) Regular and continuous contact, (b) Activities that are rights based and create awareness, (c) Sessions were held on a weekly basis and (d) Adolescents/youth groups were created to act as peer group pressures. Banglanatak.com also opined that another new trend had emerged in terms of pilgrimage from Nepal border.

- The Tourist Industry is another area that had emerged as a vulnerable sector in the travel and tourism sector. The vulnerability of boys was a threat. It was stated that young boys were found to have been trafficked from Bangladesh to West Bengal and further to Sikkim. They were quickly employed in the hotels or simply as domestic servants in the hotel industry of Sikkim. There are laws that state children below the age of fourteen are not to be employed but nevertheless these laws remain fuzzy. It is difficult to prove if these children are not a relative of the employer in which case, they are allowed to help in the family business. Examples of such are often found in Midnapore district of West Bengal such as in the tourist places of Digha and Mandarmani. Also, when the child had been absent on a regular basis from schools, supervision and monitoring of such activities were difficult to keep a check on.
- Marriageable Age: This is yet another area where proving the age of the victim is a cumbersome process. Whether the child is an adult or has attained the marriageable age is very difficult to prove in the absence of authentic documentation.
- The area of Gender Variant also opens up wide potential for exploitation especially for the LGBTQ community. The women who are masculine end up entering the sports activities, and the men that are feminine enter in begging on the traffic signals. This needs to be addressed urgently. Even during the COVID lockdown, they were found to be the most marginalized and the most stigmatized *(Forthcoming*, UN Women 2020)
- Men have also been trafficked for labour in many areas which has substantially increased at present especially in a disaster hit region which becomes not only an origin but also a destination for trafficked victims. The case of Maldives has already been discussed at length earlier where due to tsunami, many men were recruited to Maldives for reconstruction from India, Bangladesh and Sri Lanka in particular. Their plight was worse than a trafficked victim as they had sold all their assets back home to pay the agents who hired them through fraud and cheat (Dutta et al. 2015).
- The participation from the Government in terms of awareness raising in the activities has been quite active particularly in the schools, border areas and Panchayat. For example, in Cooch Behar, which is a disaster prone and extremely vulnerable area, the government is very proactive in addressing the concerns. People at the

district level have been extremely helpful. The experience of NGOs active participation shows that among the nine districts out of 23 in West Bengal, in North 24 Parganas, girls were more exposed as compared to earlier times. There have been more rescues from private places rather than from brothels. Their experience in Murshidabad, similarly, shows that how a girl who is fifteen years old was rescued three years back, and she was mentally challenged. Nevertheless, the NGOs feel that the value system has become much eroded at present with the social taboos getting fast depleted. A typical rescue operation in Punjabi Bagh, New Delhi, revealed how the present trend among the young ones prevails. Once rescued if a victim earned 5–7 thousand rupees as income per day, the victim will certainly not accept an amount which may be half of that or less than that. Thus, the child victim will be delighted to continue with the same work.

- Another shocking example was stated by the NGO 'Sanlaap'. A twelve-year-old girl from Sanlaap's rehabilitation centre listed out 'V Wash' as one of the things that she required. A 'V Wash' is a lactic acid formulation that helps maintain the ideal and delicate pH value of intimate body part and prevents infection. It was shocking for the councillors to note that at her age and mental capacity, she would demand such materials rather than toys or/and books. So, one needs to understand the psychology of the child victim and the degree of exposure she has faced within her exploitative lifetime. In another study on Reproductive Sexual Health by Child in Need institute (CINI), it was found that how the tea garden women workers had been consuming the tablets for unwanted pregnancy without understanding the side effects of the medicine. Thus, one has to understand that their maturity age has enhanced manifold while the official adult age continues to be 18 years. This has been accepted universally, although this needs to be relooked depending on the area.

Some of the other challenges faced by the NGOs include

- Networking: The activity depends upon the funding. If there are no funds, it is difficult to do networking. An NGO stated that it had developed quite a pronounced networking system. During an activity in Alipur duar, funds suddenly arrived, and the joint network activity immediately collapsed. It became altogether an individual level activity. The funding to develop the network together immediately crashed.
- Awareness Programme: When awareness programme is introduced in remote areas for the first time, it needs to be carefully implemented. Such a large intervention was organized from 2000 to 2006 by Sanlaap in some of these areas. No one had ever entered these districts to introduce any awareness programme. Even the police were not aware that anything like trafficking existed. Alas, such initiatives got taken up in a disintegrated manner and thus got washed off.
  Banglanatak.com has also been involved with awareness programme such as the 'Swayang Siddha' mentioned earlier which began in 2016. The police initiated this programme. Banglanatak.com along with the police had covered 400 schools. At least 3000 children got protected through this programme. This was also to extend to the colleges as well as the PRIs. Another programme called *Indrani*

through the Childline managed to nab about 1000 traffickers who got arrested. The main reason for children to get trafficked was abuse at home. The International Justice Mission (IJM) in Kolkata caters to online awareness in the urban areas. A total of 150 child marriages were also prevented under POSCO. A survey on the schools had revealed that things were much better now. The adolescents' group were to the next targets.

Based on several field visits undertaken earlier, it was evident that several of the NGOS had contributed significantly towards creating awareness and in pursuing rights-based approach ushering in prevention, protection and prosecution activities.

- Developing Social Integration: When schools are targeted to develop social integration between boys and girls, it is not undertaken for all schools but are restricted to only some schools. This sort of approach does not yield the desired results. This is only half-hearted effort, done merely for namesake.
- Involving The Youth: Meeting the youth members, connecting them to govt officials, e.g. BDO, District Child Protection Officer (DCPO) in Cooch Behar, Alipur Duar, and other such places are essential. According to the Head of 'Sanlaap', linking CSOs with GOs has been the main issue.

  The ICT materials were being developed by Banglanatak.com as well as others involving the youth, and the same was being implemented along the borders of India–Bangladesh and India–Nepal. The BSF and SSB have been extremely well organized, and the NGOs expressed satisfaction with their well-coordinated and all possible help. They have prevented many cases from getting trafficked. Evidence of their work was visible in the states of WB, Bihar and UP, especially in the border areas. The US Consulate too has been an important stakeholder. Along the India–Bangladesh border, Murshidabad and a few other districts are no doubt extremely vulnerable. Despite all the efforts, the networking and partnership are hugely in deficit. There is no synergy among the NGOs. Banglanatak.com expressed dissatisfaction in work ethics. It was revealed that in Nepal, there were trafficking cases to China and Korea.

The work contributed by the civil society organization has no doubt brought about visibility in the implementation of activities. It will only be proper to mention the names of a few NGOs whose work has been commendable in fighting the menace of human trafficking. 'Prajwala' based in Hyderabad, India, is devoted exclusively to eradicating forced prostitution and sex trafficking. Headed by Ms. Sunitha Krishnan the organisation actively works in the areas of prevention, rescue, rehabilitation, reintegration and advocacy to combat trafficking and restore the dignity of the victims of commercial sexual exploitation. Mr. Ravi Kant, President of 'Shakti Vahini', and his entire team have been fighting tooth and nail to locate the missing children and reach the cases to its logical end from prosecution to conviction. Similarly, it is worth mentioning NGOs like Asha Niwas, Bachpan Bachao Andolan, Prayas, STOP, Media Coalition, Butterflies and many others in Delhi and Haryana who have been working towards curbing human trafficking. The West Bengal based Civil Society Organisations include Apne Aap, Bhorukha Public Welfare Trust, Kolkata Samved, Action

Against Trafficking and Sexual Exploitation of Children (ATSEC)—India, AID Research and Training Centre (SLARTC), besides Sanlaap and Banglanatak.com. There have been some serious contribution by the NGOs in Maharashtra as well such as Prerana, Save the Children India, Church of North India, CINI besides many others. Bhoomika Vihar of Bihar, Child Rights Goa, V.M. Salgaocar College of Law, Sangath, from Goa and several others from the states of Andhra Pradesh, Karnataka, UP, north-east particularly 'Impulse' from Meghalaya, Uttarakhand, Jharkhand and Orissa have all been significant in addressing the issues of human trafficking. It would be impossible to monitor coordinate and keep a check on the victim without the help of the Civil Society Organization.

India, being a source, origin and destination of human trafficking, is surrounded by other South Asian countries such as Bangladesh, Nepal and Sri Lanka. Human trafficking is an issue of a global nature and goes beyond international borders. It is important to tackle the issue along with the neighbouring countries in complete compliance with the essence and true spirit of the definition of human trafficking. Some of the NGOs like the Association for Community Development (ACD), Bangladesh National Women Lawyers Association (BNWLA) from Bangladesh, the National Network Against Girl Trafficking (NNAGT), Office of the National Rapporteur on Trafficking/National Human Rights Commission, Forum for Protection of Public Interest (Pro Public), Forum for Women Law and Development (FWLD), National Judicial Academy (NJA), Maiti Nepal from Nepal, besides the Marga Institute, Lawyers for Human Rights and Development (LHRD), Centre for Women's Research (CENWOR) from Sri Lanka have all been involved in addressing the gruesome nature of issues related to human trafficking.

Shelter Homes

In terms of shelter homes, there are currently over 9000 registered shelter homes for children in the country. These are being monitored by an entire institutional framework set up under the Juvenile Justice (Care and Protection of Children) Act 2015. This ushers in accountability to the rehabilitative homes run both by the state and by NGOs. This is in sharp contrast to women who are survivors of trafficking but are currently denied access to any such rehabilitation, safety and support. A limited number of homes that exist ignore the minimum standards of care, hardly any regulatory or monitoring mechanism. This enhances the multiple degrees of abuse on women with impunity. There is no framework available that would audit and arrest any misuse bringing in more transparency in operation.

The women and children survivors of trafficking face an immediate sense of fear and vulnerability. They have often been trafficked and sold by their own families, and hence, returning back to them is hardly free from threats. Victims of trafficking for commercial sexual exploitation, especially women, also face socially and economically a paralysing stigma in their communities. While their survival is a struggle, they also often have to deal with trauma, depression and social exclusion. This undoubtedly will push them back into the business of exploitation that they had escaped from. In the absence of an alternative safety means of subsistence, the survivors are often left penniless and homeless. This places the responsibility on the state to ensure the safety and well-being of a victim of trafficking (The Logical Indian 2018)

There is an urgent need for providing psychological care to survivors of trafficking and to the women in the shelter homes. Severe mental health challenges such as 'significant emotional problems, ideas of hopelessness, worthlessness, crying spells, anxiety about the future, social anxiety, death wishes and suicidal ideas' are common among the women inmates (UNODC 2011). Those suffering from HIV/AIDS have even more difficult situation to face. Despite the best counselling, it has been observed that the severity of the mental trauma they undergo is an everlasting one because of the stigma attached (Field Visit to Narendrapur, Sanlaap, 2010).

The absence of regulation and monitoring mechanisms promotes ill-intentioned agencies to exploit the vulnerabilities of victims of trafficking especially the women. They are often thrown back into exploitative homes that may be operating as hubs of trafficking themselves in the garb of providing shelter. Therefore, although access to institutional care is always a measure of last resort, it is usually also the only option that a trafficked victim has for her safety and protection. The trafficking bill emphasizes that access to institutional support is the statutory right of the victim which should not and cannot be done away with.

A shelter homes is the only shelter for a victim to recuperate from their trauma and get back her sanity through the psychosocial counselling and care that is imparted at these homes. According to NGOs, one size cannot fit all. There are different shelter homes required for different types of trafficking. At least 6–7 shelter homes are required, while the number provided is far short from the demand according to the NGOs. Since 'Homes' are less, all kinds of victims are pushed into the same shelter home. The incharge with fixed mindsets lack professionalism and training. In one of the field visits, some years back (2004), a superintendent behaved in the most abusive manner rebuking the child mother who was rescued and being repatriated. The superintendent was harsh to this young victim in the presence of many, shouting her down for asking for a doctor for her baby who was suffering from high fever. She was not only rebuked but was attacked with a barrage of questions such as why she had eloped with her boyfriend in the first instance. This was in a governments home called 'Observation Home' in Delhi's *Nari Niketan*. The rescued trafficked victim was hardly sixteen years of age and a mother of two kids already. The superintendent lacked the decency and was most insensitive towards the trafficked victims and their off springs. Her tone and body language were demeaning to speak the least. They definitely need training to handle such cases and the sensitiveness of the case (Dutta et al. 2002).

The trend has not changed much over the past decades. All stakeholders need to come forward and build a structure that has all facilities such as CCTV cameras, constant and thorough monitoring and supervision as well as psychosocial counselling. It is true that in comparison, those homes maintained by the NGOs are in much better condition than the ones maintained by the government. These homes do display a sense of belonging and a chirpy atmosphere.

The challenges and opportunities of working with government actors and non-government actors have been highlighted in the form of a table (refer Table 5.1).

The discourse between the government institution and the civil society organization reveals that there is a lack of coordination between the two. A strong voluntary sector does not always have to guarantee a high degree of interaction among the

Table 5.1 Challenges and opportunities in governmental/non-governmental organizations

Actor	Challenges	Opportunities
Head of States' Offices	• Has numerous priorities to deal with • May face conflicting interests	• Turn this actor into an Anti-Human Trafficking champion • Make him/her to take a lead role in coordinating the implementation strategy for curbing trafficking during and post-disaster
Parliamentarians	• Often not involved in all stages of programme implementation • May have limited awareness of the consequences of disaster risks • May face conflicting interests	• Leverage its legislative role • Foster its advocacy role, especially for budgeting of judicial system
Judiciary	• May have limited awareness of the target • Enforcement of laws may be lacking • May face conflicting interests	• Develop synergies with laws related to good governance (e.g. disaster law, trafficking, illegal trade) as well as those necessary for the achievement of the Sendai Framework of Action and Trafficking protocol
Panchayati Raj Institutions	• May have weak capacities • Lack of funding of subnational bodies may impede in the implementation processes • Some PRI members are not well connected to development planning	• Support them in fulfilling their roles in development planning • Encourage them to integrate sustainable development objectives into plans/budgets
National documentation processes	• Data not generally captured by regular surveys • Capacity to produce policy-relevant information may be weak	• Increase investments in data and national statistical systems • Build statistical capacity to monitor the SDGs, including capacity to collect, manage and analyse data on a regular basis Civil Society Organizations

(continued)

Table 5.1 (continued)

Actor	Challenges	Opportunities
Civil Society Organizations	• Capacities may be weak, especially with respect to engagement in national development planning • Often not involved in all stages of development planning	• Engage them as SDG Champions • Involve them in all stages of development planning • Encourage them in their watchdog role (i.e. in promoting transparency and accountability) • Foster their role in information collection, information sharing and awareness raising (from policymakers to local communities)
Business and industry	• May perceive sustainable development (specifically environment management and legislation) as a barrier to their activities • Often not involved in development planning	• Mitigate the effect of their activities that have a negative impact on sustainable development • Engage them in the development planning process to provide effective and innovative solutions to achieve sustainable development and reduce poverty • Make use of this major source for financing the SDGs
Academic and research institutions	• May be disconnected from the development planning process • Capacity to produce policy-relevant information may be weak	• Leverage their innovative ideas, including new scientific approaches, to deploy sustainable solutions and appropriate technologies for achieving the SDGs • Work with them to enhance the science policy link to find sustainable solutions to development problems
Media	• May lack knowledge and attention to sustainable development issues • May lack freedom of expression	• Make use of their role in shaping the opinions of decision-makers and the general public • Work with them to encourage public involvement in national development planning • Provide them with policy-related information • Work to enhance their advocacy role in achieving the SDGs

various organizations. There can be a rigid divide between voluntary organizations and the public and private sectors. Whether a strong non-governmental organization (NGO) sector encourages governments to pursue such priorities or assist them in attaining their objectives, this vehicle of civil society has potential importance which has hitherto been largely neglected.

A healthy relationship is only conceivable when both parties have a common objective. If the government's commitment to poverty reduction is weak, NGOs will find dialogue and collaboration frustrating or even counterproductive. Likewise, repressive governments will be wary of NGOs which represent the poor or victimized. In such situations, NGOs will probably prefer to chart their own course, giving all instruments of the state as wide a berth as possible. Where the government has a positive social agenda (or even where individual ministries do) and where NGOs are effective, there is the potential for a strong, collaborative relationship. However, this does not mean the subcontracting of placid NGOs, but a 'genuine partnership between NGOs and the government to work on a problem facing the country or a region, based on mutual respect, acceptance of autonomy, independence, and pluralism of NGO opinions and positions'. (Tandon 1991). Such relations are rare, even when the conditions are met. The mutual distrust and jealousy appear to be deep-rooted as was observed during the field visit. Government fears that NGOs erode their political power or even threaten national security. While the NGOs mistrust the motivation of the government and its officials (Clark 1995).

The major problem lies in the fact that the CSOs work in independent pockets and without much synchronization with other programme that are going on in the neighbourhood. Their objectives although may be to address the major issue of human trafficking, but often, they tend to be repetitive in their approach, duplicating and supplementing rather than complementing their work. They seem to be in constant competition with each other rather than complementing their activities. The SCPCR and other state machinery make an attempt to coordinate and bring them together on a common platform. The role of the state is to harness the synergy and positivity of the various NGOs. It has been observed that during Aila and tsunami that happened, the state machinery alerted the community and had saved many orphans from being trafficked. Although the NGOs toil hard at the grass root level, but each one work within their confined arenas. A network coalition often helps especially in a cross-border situation, but they tend to remain confined within their arena. Such network coalitions are few.

Unfortunately, statistics do matter and become relevant. At the end of the day, it is the number that matters. How many were saved and how many rescues had been undertaken successfully. A lack of communication and coordination within national statistical systems (NSS) in many countries and between the NSS and international agencies complicate further a reliable data availability. International agencies that are recipients of data are not receiving a nationally sanctioned official indicator which are not certified by the NSO. This is despite the fact that an international agency is responsible for globally compiling the given indicator. Many countries also lack coordination among national data producers, which can result in reporting of inconsistent or contradictory information to international statistical agencies. As the underlying definitions and operational contexts vary, different sources can produce different data. Using different sources also means that the data is updated irregularly and the reference periods may differ (it may be fiscal or calendar year).

Many of the victims who were interviewed often disclosed that they prefer going back to the illegal trade due to the red-tapism and inhuman living conditions in the shelter homes. As mentioned earlier, some of the NGOs were convinced that one of the main reasons for children to get trafficked was abusive parents. Sometimes the shelter homes have no respite for them. The same reason that is abuse prevalent in the shelter homes compels them to run away! And now with new trends emerging such as online trafficking, higher demand for young boys as waiters to work in restaurants and small hotels, enhanced demand for labour in disaster hit areas, compel the victims to get trafficked and fall prey in the hands of the traffickers. In 2020 a massive number of young boys from Bihar were found working under inhuman conditions in the bangle industry of Jaipur (*Forthcoming* Dutta 2020).

Funding is often difficult to obtain for implementation of a strategy and so is developing the networking and coalition among the NGOs. Besides funding, there are also structural issues including difficulty in getting ministries and members of parliament to develop a feeling of ownership over the strategy adopted and its implementation. This has often been pointed out by the NGOs about the parliamentarians. The inadequacy of institutions is in terms of perceiving the social and economic realities and their impacts on the ground, the difficulties in coordinating policies and initiatives in efforts towards achieving the targets (UNDP 2017). Some of the NGOs do struggle to collect reliable and adequate data on the effectiveness of policies and initiatives. The lack of a systematic data collection and the fragmented nature of the targets achieved becomes a key reason for not obtaining the desired visibility of an otherwise well-meaning programme. The role of parliament is critical for any implementation strategy through their legislative, budgetary and oversight functions. Parliamentary approval is a must for all legislations.

Thus, the institutional environment provides the framework in which an NGO operates, but an NGO can also establish formal rules and informal norms of its own that in turn influence other actors over time, in the society. The influence of NGOs when they act alone in the institutional setting is washed away as compared to their influence when they act in tandem with host government policy? How do they affect the local environment that is perceived by foreign investors? The answers to the above questions can be obtained by examining the relationship among actors in three important sectors of the society, namely the NGOs, host government and business. The convergence between disaster risk reduction, sustainable development and combating human trafficking presents a unique opportunity for increased coherence and global impact. The global policy agenda incorporates a common message: understanding hazards, how they interact and managing exposure and vulnerability that become imperative for development to be sustainable.

References

Clark, John. 1995. *The Relationship Between the State and the Voluntary Sector*. The NGO Café. https://www.gdrc.org/ngo/ncafe-ks.html.

Dutta, Mondira and Bupinder Zutshi. 2002. '*Rescued Trafficked Children from Commercial Sexual Exploitation—A Situational Analysis and Their Rehabilitation—A Case Study of the cities of Delhi, Mumbai and Kolkata in India*', United Nations Human Rights Commission, Geneva, Switzerland, April 2002.

Dutta, M. 2015. '*Understanding Maldives in the Context of Trafficking*' in Development and Regional Cooperation in Central and South Asia: Euro-Asian Perspectives, Edited By Henrik Berglund, Mondira Dutta & Per Hilding, Pentagon Press, Oct 2015, New Delhi, ISBN: 978-81-8274-864-4, 9788182748644.

Dutta, Mondira. 2020. *Impact of COVID—19 on Trafficked Children in Bihar*, sponsored by World Vision, Oct 2020 (Forthcoming)

Lester Robert, T. 2004. *Corporate Governance and Environmental Performance*, Gerencia Ambienta Int'l (Jan. 1, 2004). https://www.environmental-expert.com/articles/corporate-governance-and-environmental-performance-3494.

Ministry of Home Affairs. *A Comprehensive Scheme for Establishment of Integrated AHTUs and ToT*, Government of India Page 1 of 12 Ministry of Home Affairs/Grih Mantralaya Government of India/Bharat Sarkar Centre-State Division North Block, New Delhi. https://mha.gov.in/sites/default/files/Scheme-AHTU-SS-271011.pdf.

NALSA. 2018. *Compensation Scheme for Women Victims/Survivors of Sexual Assault/Other Crimes—2018*, National Legal Services Authority. https://wcd.nic.in/sites/default/files/Final%20VC%20Sheme_0.pdf.

Swayang Siddha. www.swayangsiddha.org.

Tandon, Rajesh. 1991. *NGO Government Relations: A Source of Life or a Kiss of Death*. New Delhi, India: Society for Participatory Research in Asia.

The Logical Indian. 2018. *Victims of Human Trafficking have the Right to Shelter and Safety* (18 Dec 2018). https://thelogicalindian.com/opinion/human-trafficking-victims/.

The Print. 2020. https://theprint.in/india/india-had-38503-victims-of-trafficking-in-2011-19-only-77-have-got-compensation/365761/. March 2020.

Times of India. 2021. '*She's at the Plough*'. 16 Jan 2021.

UNDP. 2017. *Institutional and Coordination Mechanisms*. https://sustainabledevelopment.un.org/content/documents/2478Institutional_Coordination_Mechanisms_GuidanceNote.pdf.

UNODC, 2011: UNODC & National Institute of Mental Health & Neuro Sciences, 2011: Psychosocial Care for Women in Shelter Homes, https://www.unodc.org/documents/human-trafficking/2011/Psychosocial_care_for_women_in_shelter_homes.pdf

UN Women. 2020. '*Socio Economic Impact of COVID—19: Gender Perspectives*', UN Women in collaboration with NITI Aayog, By Nath Madhubala and Mondira Dutta, July–October 2020 (Forthcoming)

Chapter 6
Conclusion

India's porous border is shared across seven other countries. Many of them are not even fenced. The connivance of the traffickers and sometimes the border police from either side take advantage of such non-fenced borders and do cross over to the Indian side. Many times, young girls from Nepal, Bangladesh, Myanmar and even as far as Uzbekistan are sold off to traffickers out of a situation of political instability and economic compulsions. At the micro-level, studies have confirmed cases of trafficking that has taken place during and after a disaster. Several hundred thousands of men from Bangladesh, India and Sri Lanka had been trafficked to various south Asian countries and even from SE Asia and Central Asia following a tsunami, floods, earthquake or even during ethnic cleansing in search of livelihood options. The link between disasters and human trafficking is an essential link which has been ignored and not many researches have come forward to study on this vital topic. Disasters not only promote social exclusion of the vulnerable communities but leads to institutionalizing, social sanctioning and marginalization of the victims. Human trafficking particularly that of women and girls leave them stigmatized which compel them to carry a gender stereotype role in the society. Women usually consider themselves as responsible for retaining the family honour, take care of their children during a crisis and protect themselves from societal shame. It is therefore critical to identify the major stakeholders. This consists of a range of institutions consisting of both government and non-government actors. It is of extreme significance to revisit and study the major national and sector development policies. These are relevant for ushering in the SDGs and their smooth implementation. Thus, identifying the challenges help in better articulation of their actions on the ground. This enables to be alert in the understanding of political consequences that may impair the implementation process of the SDGs by 2030.

Poverty and the low economic status already identifies the community who are the vulnerable marginalized groups making them a prey to the impact of disasters even more. The low economic status combined with a lack of livelihood options leaves them to fend for themselves during a disaster. There is a lack of awareness and a complete ignorance to the policies and schemes available for the grassroots. Such

M. Dutta, *Disaster and Human Trafficking*,
https://doi.org/10.1007/978-981-16-1630-3_6

schemes rarely reach the actual and needy. This becomes even more complex and difficult in the case of mass scale illiteracy and low literates leaving them vulnerable to further exploitation and a prey to getting trafficked. This is more so among women and girls who therefore continue to concentrate in the peripheral areas of work culture. Seldom does one find, women representing the core group of policymakers and decision-making bodies. Awareness programmes are not only a necessity for the women but for men as well.

Vulnerability to trafficking is related to deprivation indices like food insecurity, migration, caste and class issues, social insecurity, economic insecurity and above all areas that are disaster prone. Disasters enhance these deprivation indices manifold. Moreover research studies often remain confined and are rarely shared among the concerned stakeholders. Ministries thus are unable to imbibe the preventive measures into their ongoing schemes. A capacity build of government institutions no doubt would converge their synergy to usher in greater success of the ongoing schemes at the various ministries impacting people's lives. Safe migration procedures are dependent on proper development of tool kits and publicity material of easy understanding. This needs to be initiated for creating the necessary awareness and knowledge sharing mechanisms. For achieving the SDGs leading to gender empowerment, it is important to promote the concept of public private partnership in a restricted and modified manner in the targeted areas.

The present study reveals how closely disaster and human trafficking are related. While there are evidences of research on human trafficking or on disaster risk reduction, but there are very few studies that show the relationship between human trafficking as a result of disasters. Research on human trafficking has significantly increased, especially after the passing of the Trafficking Victims Projection Act of 2000, but it requires much more intensive research. In the present times, the subject has become quite complex and has a whole lot of implications on the magnitude and types of human trafficking as a result of the enhanced technology, disasters and other vulnerabilities. Therefore, it needs a thorough understanding of indicators that impact people in getting trafficked. Future research need to include an analysis on relief efforts following a natural disaster. Some of the important gaps that exist have emerged from the present study. These gaps need to be understood and studied thoroughly for a proper strategy to be visualized.

Capturing the magnitude in terms of numbers is most important. It is difficult to collect data on human trafficking itself, leave alone as an impact of disasters. Without statistics, no study can be thorough or complete for any policy recommendations. While there are several case studies that one comes across during a disaster throughout the world, but there are no structured data available on human trafficking other than the TIP report which do not really throw light on the magnitude of human trafficking. Without proper data, any initiative will remain like half-baked cake which is neither fit to eat nor process and thus can never address the real issues. Needless to say, availability of proper data would allow aid workers and governments to function more efficiently. The much-needed information on how to be better prepared will go a long way in preventing increase in human trafficking particularly during and post-natural disasters. Initiatives such as alternative placement for people affected or the time required for sending the children back to school post a disaster are all indirectly or directly related with the effectiveness of combatting human trafficking. All such efforts cannot be studied in solitude. Future research needs to incorporate the various other causal events in relation to human trafficking. Other issues such as ethnic cleansing, conflicts, political unrest are also important factors that are yet under researched about how they enhance human trafficking. Identifying such factors of vulnerability during a conflict, ethnic clash or a post-disaster scenario are of significance for enhancing human trafficking. Simultaneously collection of data during, before and after a disaster permits the researchers to understand the mitigation effects of a disaster and that of the risk reduction policies. The impact changes in the levels of different types of human trafficking are all a learning experience. Such results could be compared with the results from other vulnerable indicators that could throw light on the magnitude of the severity of these calamities on human trafficking. Unfortunately, such studies are seldom undertaken from a holistic perspective. It is only with the help of a robust data availability that all kinds of analysis can be undertaken. A database is the first step in eradicating a phenomenon and observing the trend pattern. With the availability of a structured data, the target to be achieved becomes more focused and achievable. It would not be accurate to state that there are no available statistics for human trafficking during and post-disaster, but these are mostly available in a scattered manner and needs an effort to compile this information and be stored in a structured manner by the international organizations and national and local NGOs. In the current scenario, data can be collected digitally allowing for small and large samples depicting the reliability of the data. There are plenty of evidence available through primary surveys that have been undertaken at the grass-root level by NGOs and researchers. In fact, the year 2018 had faced some of the horrendous disasters throughout the world. Unfortunately, there is a deficit of data on human trafficking from these vulnerable areas during and post-disaster. By mere observation of the number of people killed, displaced or/and missing, it reflects the level of vulnerability and desperation that existed among the people. Undoubtedly, the greater the vulnerability, the greater is the risk of falling prey to human trafficking. Therefore, there exists an abject lack of relevant data related to trafficking, data which is precise, up-to-date and dependable. Lack of this data-led knowledge base is what dilutes the responses towards the combat procedures and strategies of trafficking greatly. It is crucial for a scientific collection, tabulation and analysis of the existing, scattered data bases, which should be integrated, monitored and updated on a real-time basis. Such data will not only provide historical trends, but also flag off potential divergences and emerging patterns. It would help in setting up a communication channel—both at the community level and among those waging the battle against trafficking during and after disaster. Such channels should ensure perennial and unhindered flow of information so that all stakeholder efforts can be strengthened with the information edge.

Besides establishing a strong communication channel, the data availability will enhance in creating the necessary awareness. The awareness also would ideally contribute to effective communication. Thus, communication will aim at spreading awareness and vice versa. This in turn leads to co-opting of local communities to arrest potential trafficking at the grassroots—at ground zero on the one hand and to educate the vulnerable who are at risk on the other. The more effective the communication, the larger will be its spread, increasing its efficacy. Moreover, at a higher level, this will imbibe the element of inclusiveness. The greater co-ordination among various organizations, both governmental and non-government, across man-made borders, will have to be worked upon so that the response not only unifies effectiveness, but also helps plug the loopholes that are responsible for the system failures. The aim of this entire effort should also be for the optimal utilization of the scarce resources that are in the command of various stakeholders for maximization of end results.

India has been on the forefront in terms of framing some important laws to fight human trafficking, undertake disaster risk reduction initiatives and establish laws to strengthen the implementation of sustainable development goals. The Hyugo Framework of Action was established in 2005, for a period of ten years followed by the Sendai Framework of Action in 2015 for a period of fifteen years. This was followed by the Disaster Management Act of India, established on 23 December 2005 providing an effective management of disasters and matters connected with it. If one looks back at the laws for combatting human trafficking, it was way back in the year 2000 that the Palermo Protocol on Trafficking was formed. All these important laws and the subsequent policy recommendations that emerged from it have been built in solitude ignoring the cross links that need to be imbibed within these laws. Individual Protocol and Framework of Actions have their own strength, but the implementation holds better when the synergy of all these actions are compatible with each other to address the overlapping areas. The international protocols are important to be followed, but these essentially has to be not only need based but context and area specific as well. Every region has its own needs and requirements. Therefore, the laws and policies framed must have the adaptability and the capacity to imbibe certain needs based and context specific modifications as and when required. There cannot be a blanket approach for all the areas concerned. Hence, it is important to weave together the synergy among these protocols within the perspective of the present development agenda of Sustainable Development Goals (SDG). Since a large proportion of trafficking happens for labour trafficking and trafficking for commercial sexual exploitation, it is important that the areas concerned be identified and specific laws be framed to address how a disaster impacts the migration process and displacements that take place. The present study has shown how the legislation that was passed on human trafficking has impacted the various levels and types of human trafficking. Governments get strengthened by achieving vital information on laws that are most effective. Those laws which are especially able to combat human trafficking particularly during and post-disaster. However fast tracks need to come up urgently. Only these can regulate both the crime of human trafficking and the prosecution and conviction that is to be meted out to those that are found guilty of trafficking in persons. The gap between prosecution and conviction need to be addressed on a war footing. Research tends to get focused on factors that enhance the supply of human trafficking victims. Notwithstanding that the supply would not remain sustainable unless there was not a corresponding demand for that supply.

Thus, the target areas also need to incorporate the demand areas as well. Research needs to focus on what motivates customers for sex and labour trafficking. This would enable the strategy makers to assess how to curb and eliminate the demand factor in human trafficking.

A huge potential research needs to focus around assistance that are given to human trafficking victims. This warrants a visit to the trafficked survivors in person in order to understand their plight and experiences in the entire journey of their life till after escaping their traffickers. This is significant for developing laws to combat trafficking. It is important to understand the kind of assistance that is required by these survivors. This would be the best way to guide organizations in integrating the survivors of human trafficking back into society.

Organisations that deal with aid programmes will be benefitted by understanding into the nature and type of programs that is most helpful for the survivors. The efforts of the aid agencies can thus focus their efforts on increasing the available funds to such areas, making special need based services widely available to the survivors. Sometimes, the international and inter-regional laws including the intra-regional ones can hamper in addressing the real issues. On several occasions, it has been found that instead of repatriation, the victims land back into the brothels, as a result of red tapism and long duration of waits in fulfilling protocols and procedures that go on for years and years.

Under the SDG development agenda, a command-control view has to be taken of the domain so as to ensure the long-term sustainability of the efforts. Trafficking is not a one-off case, it is as dynamic as the demands that lead to its being—the response too therefore has to be based on the ground realities, consistent in action and surgically precise in terms of thought and content. This can be done only by a system that collects, analyses and acts on raw data that is relevant and precise. The systems are mostly in place—the rules, regulations, delivery mechanisms. What is conspicuous in its absence, however, is the last mile integration—a cohesive, all-out attack at the very roots of trafficking. And, this can be achieved only if we are able to educate and empower the vulnerable; organize resistance at the community levels; motivate the enforcers into positive action; deploy scarce resources for multiplier effects and ensure that the system of vigilance is relentless in its sustainability.

Let not the role of the civil society organization be underscored. The NGOS have a very important role not merely as service providers for the community but also are the major players themselves. They can be highly empowered with resources and the potential to influence policymakers. There are institutions that have received ample empirical and theoretical attention from the civil society organization. Further, NGOs have become new organizational forms and vehicles delivering social services such as poverty relief and environmental protection. The civil society counterparts of many multinational enterprises (MNEs) and governments have influenced corporate strategy. The CSOs have managed to get commitment from many corporate executives towards social objectives. In fact corporate social responsibility has become a buzz word among the firms in seeking competitive advantage. They respond to pressures from the—moral marketplace and have caused many corporate executives towards such commitments despite there being no apparent economic benefit to the firm or other individual.

A strategic thinking is required to break the cycle of the existence of vicious circle of disaster management and development. It need not be emphasized that disasters exacerbate the pre-existing vulnerabilities which are often ignored in the disaster risk reduction policies. An analysis of data over 20 years (1999–2019) in South Asia and Central Asia shows an absolute consistency with this conceptual model that, disasters hit most where the vulnerable exists and transforms it into a hazard. Under a most precarious situation when the entire system seems to be disrupted and collapse, communication though radio remains as the best option that can pave the way to reach the needy and create the necessary awareness.

Based on the study, the following recommendations may be considered.

- A systematic data bank needs to be created based on primary survey and case studies. The availability of reliable data is the first priority in addressing the issues of human trafficking particularly if this data is qualified within the framework of disaster provoked. The type of human trafficking, the magnitude and the rehabilitation measures introduced from time to time need to be studied and documented in a systematic manner and not in piece meal.
- Despite laws existing within India, there needs to be a continuity that can imbibe the Palermo Protocol with the DMA within the perspective of the SDGs. It ought to highlight and address the cross-cutting links that emerge as a result of a difficult situation. As one sieves through the various laws, it is amply clear that what India needs is not another law but an understanding into the issues and modifying the existing laws to interlace the cause and effect relationship that gets triggered off due to a disaster or a conflict or ethnic cleansing. An alignment of the major global policy instruments for facilitating and encouraging better awareness in disaster risk reduction (DRR) is urgently needed. Such a law will indeed have a rippling multiplier's impact on achieving the sustainable development goals (SDG).
- The shelter homes and protective measures need to be victim friendly with proper trained professionals and personnel, who are in a position to impart psycho-social counselling and maintain law and order situation within the shelter homes, until the victim is repatriated back to their original place of stay. The exploitative situation that sometimes rises needs to be visualized and addressed in a victim centric manner.
- Networking among all the stakeholders cutting across all cross sections of the society is a must for harnessing the synergy of all concerned in order to curb the human trafficking particularly among the children and women.

Annexure I: Advisory on Combating Human Trafficking in India, 2009

F.NO.15011/6/2009-ATC (Advisory)
GOVERNMENT OF INDIA/BHARAT SARKAR
MINISTRY OF HOME AFFAIRS/GRIH MANTRALAYA
NORTH BLOCK NEW DELHI /CS DIVISION

New Delhi, the 09.09.2009

OFFICE MEMORANDUM

Subject: **Advisory on Preventing and Combating Human Trafficking in India**

Introduction:

The Trafficking in Human Beings (THB) is a crime committed in order to target, lead or drive a human being into an exploitative situation with the aim to make profits. Such exploitation may take many forms, for example commercial sexual exploitation, child labour, forced labour, bonded labour or illegal organ removal etc. The country is witnessing cross-border as well as internal (intra-country) trafficking.

Human Trafficking and Indian Laws:

Trafficking in Human Beings (THB) is prohibited under the Constitution of India under Article 23 (1). Following specific legislations deal with Trafficking in Human Beings (THB)

- Laws relating to trafficking in women and children being administered by the MWCD (wcd.nic.in)
    i. Immoral Traffic (Prevention) Act, 1956,
    ii. Prohibition of Child Marriage Act (PCMA), 2006.
- The "Bonded Labour System (Abolition) Act, 1976", being administered by Ministry of Labour and Employment (labour.nic.in), provides for abolition of the system of bonded labour and the rehabilitation of released labourers. Child Labour (Prohibition and Regulation) Act, 1986 is also being administered by Ministry of Labour.

M. Dutta, *Disaster and Human Trafficking*,
https://doi.org/10.1007/978-981-16-1630-3

- Further, commercial dealing in human organs is a punishable offence under the Transplantation of Human Organs act, 1994, being administered by Ministry of Health and family Welfare (mohfw.nic.in). The appropriate authorities appointed under the Act are responsible and empowered to check the illegal activities of human organs traffickers.
- Specific Sections in the IPC, e.g., Sections 372 and 373 dealing with selling and buying of girls for the purposes of prostitution.

'Public Order' and 'Police" as per the 7th Schedule of the Constitution of India, are State subjects and, as such, detection, registration, investigation and prevention of crime is primarily the responsibility of the State Governments. However, Central Government supplements the efforts of the State Governments by providing policy guidelines, financial assistance for modernization of the State Police Forces in terms of weaponry, communication, equipment, mobility, training and other infrastructure under the Scheme of Modernization of State Police Forces

A working Group comprising of Directors General of Police of some of the affected States was constituted in 2004 by MHA to study the issues relating to cross border trafficking. The recommendations of this group were sent to the State Governments and they were advised to evolve a comprehensive strategy for effectively dealing with the problem of trafficking. Also an

"Integrated National Plan of Action to Prevent and Combat Trafficking in Human Beings. Specially Women and Children" (*nhrc.nic.in/planofaction.doc)*, which has been worked out through a consultation process of all related Ministries and other stakeholders, has been adopted by Government of India in the Ministry of Women and Child Development. This plan deals with all aspects of prevention, rescue, registration of cases, investigations, prosecution, conviction, cross border trafficking issues, rehabilitation, repatriation and reintegration of victims etc. Based on these the recommendations of DGPs and the integrated action plan stated above the State Governments may evolve a holistic approach towards combating Trafficking in Human Beings (THB), encompassing all aspects of prevention, rescue and rehabilitation. Convergence should be adopted between various state departments and stakeholders for effective of handling of crime of Trafficking in Human Beings (THB).

Following key points of advice have been worked out in collaboration with the related Ministries of Women and Child Development, Labour and Employment, and Health and family Welfare where the assistance/ action by the State Government/ Police would be required for the effective implementation/ enforcement of laws relating to Trafficking in Human Beings (THB):

1. **Constitution of the State Advisory Committee for Preventing and Combating Trafficking of Women and Children for Commercial Sexual Exploitation.**

   According to the Supreme Court order dated 2/05/09 (Vishal Jeet Vs Union of India), every State Government should set-up a State Advisory Committee for Preventing and Combating Trafficking of Women and Children for Commercial Sexual Exploitation. Ministry of Women & Child Development (MWCD) has already issued an advisory in this regard to all the State Governments.

2. **Implementation of Immoral Traffic (Prevention) Act (ITPA), 1956.**

   2.1. Since ITPA is the main Act that can be used to book trafficking for commercial sexual exploitation, its implementation is essential for counter-trafficking. Under Section 23, the State Government may, by notification in the Official Gazette, **make rules for carrying out the purposes of the Act.** Such rules may be formulated, notified and intimated to MWCD with a copy to MHA.

2.2. Under Section 13, the State Government may **appoint 'Special Police Officers (SPOs)'** and the 'Non-official advisory bodies' to advise the SPOs for dealing with offences under the Act.

2.3. Under Section 21, the State Governments may set-up 'Protective homes' and 'Corrective institutions' for ensuring proper implementation of the provisions of the Act. **The information regarding these homes may be circulated to all Police Stations and officers dealing with the trafficking cases.**

2.4. Under Section 22-A, the State Government may, by notification in the Official Gazette, and **after consultation with the High Court, establish one or more Courts** for providing speedy trial of the offences under the Act.

2.5. It is generally noticed that sections 8 and 20 of ITPA, which focuses on the victims, are more often invoked as a result of which the victim is re-victimized and the exploiters are not punished. It is, therefore, advised that sections 3, 6 and 7 which pertains to pimps, brothel owners, clients who are actual perpetrators of the crimes need to be invoked rather than sections 8 and 20. **Law enforcement agencies need to adopt a victim centric approach in the investigations.**

present status sent to this Ministry within a month.

12. This advisory is being issued in consultation with the Ministry of Women and Child Development and Ministry of Labour and Employment.

The receipt of this letter may kindly be acknowledged immediately.

Yours faithfully,

(Nirmaljeet Singh Kalsi)
Joint Secretary to the Government of India
Ministry of Home Affairs, North Block
New Delhi - 110001
Tel. No. 23092630

To,

The Chief Secretaries &

The Principal Secretary / Secretary (Home)

All State Governments and Union Territory Administrations – for information and necessary action.

Copy for information and necessary action to:

i. The DGs / IGs (In-charge of Prisons)/ - All State Governments / UTs for information and necessary action.

ii. Ministry of Women and Child Development (Mrs. Manjula Krishnan, Advisor & Joint Secretary, MWCD, Ms. P. Bolena, Joint Secretary) Shastri Bhawan, New Delhi.

iii. Ministry of Labour (Shri S.K. Dev Verman, Jt. Secy.), Shram Shakti Bhavan, New Delhi.

iv. Ministry of Social Justice and Empowerment (Sh. D.V.S. Ranga, Joint Secretary), Shastri Bhawan, New Delhi.

v. Ministry of Overseas Indian Affairs (Shri G. Gurucharan, Jt. Secy.), New Delhi.

vi. Ministry of External Affairs, (Joint Secretary SAARC and Joint Secretary UNES) South Block, New Delhi.

vii. Chairperson, National Commission for Women, 4, Deen Dayal Upadhyaya Marg, New Delhi-110 002.

viii. Chairperson, National Commission for Protection of Child Rights, 5th Floor, Chandralok Building, Janpath, New Delhi-110 001.

ix. Chairperson, National Human Rights Commission, Copernicus Marg, New Delhi.

x. Director General, NCRB, RK Puram, New Delhi.

xi. Director General, BPR&D, New Delhi.

xii. Director General Border Security Force, New Delhi

xiii. Director, CBI, New Delhi.

xiv. JS (UT)/ JS (NE) /JS (K), MHA, North Block, New Delhi.

xv. Under Secretary (Parliament), MHA, North Block, New Delhi.

(Nirmaljeet Singh Kalsi)
Joint Secretary to the Govt. of India

Annexure II: Advisory on Preventing and Combating Human Trafficking in India—Dealing with Foreign Nationals, 2012

MOST IMMEDIATE

No. 14051/14/2011-F.VI
Government of India
Ministry of Home Affairs
(Foreigners Division)

Dated 1st May, 2012

OFFICE MEMORANDUM

Sub: Advisory on preventing and combating human trafficking in India - dealing with foreign nationals.

The undersigned is directed to refer to this Ministry's Office Memorandum No. 15011/6/2009-ATC (Advisory) dated 09.09.2009 on the above mentioned subject (copy enclosed). It has come to the notice of this Ministry that foreign nationals are associated in some instances of human trafficking among women and children.

2. Further to the detailed procedure outlined in the above mentioned Office Memorandum, it has been decided with the approval of the competent authority that in cases of foreign nationals who are apprehended in connection with human trafficking, the State Governments / UT Administrations may follow the following procedure : -

Contd...2...

M. Dutta, *Disaster and Human Trafficking*,
https://doi.org/10.1007/978-981-16-1630-3

(i) Immediately after a foreign national is apprehended on charges of human trafficking, a detailed interrogation/investigation should be carried out to ascertain whether the person concerned is a victim or a trafficker.

(ii) The victims and the persons actually involved in human trafficking should be treated differently by the police authorities. This is in line with the SAARC Convention which advocates a victim-centric approach.

(iii) Missions/Posts in India may be informed of the arrest/detention of the foreign national by the concerned state or other authorities through CPV division in the Ministry of External Affairs(MEA) or the concerned territorial Division in MEA.

(iv) It is seen that in general, the foreign victims of human trafficking are found without valid passport or visa. If, after investigation, the woman or child is found to be a victim, she should not be prosecuted under the Foreigners Act. *If the investigation reveals that she did not come to India or did not indulge in crime out of her own free will, the State Government / UT Administration may not file a charge sheet against the victim. If the chargesheet has already been filed under the Foreigners Act and other relevant laws of the land, steps may be taken to withdraw the case from prosecution so far as the victim is concerned.* Immediate action may be taken to furnish the details of such victims to the Ministry of External Affairs (Consular Division), Patiala House, New Delhi so as to ensure that the person concerned is repatriated to the country of her origin through diplomatic channels.

(v) During the interim period, pending repatriation, the victim may be taken care of in an appropriate children's home, or "Ujjawala" home or appropriate shelter home either of the State Government concerned or of any NGO aided by the Government of India / State Government.

Contd…2…

(vi) If the investigation reveals that the person is actually a trafficker, he/she may be charge-sheeted under the Immoral Trafficking Prevention Act and the Foreigners Act and due process of law should be followed in such cases.

(vii) In order to ensure better conviction rates of perpetrators of the crime of trafficking, prosecution should be based on documentary, forensic and material evidence. State Governments are advised to encourage the law enforcement agencies to investigate the cases in a manner that they are able to build fool proof cases against the traffickers, so that convictions can be guaranteed. Use of fast-track courts and video conferencing to the extent possible also need to be ensured. Please refer to para 7 of the enclosed Advisory dated 9.9.2009.

3. All other instructions contained in this Ministry's Advisory dated 09.09.2009 including reporting to the Anti Human Trafficking Nodal Cell in MHA will be applicable in the case of foreign nationals associated with human trafficking, whether they are women or children(children means both boys and girls upto 18 years of age).

4. You are requested to issue suitable directions to all concerned under intimation to this Ministry.

5. The receipt of this Office Memorandum may kindly be acknowledged.

(G.V.V. Sarma)
Joint Secretary to the Govt. of India

To

The Chief Secretaries/Principal Secretaries/ Secretary (Home) of all State Governments and Union Territory Administrations.

Annexure III: TIP Report 2019: Country Narrative (India)[1]

India: TIER 2

The Government of India does not fully meet the minimum standards for the elimination of trafficking; however, it is making significant efforts to do so. The government demonstrated overall increasing efforts compared to the previous reporting period; therefore, India remained on Tier 2. These efforts included convicting traffickers, initiating a high-profile investigation into one case that allegedly involved officials complicit in sex trafficking at a government-funded shelter and continuing to India raise awareness of trafficking. The Supreme Court oversaw a key shelter abuse case and encouraged all states to review their shelter homes given concerns regarding the overall level of oversight. The lower house of parliament passed the Trafficking in Persons (Prevention, Protection and Rehabilitation) Bill that was aimed at strengthening investigations and coordination of victim services, but it was not taken up by the upper chamber during the reporting period. However, the government did not meet the minimum standards in several key areas. The government took some action following reports of government complicity in forced labour and sex trafficking, although the systemic failure to address forced labour and sex trafficking in government-run and government-funded shelter homes remained a serious problem. The government did not report information on investigations, prosecutions, and convictions of traffickers or on trafficking victims identified and referred to care. NGOs reported government law enforcement and victim identification efforts were limited compared to the scale of the problem. Authorities sometimes penalized victims for unlawful acts their traffickers compelled them to commit. The government's efforts to address bonded labour remained insufficient compared to the scale of the problem, and in the majority of reported cases officials did not follow the law requiring provision of release certificates and compensation to bonded labourers removed from exploitation, which prevented victims from accessing government services and in some cases led to their re-victimization.

[1]https://www.state.gov/wp-content/uploads/2019/06/2019-Trafficking-in-Persons-Report.pdf.

M. Dutta, *Disaster and Human Trafficking*,
https://doi.org/10.1007/978-981-16-1630-3

Prioritized Recommendations

Increase investigations, prosecutions and convictions of all forms of trafficking, including bonded labour.

- Vigorously investigate allegations of official complicity in human trafficking and sentence perpetrators to significant prison terms.
- Develop and immediately implement regular monitoring mechanisms of government-run and government-funded shelters to ensure appropriate quality of care, and promptly disburse funding to shelters that meet official standards for care.
- Improve central and state government implementation of protection programmes and compensation schemes for trafficking victims to ensure they receive benefits, and release certificates and compensation in a timely manner.
- Establish Anti-Human Trafficking Units (AHTUs) in all districts with clear mandates, dedicated funding and specially trained staff.
- Increase efforts to proactively identify victims by dissemination and implementation of standard operating procedures (SOPs) for victim identification and referral, and train officials on their use.
- Cease inappropriate penalization of trafficking victims.
- Amend the definition of trafficking in Section 370 of the Penal Code to include forced labour trafficking and ensure that force, fraud or coercion is not required to prove a child sex trafficking offence.
- Cease forcible detention of adult trafficking victims in government-run and government-funded shelters.
- Eliminate all recruitment fees charged to workers.
- Increase oversight of, and protections for, workers in the informal sector, including home-based workers.
- Lift current bans on female migration through agreements with destination countries that protect Indian workers from human trafficking.
- Develop a national action plan to combat trafficking.
- Provide rehabilitation services for child soldiers associated with non-state armed groups.
- Provide anti-trafficking training for diplomatic personnel.

Prosecution

The government did not report law enforcement data during the reporting period, rendering it impossible to compare efforts with the previous year. Indian law criminalized sex trafficking and some forms of labour trafficking. Section 370 of the Indian Penal Code (IPC) criminalized trafficking offences that involved exploitation that included any act of physical exploitation or any form of sexual exploitation, slavery or practices similar to slavery, and servitude. The law did not explicitly address labour trafficking. The recruitment of children younger than age 18 by non-state armed groups was not criminally prohibited. Section 370 prescribed penalties ranging from seven to 10 years' imprisonment and a fine for offences involving an adult victim, and 10 years to life imprisonment and a fine for those involving a child victim; these penalties were sufficiently stringent and, with respect to sex trafficking, commensurate with those prescribed for other serious crimes, such as kidnapping. Inconsistent with international law, Section 370 required a demonstration of force, fraud or coercion to constitute a child sex trafficking offence and therefore did not criminalize all forms of child sex trafficking. However, Sections 372 and 373 of the IPC criminalized the exploitation of children through prostitution without requiring a demonstration of such means, thereby addressing this gap. These sections prescribed penalties of up to 10 years' imprisonment and a fine, which were also sufficiently stringent and commensurate with those prescribed for other serious crimes, such as kidnapping. Section 370 criminalized government officials' involvement in human trafficking and prescribed penalties up to life imprisonment and a fine. Bonded labour was specifically criminalized in the Scheduled Castes and Scheduled Tribes (Prevention of Atrocities) Act, which prescribed sufficiently stringent penalties of up to five years' imprisonment. The Bonded Labor System (Abolition) Act (BLSA) prescribed penalties of up to three years' imprisonment, which were not sufficiently stringent. The Juvenile Justice Act and other sections of the IPC criminalized many forms of forced labour; however, these provisions were unevenly enforced, and some of their prescribed penalties were not sufficiently stringent, allowing for only fines or short prison sentences. The government frequently used the Immoral Traffic Prevention Act (ITPA) and various provisions of the IPC to prosecute sex trafficking, which prescribed penalties that were sufficiently stringent and commensurate with other serious crimes, such as kidnapping. In July 2018, the lower house of parliament passed the Trafficking in Persons (Prevention, Protection, and Rehabilitation) Bill. Some NGOs noted that the draft Trafficking in Persons Bill demonstrated that the government understood the trafficking problem, was aware of the gaps in the existing response to trafficking and was willing to address them in a coordinated way. The bill lapsed while pending in the upper house of parliament and did not pass during the reporting period. The government did not report anti-trafficking law enforcement data during the reporting period. The National Crimes Record Bureau (NCRB) did not issue the 2017 Crime in India Report due to a change in methodology that was intended to increase the amount of data collected, including on trafficking cases. Media reported the government initiated 11 trafficking investigations involving at least 52 suspected traffickers (nine cases of sex trafficking, one of forced labour and one case where the type of alleged trafficking was unknown), concluded six investigations and prosecutions from previous years and convicted 19 traffickers. Sentences for convicted traffickers ranged from probation to life imprisonment. Five of the six completed cases involved sex trafficking and resulted in the conviction of 16 traffickers and the acquittal of one suspect; the sixth case, for bonded labour, resulted in conviction of three traffickers.

The Delhi Commission for Women reported that 15 prosecutions were pending trial at the end of 2018; it was unclear if there was overlap between these cases and trafficking cases reported by media. During the previous reporting period, the government released the 2016 Crime in India Report, which reported investigation of 5217 trafficking cases, completion of prosecution in 587 cases, conviction of traffickers in

163 cases and acquittal of individuals in 424 cases. It separately reported 114 investigations, 13 case prosecutions and three convictions for bonded labour under the BLSA. The acquittal rate for 144 trafficking cases was 72% in 2016. Media reported that the police filed First Information Reports (FIRs) in additional trafficking cases during the reporting period, although it was unclear if they were actively investigating these cases. NGOs continued to comment that available law enforcement data did not reflect the large scale of human trafficking in India, as police did not always file FIRs to officially register a complaint and settled many other cases at the complaint stage. Some authorities in West Bengal and Jharkhand allegedly ordered police to register trafficking cases as ‘missing persons’ to reduce the number of trafficking cases in official statistics. NGOs also stated that law enforcement efforts, especially against bonded labour, remained low compared to the scale of the problem, and some police dissuaded labour trafficking victims from pursuing charges against their employers. NGOs noted several states showed some political will to address bonded labour abuses with improved awareness of the issue. NGOs reported the Ministry of Home Affairs (MHA) established a new Women Safety Division and conducted police trainings and judicial collegiums related to trafficking. AHTUs served as the primary investigative force for human trafficking crimes. The government did not report how many AHTUs operated during the reporting period, compared to 264 AHTUs in the previous reporting period. However, some AHTUs lacked clear mandates, were not solely dedicated to trafficking and sometimes received requests for assistance after a delay of several months, which limited the effectiveness of investigations. In a few cases, police reportedly released alleged sex traffickers immediately on bail and prioritized investigation of other crimes. An NGO reported some district magistrates mediated cases of bonded labour to secure back wages for bonded labourers in lieu of referring suspects for criminal prosecution. Court backlogs, inadequate preparation, lack of funding and a lack of prioritization of trafficking delayed cases increased the length of trials and sometimes resulted in acquittals. Some police training centres included anti-trafficking training in their regular curriculum. State and local governments partnered with NGOs and international organizations to train police, prosecutors and judicial officers on human trafficking. A lack of full accountability for misconduct and corruption continued at various levels of government, contributing to widespread impunity. NGOs reported that in a number of instances police refused to register FIRs for cases in which officials were the alleged perpetrators. Unofficial village caste councils were reported to pressure lower-caste female sex trafficking victims not to pursue criminal cases. In the past, some law enforcement officers reportedly received bribes from sex trafficking establishments and sexual services from victims in exchange for alerting the traffickers of forthcoming raids, and there was no indication this practice had ceased. Police initiated one investigation into a sex trafficking ring that allegedly involved an official, and the investigation was ongoing at the close of the reporting period. Some Indian immigration officials in New Delhi and Mumbai reportedly accepted bribes to allow traffickers to transport Nepali women to the Gulf or Malaysia without proper documentation, where some women were victims of forced labour. During the reporting period, several junior police officers in Kerala alleged forced labour by senior officers. The Chief Minister

vowed to end the practice, and authorities temporarily transferred one official but did not file formal charges or take action against the other accused. While serious challenges in oversight of government-run and government-funded shelters continued during the year, some of these cases drew the Supreme Court's attention to the issue, and NGOs reported some subsequent positive actions by some state governments. Lack of investigations into suspected trafficking crimes and broader physical and sexual abuse of trafficking victims at government-run and government-funded shelters due to widespread negligence created an atmosphere of impunity for shelter employees and government officials to engage in trafficking.

Victims alleged in a few cases government officials facilitated trafficking and, in three cases, were clients of shelter residents exploited in sex trafficking. In one government-funded shelter for victims of child labour and abandonment, at least five girls died after sex trafficking, and traffickers buried them on the shelter's premises; victims alleged both government and NGO officials facilitated the sex trafficking and were among the clients of the victims at that shelter. A report commissioned by the Bihar state government noted abuse 'varying in forms and degrees of intensity' was reported to be prevalent in almost all 110 government-funded women and child care institutions surveyed, and the report noted 'grave concerns' in 17 institutions that required immediate attention. NGOs commended the Bihar government for undertaking the study and allowing the investigator full authority and independence to report on all institutions in the state. The Bihar state government initially investigated some of the allegations, but the Supreme Court called the government's overall inaction on the cases 'very shameful' and noted the state had been 'very soft' and 'very selective' in investigating alleged perpetrators. However, the Bihar state government did arrest the husband of a local political leader implicated in one of the shelter cases and took over the operations of all shelters in the state. In November, due to the pace of investigations into the other cases, the Supreme Court ordered the Central Bureau of Investigation (CBI) to take over investigation of the additional 16 shelters in Bihar with the 'gravest concerns' of abuse, in addition to the shelter it had already begun investigating. As of January 2019, the CBI had initiated investigations into nine of the 17 homes, and the Supreme Court was monitoring the cases.

Media and NGOs reported other cases of abuse, including trafficking, in other government-run, government-funded and private shelters across in four other states. In at least two cases allegedly involving sex trafficking in government-funded shelters, lawyers and media reported government officials impeded the investigation. In Deoria, despite 20 letters from the district government to cease sending vulnerable women and children to a shelter operating without proper registration, three police superintendents sent at least 405 girls to the shelter over two years, where shelter employees exploited many in sex trafficking. Furthermore, a home department official reportedly tried to investigate the shelter but received an order from a superior not to do so. In response, the state government requested a report from all shelter homes in the state, initiated investigations, and arrested the owner of the shelter. In a separate case in Agra, October 2018, a judge convicted the government-run shelter warden with a sentence of life imprisonment for selling shelter residents into sex trafficking, some of whom police had initially removed from sex trafficking and sent to the shelter for rehabilitation. The initial police lead on the investigation, however, had alleged the involvement of multiple traffickers, but authorities transferred him before he named additional suspects. A senior government official claimed the warden had avoided investigation for 10 years due to political connections. After the issuance of the Bihar report and Deoria case, the Supreme Court encouraged the National Commission for Women and state-level institutions to audit the status of shelter homes across India, and Uttar Pradesh issued interim guidelines for the management of shelter homes and ordered the inspection of all homes in the state. The Delhi government also initiated a review of all of its shelter homes during the year. The government did not report the outcomes of any of these inspections or if any other states undertook such inspections.

Protection

The government decreased victim identification and protection efforts. The government did not report comprehensive data on victim identification efforts during the reporting period. Media indicated the government and NGOs, at times in partnership, identified at least 1172 trafficking victims during the reporting period, including men, women and children exploited in forced labour and sex trafficking. The Railway Protection Force intercepted 244 children from dangerous situations, including potential trafficking. Between January and November 2018, the Andhra Pradesh and Telangana police identified 858 trafficking victims; it was unclear how much overlap existed between this data and cases reported by media. Through the 2016 Crime in India Report, the government reported identifying 22,955 victims the previous reporting period. A 2009 MHA non-binding directive advised state officials to use SOPs for proactive victim identification and referral to services. Not all 29 states employed SOPs, although at least one state worked with civil society to establish SOPs for its child welfare committees. In December 2017, the National Human Rights Commission created and published SOPs for combating human trafficking. According to the commission, awareness and implementation of the SOPs were more common in urban centres due to closer supervision by senior police officials. NGOs noted some police relied on NGOs to report victims to the police for action. In some cases, poor interstate coordination impeded victims' ability to obtain services and participate in civil and criminal cases upon return to their home states. The Odisha Labor Department took steps to improve interstate coordination on labour trafficking cases by establishing help desks, located in the capital cities of Telangana and Andhra Pradesh, as well as Delhi, to identify trafficking victims from Odisha. The Ministry of Women and Child Development (MWCD) continued to support some broad national child protection mechanisms, including a hotline for children in need of assistance, a system to identify missing children and rescue operations for missing children. The NCRB drafted a memorandum of understanding with the US National Center for Missing and Exploited Children to share data on missing and exploited children, which received cabinet approval on February 28. The government did not report how many trafficking victims it assisted or referred to care during the reporting period. The government could refer adult female and child trafficking victims to government-run shelters, government-funded shelters run by NGOs or private organizations, or privately run shelters. NGOs continued to report that the number of government-run and government-funded shelters was insufficient and overcrowding compromised victim rehabilitation. Both government- and NGO-run shelters faced serious shortages of financial resources and trained personnel, particularly counsellors and medical staff. No shelters were available for adult male trafficking victims. Government child welfare committees generally returned child trafficking victims to their parents or placed them in privately run shelters, government-run juvenile justice homes (some of which may have housed child victims with children accused of crimes) or government-run women and children's homes, some of which allowed routine abuse as noted above. Children largely received the same services as adults. MWCD continued to fund NGO- and government-run shelter and rehabilitation services for women and children through the Ujjawala programme for female sex trafficking victims (operating 148 shelters as of July 2018) and the Swadhar Greh programme for women in difficult circumstances (operating 518 shelters as of July 2018).

The central government did not report its budgets for the Ujjawala and Swadhar Greh programmes in 2018–2019, but initial estimates signalled a potential decrease for the Ujjawala programme and a larger decrease for the Swadhar Greh programme. MWCD ran One-Stop Centers for female victims of crime that female sex trafficking victims could access. It did not report if these centres assisted any trafficking victims during the reporting period, and some NGOs reported the centres were ineffective and difficult to access. In some cases, trafficking victims were detained in shelter homes, including in the homes described above that allowed routine physical and sexual abuse. During the reporting period, the Ministry of Railway issued a circular to stationmasters nationwide allowing the use of station funds to cover child protection expenses for vulnerable children such as trafficking victims. NGOs relied primarily on donor contributions, although some received government funds. The disbursal of government funding to NGOs was sometimes delayed for multiple years. During the reporting period, media, NGOs and authorities documented a persistent lack of oversight and negligence in government-run, government-funded and privately run shelters that sometimes resulted in abuse and trafficking of residents. The National Commission for the Protection of Child Rights estimated 1300 of India's approximately 9000 shelters for vulnerable people were not registered with the government and operated with little or no oversight. In several cases, government-funded shelter homes continued to operate despite significant gaps in mandatory reporting and allegations of abuse, at times due to alleged political connections. Police documented at least 156 residents—including sex trafficking victims—missing from six shelters as of March 2019; at least one shelter owner had reportedly sold some of the women and girls for prostitution. In another case, 30 girl residents of a shelter were reportedly exploited in sex trafficking. Due to unsafe conditions and forcible detention in government-run and government-funded shelters, some sex trafficking victims—including children—ran away, and at least one attempted suicide in the shelter during the reporting period. In one case, the Bihar's Child Rights Commission visited a government-funded shelter home in November 2017 and requested officials remove children from the home due to the unacceptable conditions. The district magistrate ordered the home to initiate shutdown procedures in December 2017, but it operated until June 2018, when authorities uncovered shelter employees had exploited approximately 30 girl residents in sex trafficking. In September 2018, the Bihar state government announced that it would assume management of all government-funded and NGO-run shelters by December 2018 and cancelled the licences of at least 50 NGOs that had been operating shelters in the state. The central government committed to audit all shelter homes for children, which also cared for trafficking victims, and the Supreme Court ordered all states to complete their respective audits by September 2018; as of September 2018, however, authorities had only surveyed approximately one-third of shelters. In September 2018, the Supreme Court ordered the MWCD to formulate a child protection policy to prevent abuse in government-run and government-funded shelter homes. MWCD began drafting the policy, in consultation with NGOs and activists. The Supreme Court further implored MWCD to present an update on incidents of child sexual abuse in all shelter homes; MWCD did not produce the report by the close of the reporting period. NGOs noted concern for children transferred from NGO shelters to government shelters, as the scale of abuse and concerns regarding limited oversight were reportedly similar in both institutions. While the government had a programme to compensate and provide services to former bonded labourers, it failed to fully implement the programme, and overall efforts were insufficient to the scale of the problem. The central government had a programme through which bonded labour victims could obtain assistance and compensation upon conviction of their trafficker to obtain full benefits, although delays in implementation led to many victims returning to bonded labour. In 2016, the government amended the programme to include female sex trafficking and child forced labour victims as recipients and to authorize local district authorities to provide immediate monetary assistance up to 20,000 Indian rupees (INR) ($287) to a victim released from bonded labour without a release certificate, regardless of the status of the related court case. The release of the overall compensation amounts (between 100,000 INR [$1430] and 300,000 INR [$4300] based on the victim's demographics) remained contingent on issuance of a release certificate and the conviction of the trafficker or administrative processes that could take several years to conclude. Implementation of this programme, however, remained inadequate. Since 2016, the government has not reported providing full compensation to any former bonded labourers. Former bonded labourers were also entitled to 'release certificates' enabling them to receive government-funded services. The disbursal of such certificates, however, varied greatly between states; some victims received certificates at or soon after their rescue, especially in areas with significant coordination between the government and NGOs. Other victims experienced lengthy delays before obtaining certificates. NGOs reported some officials in Uttar Pradesh treated bonded labour cases as labour exploitation, which meant victims were not identified as bonded labour victims, did not receive 'release certificates' and were not eligible for government compensation or services. One NGO reported that among the 537 victims it successfully removed from bonded labour during the reporting period, the government only provided release certificates to 29, therefore preventing the remaining 508 from obtaining full compensation and services. The Telangana state government, in collaboration with Odisha government officials and NGOs, opened eight Odia language schools that educated approximately 870 former victims of child labour and children of migrant workers.

District governments provided stipends for volunteer teachers, meals and some materials. Judges could order compensation for victims of all forms of trafficking through other government programmes and did so on an ad hoc basis. Prosecutors used protective courtroom procedures for some trafficking victims during the reporting period, including the creation of child-friendly courts in Telangana and West Bengal. Videoconferencing was used by Hyderabad and Mumbai's anti-trafficking court in at least one case to allow testimony from victims who had returned to Bangladesh. Many victims were reluctant to participate in trials against their traffickers due to inadequate witness protection and the lengthy judicial process. Female victims of sex trafficking faced systemic barriers in pursuing justice, including victim blaming by law enforcement, challenges to successfully filing FIRs and poor access to services. Police and court officers did not always follow the victim protection measures enshrined in law. Moreover, NGOs reported that judges closed many cases because the government did not provide adequate financial assistance to enable victims to participate in trials. Foreign victims had the same access to shelter and services as Indian nationals. Government policy on foreign victims dictated their return to their country of origin at the earliest possible time. Authorities detained foreign sex trafficking victims in government-run or government-funded shelters until deportation. At times, both repatriation of foreign victims seeking to return home and deportation of victims could take years due to a number of constraints. The government provided some funding to NGOs to repatriate child trafficking victims but did not offer any financial assistance for repatriation of adult trafficking victims. During the reporting period, the government secured the release and assisted with repatriation of Indian forced labour victims from Saudi Arabia and Iraq. Some law enforcement continued to penalize trafficking victims for unlawful acts their traffickers compelled them to commit, including prostitution and immigration violations. The government required Indians who received a visa from a foreign government indicating the person was a trafficking victim in the foreign country or was a family member of a victim to provide documentation of the trafficking experience in order to renew their passports. In 2016 and 2017, the government stamped the passports of some recipients of the foreign government's visas, for both trafficking victims and their eligible family members, identifying them as trafficking victims involved in a particular investigation or civil or criminal case. While the stamp-requested authorities permit the visa holder to travel without hindrance, some NGOs familiar with this practice noted it made some victims fearful of reprisal and penalization and served as a deterrent to victims interacting with authorities. Some victims previously cited lengthy delays, requests from the government for private or otherwise sensitive information, and inconsistent application of the policy when attempting to renew their passports.

Prevention

The government maintained modest efforts to prevent human trafficking at the state level. The government's interministerial committee, chaired by MWCD, did not report meeting during the reporting period; it had met in the previous reporting period. The government did not have a national action plan to combat trafficking. The Ministry of Railways had 84 child help desks at stations to provide immediate support to unaccompanied children who might have been vulnerable to trafficking—an increase from 62 desks the previous year. In some states, police and NGOs noted government agencies largely lacked anti-trafficking preventative measures. Some state governments conducted anti-trafficking awareness campaigns. West Bengal expanded its Swayangsiddha Initiative to all 23 districts, reaching 200,000 students in 500 schools to share information on human trafficking and child rights. The government registered foreign recruitment agencies and Indian migrant workers through the eMigrate system. The government required migrant workers going to 16 specific countries, including many in the Middle East, to receive emigration clearance before departure; it did not allow emigration to Iraq. The Ministry of External Affairs (MEA) drafted an emigration bill that required all Indian nationals seeking education or employment overseas to register with the government, provided for enhanced pre-departure trainings and migrant resource centres, and prescribed more stringent penalties for recruitment agency violations; the bill was pending submission to parliament at the close of the reporting period. The government maintained its ban on females younger than age 30 from working in 17 countries. The UN and members of civil society argued any ban on migration increased the likelihood of illegal migration and therefore heightened vulnerability to human traffickers. MEA operated five centres nationwide and a 24/7 helpline to provide counselling and other resources to those considering migrant work. MEA's Indian Community Welfare Fund (ICWF), accessible to all Indian missions abroad and funded primarily via overseas consular fees, offered shelter, legal assistance and repatriation for migrant workers in distress, as well as awareness measures and hotlines. MEA did not report data on utilization of this fund during the reporting period. The government permitted licensed foreign employment recruiters to charge migrant workers up to 20,000 INR ($287) for recruitment fees and costs; however, observers stated employers frequently charged migrant workers more than the maximum, thereby increasing debt and vulnerability to labour trafficking. Unregistered subagents operated widely without oversight. MEA received 231 complaints from January to June 2018 against recruitment agencies and agents and referred the cases to state governments for investigation. Some states regulated some aspects of work in the informal sector, including domestic work. The central government could provide reimbursement of 450,000 INR ($6450) to any district that conducted a census of bonded labour, but no district reported utilizing this incentive during the year. Despite India being a destination for child sex tourism, the government did not report measures to reduce child sex tourism. The government made efforts to reduce the demand for commercial sex. The government did not provide information about any training provided to its troops prior to their deployment as peacekeepers or to its diplomatic personnel. During the reporting period, a domestic worker filed a civil lawsuit in a federal court in New York seeking damages from a former Indian consular officer previously posted at the New York consulate, whom the domestic worker alleged subjected her to forced labour in 2013–2014.

Trafficking Profile

As reported over the past five years, human traffickers exploit domestic and foreign victims in India, and traffickers exploit victims from India abroad. Forced labour, including bonded labour, constitutes India's largest trafficking problem; men, women and children in debt bondage—sometimes inherited from previous generations—are forced to work in agriculture, brick kilns, rice mills, embroidery factories and stone quarries. Most of India's trafficking problem is internal, with traffickers targeting those from the most disadvantaged social strata. Experts estimate there are more than eight million bonded labourers in the country. In addition to bonded labour, traffickers exploit children in forced labour agriculture; construction; domestic service; garment, steel and textile industries, including tanneries and zari factories; begging; biscuit factories; carpet making; floriculture; fish and ginger farms; glass manufacturing; pickling; ship breaking; and wire manufacturing for underground cables. Forced begging ringleaders sometimes maim children to earn more money. Traffickers have coerced poor parents to give up their children and forced the children to work and in one case steal in large cities. Multiple organizations note physical violence against trafficking victims—in both forced labour and sex trafficking—is particularly prevalent in India. Unregulated work placement agencies reportedly use false promises of employment to lure adults and children into sex trafficking or forced labour. Some traffickers force women and girls to conceive and deliver babies for sale. In some cases, the 'Provident Funds' or 'Sumangali' scheme in which employers pay young women a lump sum for education or a dowry at the end of multi-year labour contracts, often in Tamil Nadu's spinning mill industry, may amount to bonded labour, and some employers subject these women to sex trafficking. Maoist groups, particularly in Chhattisgarh and Jharkhand, allegedly continued to recruit children, and three incidents of child recruitment by separatist groups were reported in the state of Jammu and Kashmir. NGO observers reported children as young as age 12 were members of Maoist youth groups and allied militia. The children reportedly handled weapons and improvised explosive devices (IEDs). Maoists reportedly held children against their will and threatened severe reprisals, including the killing of family members, if the children attempted to escape. Maoist groups sometimes used children as human shields in confrontations with security forces. Several women formerly associated with Maoist groups reported that sexual violence, including rape and other forms of abuse, was a practice in some Maoist camps. Some female child soldiers reported commanders recruited and used them in part for sexual exploitation, including practices indicative of sexual slavery. Some parents in Jharkhand send their children to Bihar and Gujarat to avoid abduction and recruitment by armed groups; the children often work on farms and in brick kilns, sectors that render them vulnerable to forced labour. Unverified reports allege national security forces also use children as informants and spies. Experts estimate millions of people are sex trafficking victims within India. Traffickers exploit women and children in sex trafficking in religious pilgrimage centres and in tourist destinations.

Traffickers subject women and girls—predominately from Nepal and Bangladesh and, to a lesser extent, from Europe, Africa and Asia—to sex trafficking in India. Traffickers exploit Indian and Nepali women and girls in India as 'orchestra dancers', where girls work for dance groups hired to perform at public functions but are subsequently subjected to sex trafficking. Traffickers use online technology to facilitate sex trafficking and fraudulent recruitment. Some traffickers kidnap children from public places, entice girls with drugs and force girls as young as five years old in sex trafficking to take hormone injections to appear older. Some corrupt law enforcement officers protect suspected traffickers and brothel owners from law enforcement efforts and take bribes from sex trafficking establishments and sexual services from victims. Some traffickers have bribed police to release child sex trafficking victims back into traffickers' custody. In addition to traditional red light districts, dance bars, spas and massage parlours, traffickers increasingly exploit women and children in sex trafficking in small hotels, vehicles, huts and private residences. India is a source for child sex tourists and a destination for child sex tourism. Traffickers arrange sham marriages within India and Gulf states to subject females to sex trafficking. Media, NGOs and government authorities documented physical and sexual abuse of trafficking victims in government-run, government-funded and privately run shelters, as well as cases of shelters forcing vulnerable male, female and child residents into forced labour and sex trafficking. Victims alleged government officials' involvement in some of the cases, including facilitating trafficking and—in at least three cases—as clients of victims in sex trafficking. Traffickers exploit some Indian migrants who willingly seek employment abroad in construction, domestic work and other low-skilled sectors to forced labour in the Middle East and other regions, often following recruitment fraud and exorbitant recruitment fees. News articles reported Indian males in labour trafficking in Malaysia, Armenia and Portugal during the reporting period. Girls from north-east India are vulnerable to trafficking as they transit Burma to circumvent the Indian government's emigration clearances. During the reporting period, new reports emerged of Zambian traffickers bringing Indian children to Zambia through illegal adoption for domestic servitude. Traffickers subject some Indian, Nepali, Bangladeshi and Afghan women and girls to labour and sex trafficking in major Indian cities and exploit Rohingya, Sri Lankan Tamil and other refugee populations in sex and labour trafficking. Some traffickers bribe Indian immigration officials in New Delhi and Mumbai to allow them to transport Nepali females to the Gulf or Malaysia without proper documentation for forced labour. Traffickers subject some boys from Bihar and Uttar Pradesh to forced labour in embroidery factories in Nepal. Employment agents recruit boys from Assam for construction work in Nepal, where workers are undocumented and vulnerable to forced labour.

Annexure IV: Links of Disaster Risk Reduction (DRR) with Sustainable Development Goals (SDGs)

Sustainable development goal	Related disaster risk reduction (target)	Suggested indicators
Goal 1: End poverty in all its forms everywhere	Target 1.5: By 2030, build the resilience of the poor and those in vulnerable situations and reduce their exposure and vulnerability to climate-related extremes and other economic, social and environmental shocks and disasters	• Number of deaths, missing and affected people due to hazardous events per 100,000 [Sendai Framework Target (a) and (b)] • Direct economic loss due to hazardous events in relation to global gross domestic product. [Sendai Framework Target (c)]
Goal 2: End hunger, achieve food security and improved nutrition and promote sustainable agriculture	Target 2.4: By 2030, ensure sustainable food production systems and implement resilient agricultural practices that increase productivity and production, that held to maintain ecosystems, that strengthen capacity for adaptation to climate change, extreme weather, drought, flooding and other disasters and that progressively improve land and soil quality	• Direct agricultural loss due to hazardous event
Goal 3: Ensure healthy lives and promote well-being for all at all ages	Target 3.d: Strengthen the capacity of all countries, in particular developing countries, for early warning, risk reduction and management of national and global health risks	

(continued)

M. Dutta, *Disaster and Human Trafficking*,
https://doi.org/10.1007/978-981-16-1630-3

(continued)

Sustainable development goal	Related disaster risk reduction (target)	Suggested indicators
Goal 4: Ensure inclusive and equitable quality education and promote lifelong learning opportunities for all	Target 4.7: By 2030, ensure that all learners acquire the knowledge and skills needed to promote sustainable development including, among others, through education for sustainable development and sustainable lifestyles, human rights, gender equality, promotion of a culture of peace and non-violence, global citizenship and appreciation of cultural diversity and of culture's contribution to sustainable development	
	Target 4.a: Build and upgrade education facilities that are child, disability and gender-sensitive and provide safe, non-violent, inclusive and effective learning environments for all	Number of safe educational facilities
Goal 6: Ensure availability and sustainable management of water and sanitation for all	Target 6.6: By 2020, protect and restore water-related ecosystems, including mountains, forests, wetlands, rivers, aquifers and lakes	
Goal 9: Build resilient infrastructure, promote inclusive and sustainable industrialization and foster innovation	Target 9.1: Develop quality, reliable, sustainable and resilient infrastructure, including regional and trans-border infrastructure, to support economic development and human well-being, with focus on affordable and equitable access for all	• Damage to critical infrastructure due to hazardous events [Sendai Framework Target (d)] • Number of countries that adopt and implement critical infrastructure protection plan
	Target 9.a: Facilitate sustainable and resilient infrastructure development in developing countries through enhanced financial, technological and technical support to African countries, least developed countries, landlocked developing countries and small island development states	

(continued)

(continued)

Sustainable development goal	Related disaster risk reduction (target)	Suggested indicators
Goal 11: Make cities and human settlements inclusive, safe, resilient and sustainable	Target 11.1: By 2030, ensure access for all to adequate, safe and affordable and basic services and upgrade slums	
	Target 11.3: By 2030, enhance inclusive and sustainable urbanization and capacity for participatory, integrated and sustainable human settlement planning and management in all countries	
	Target 11.4: Strengthen efforts to protect and safeguard the world's cultural and natural heritage	
	Target 11.5: By 2030, significantly reduce the number of deaths and the number of people affected and substantially decrease the direct economic losses relative to global gross domestic product caused by disasters, including water-related disasters, with a focus on protecting the poor and people in vulnerable situations	• Number of deaths, missing and affected people due to hazardous events per 100,000 [Sendai Framework Target (a) and (b)] • Direct economic loss due to hazardous events in relation to global gross domestic product. [Sendai Framework Target (c)]
	Target 11.b: By 2020, substantially increase the number of cities and human settlements adopting and implementing integrated policies and plans towards inclusion, resource efficiency, mitigation and adaptation to climate change, resilience to disasters, and develop and implement, in line with the Sendai Framework for Disaster Risk Reduction, 2015–2030, holistic disaster risk management at all levels	• Percentage of local governments that adopt and implement local DRR strategies in line with the Sendai Framework for Disaster Risk Reduction, 2015–2030 [Sendai Framework Target (e)]

(continued)

(continued)

Sustainable development goal	Related disaster risk reduction (target)	Suggested indicators
	Target 11.c: Support least developed countries, including through financial and technical assistance, in building sustainable and resilient buildings utilizing local materials	
Goal 13: Take urgent action to combat climate change and its impacts	Target 13.1: Strengthen resilience and adaptive capacity to climate-related hazards and natural disasters in all countries	• Number of deaths, missing and affected people due to hazardous events per 100,000 [Sendai Framework Target (a) and (b)] • Direct economic loss due to hazardous events in relation to global gross domestic product [Sendai Framework Target (c)]
	Target 13.2: Integrate climate change measures into national policies, strategies and planning	• Number of countries that adopt and implement national DRR strategies in line with the Sendai Framework for Disaster Risk Reduction, 2015–2030 [Sendai Framework Target (e)] • Number of countries that integrate climate and disaster risk into development planning
	Target 13.3: Improve education, awareness raising and human and institutional capacity on climate change mitigation, adaptation, impact reduction and early warning	• Number of countries that have multi-hazard early warning system [Sendai Framework Target (g)] • Number of countries that have multi-hazard national risk assessment with results in an accessible, understandable and usable format for stakeholders and people [Sendai Framework Target (g)]

(continued)

(continued)

Sustainable development goal	Related disaster risk reduction (target)	Suggested indicators
	Target 13.a: Implement the commitment undertaken by developed country parties to the United Nations Framework Convention on Climate Change to a goal of mobilizing jointly $100 billion annually by 2020 from all sources to address the needs of developing countries in the context of meaningful mitigation actions and transparency on implementation and fully operationalize the Green Climate Fund through its capitalization as soon as possible	
	Target 13.b: Promote mechanisms for raising capacity for effective climate change-related planning and management in least developed countries, including focusing on women, youth and local and marginalized communities	
Goal 14: Conserve and sustainably use the oceans, seas and marine resources for sustainable development	Target 14.2: By 2020, sustainably manage and protect marine and coastal ecosystems to avoid significant adverse impacts, including by strengthening their resilience, and take action for their restoration in order to achieve healthy and productive oceans	• Number of deaths, missing and affected people due to hazardous events per 100,000 [Sendai Framework Target (a) and (b)] • Direct economic loss due to hazardous events in relation to global gross domestic product [Sendai Framework Target (c)]
Goal 15: Protect, restore and promote sustainable use of terrestrial ecosystems, sustainably manage forests, combat desertification, halt and reverse land degradation and halt biodiversity loss	Target 15.1: By 2020, ensure the conservation, restoration and sustainable use of terrestrial and inland freshwater ecosystems and their services, in particular forests, wetlands, mountains and drylands, in line with obligations under international agreements	

(continued)

(continued)

Sustainable development goal	Related disaster risk reduction (target)	Suggested indicators
	Target 15.2: By 2020, promote the implementation of sustainable management of all types of forests, halt deforestation, restore degraded forests and substantially increase afforestation and reforestation globally	
	Target 15.3: By 2030, combat desertification, restore degraded land and soil, including land affected by desertification, drought and floods, and strive to achieve a land degradation neutral world	• Direct agricultural loss due to hazardous events • Number of countries that have multi-hazard early warning system [Sendai Framework Target (g)] • Number of countries that have multi-hazard national risk assessment with results in an accessible, understandable and usable format for stakeholders and people [Sendai Framework Target (g)]
	Target 15.4: By 2030, ensure the conservation of mountain ecosystems, including their biodiversity, in order to enhance their capacity to provide benefits that are essential for 19 Sustainable Development Goals	
	Target 15.9: By 2020, integrate ecosystem and biodiversity values into national and local planning, development processes, poverty reduction strategies and accounts	

Source UNISDR, Disaster risk reduction and resilience in the 2030 agenda for sustainable development, https://www.preventionweb.net/files/46052_disasterriskreductioninthe2030agend.pdf

Annexure V: Field Visit Survey, November 2018, Kolkata, West Bengal

Date	Time	Organization	Names of stakeholders interviewed
12 November 2018	10 am	Sanlaap	Mr. Souvik Basu, Ms. Shruti Roy Choudhury, Ms. Tapati Bhoumik, Mr. Pinaki Ranjan Sinha
13 November 2018	10 am	State Commission for Protection of Child Rights, West Bengal (SCPCR), Ulto Danga	Ms. Ananya Chatterjee Chakraborty, Chairperson
14 November 2018	11:30 am	West Bengal Task Force	Ms. Madhumita Haldar, Director
14 November 2018	2:00 pm	Trafficked Women Victims (FGD)	22 women victims who work in the Kolkata brothels
15 November 2018	10 am	https://www.Banglanatak.com	Ms. Ananya Bhattacharjee
15 November 2018	2 pm	Meeting the 'second-generation' victims	Child victims (7) and school teachers (2) working in the area
16 November 2018	11:30 am	ADM, South 24 Parganas	Mr. Sagar Chakravarti and Team
16 November 2018	2 pm	State Legal Services, (SLS)	Mr. Balaram Ms. Durba Khaita
16 November 2018	4 pm	AHTU, WB	Mr. Azizul Haq Ms. Neloo Sherpa
17 November 2018	10 am	DM South 24 Parganas	Mr. Ratnakar Rao, IAS (*could not contact despite several attempts*)

M. Dutta, *Disaster and Human Trafficking*,
https://doi.org/10.1007/978-981-16-1630-3

The manufacturer's authorised representative in the EU is Springer Nature Customer Service Centre GmbH, Europaplatz 3, 69115 Heidelberg, Germany. If you have any concerns regarding our products, please contact ProductSafety@springernature.com

Printed and bound by CPI Group (UK) Ltd, Croydon, CR0 4YY
30/09/2026
02225297-0003